FIRE, RADIANCE, & LOVE

Fire Radiance & Love

W. HERBERT BROWN

Tyndale House Publishers, Inc. Wheaton, Illinois

Originally printed under the title
Pentecostal Fire, Radiance, and Love
by Southern Bible Testimony, Inc.,
Bryson City, North Carolina.

Library of Congress Catalog Card Number 78-65909
ISBN 0-8423-0867-9, paper

First Tyndale House printing, February 1979
Printed in the United States of America.

To All Who Are
Determined
to Blaze with Holy Fire

(Especially my good friends in Swain County)

O Thou who camest from above
    Thy pure celestial fire to start,
Help me Thy flame of sacred love
    To spread throughout my yielded heart.

There let it for Thy glory burn
    With inextinguishable blaze;
And trembling to its source return
    In humble prayer and fervent praise.

Jesus, confirm my heart's desire
    To work, and speak, and think for Thee;
Still let me guard Thy holy fire
    And still stir up Thy gift in me.

Ready for all Thy perfect will,
    My acts of faith and love repeat,
Till death Thy endless mercies seal,
    And make the sacrifice complete.

                    —Charles Wesley (alt.)

Contents

The Spirit in the Pentateuch—
Divine Immanence

WHY STUDY GOD THE SPIRIT in the Old Testament? Because, otherwise, we could not rightly understand or fully appreciate much of what the New Testament has to say about Him, or rather what He has to say about himself in the New Testament. What we learn about Him in the New Testament largely has the Old Testament as its basis. For instance, we would certainly miss the prophetic significance of Luke 4:18, 19— "The Spirit of the Lord is upon me. . ."—if we had no previous knowledge of Isaiah 61:1, 2. Or take Acts 2:16–21: "But this is that which was spoken by the prophet Joel. . . ." The New Testament gives no explanation of these passages. We must refer to their backgrounds in the Old Testament. Furthermore, the Scriptures of the apostolic churches were almost totally the Old Testament Scriptures. Therefore we turn eagerly to the Old Testament—to study the Holy Spirit verse by verse. There we discover that the Spirit mentions himself directly only fourteen times in the first five books. According to the Authorized Version, there are only two direct references, Genesis 1:2 and 41:38; but the American Standard Version contains ten other instances where *spirit* is capitalized: Genesis 6:3; Exodus 31:3; 35:31; Numbers 11:17, 25 (twice), 26, 29; 24:2; and 27:18. Other authorities believe, furthermore, that Exodus 28:3 and Deuteronomy 34:9 should be added to this list.

9

I. GENESIS—THREE REFERENCES

1:2   *And the earth was without form, and void; and darkness was upon the face of the deep. And the Spirit of God moved upon the face of the waters.*

This first reference to the Spirit pictures Him as the great Agent of the Godhead in creation. Theologians use related passages to bring out chief details of the picture as follows: everything was *brought forth* out of nothing by the power of the Father (Heb. 11:3). *arranged* for God's glory by the power of the Son (John 1:1–3), and *caused to develop according to its nature* by the power of the Spirit (Gen. 1:2). Thus "in the beginning" the Triune God "created the heavens and the earth."

That is, God the Spirit, acting as the completing Agent in all things, imparted energy and motion to improve the desolate, gloomy, uninhabited condition of things. He "moved," "brooded," "fluttered" over the original chaos until a beautiful and fruitful earth was formed and inhabited. The crown of His creative activity. of course. was man, a full-grown, highly intelligent person existing in the moral and spiritual image and likeness of God.

Think of it. We are told, for instance, that our sun is an average star in weight and size a round ball of blazing gases, a veritable atomic furnace large enough to contain 1,400,000 earths. This verse 2 teaches us, then, that the Spirit of God developed it out of what the Father brought forth and the Son arranged. And our sun is only one of the billions of stars. Again we are told there are about 800.000 kinds of animals and 250.000 kinds of plants living on earth today. This verse declares the Spirit of God developed and perfected them, too. For by His Spirit God creates and sustains all animate and inanimate things (Ps. 104:30).

Actually, the term "Spirit of God" in Genesis 1:2 stands for God's invisible energy and power, His own presence as a spiritual Being (Ps. 139:7). The personality of the Spirit is not set forth at first; that will be unfolded later in Scripture. Here we understand that while God was above and beyond

His creation, transcendent, He was also present and omnipresent within it, immanent. For example, the very life of man was God's gift produced in man by His Spirit (Gen. 2:7). Right from the very beginning God, by His Spirit, made himself known in history and human experience. A free, purposive, personal God—not an impersonal force—acted. God, an infinite Being, cared for you and me.

This first reference to the Spirit should become for us a "front-door key" to His work in Christian experience. It can, in this way: consider the Hebrew word translated "moved" in Genesis 1:2. It is translated "flutter" in Deuteronomy 32:11, 12: "As the eagle stirreth up her nest, fluttereth over her young, spreadeth abroad her wings, taketh them, beareth them on her wings: so the Lord alone did lead him." Thus the eagle stirs her nest to make the fat and lazy eaglets so uncomfortable that they become willing to launch out and fly. She plucks out the soft lining of rabbit, goat and sheep skins—animals which she has destroyed—and makes bare the briars and thorns and sharp sticks.

This illustrates the Spirit's method with those who are destined to become God's "eagles." All the patriarchs and prophets had their nests stirred, all the apostles, all the reformers. The Holy Spirit will not only stir your nest, but will "flutter" over you—to draw your attention to Christ, to get you to look away to Christ. The mother bird might flutter all day long, but the young birds would never look up while lying on soft fur. But when it becomes all thorns and briars and sharp sticks, they look up, look for a better resting place. Then the time has come for the mother eagle "to spread abroad her wings."

In your case the time has come for the Spirit to unfold to you the magnitude of Christ—His beauties, His wisdom, His power, His majesty, His glory. The eagle will spread out her wings from tip to tip and lay them flat down, and the young bird will step out and put its claws in her wings and hold on to her feathers. When she shakes her wings, the eaglet takes stronger hold. Then she sails away through the dizzy heights.

The little bird can look back and see the tree and the nest, but around and around the mother goes, spiraling into the clear, blue sky.

After she's soared one thousand, two thousand, three, four, five thousand feet, she gives a sudden lurch, and off falls the eaglet. Oh, how it tumbles and rolls, and puts out its wings and beats the air! The mother bird watches until the young bird is about halfway down to death; then she shoots down like a bullet to rescue her baby. But when it's on her wings again. around and up she goes, repeating the frightening lesson until the eaglet becomes an eagle.

This is what the Holy Spirit did to the early Christians in Jerusalem. He "stirred their nest" and they "went everywhere preaching the word." Otherwise. they never would have gone fifty miles.

6:3 *And the Lord said, My Spirit shall not always strive with man, for that he also is flesh: yet his days shall be an hundred and twenty years.*

The Hebrew word translated "strive" means primarily *to rule*. Until Noah's day God's Spirit, in a relative sense, ruled the human race. But there came a time when God "gave them up to uncleanness ... vile affections ... a reprobate mind" (Rom. 1:24–28). Thereafter He executed judgment whenever their iniquities became "full" (Gen. 15:16).

Although the Spirit no longer strives with the race as such. He does restrain lawlessness (II Thess. 2:6, 7) and convict of sin (John 16:7–11). That God's Spirit may sometimes leave off convicting individuals is implied in many Scriptures, such as Zechariah 7:12; Hosea 4:17; Matthew 12:31. 32; 23:32; Ephesians 4:19; I Thessalonians 2:16; I Timothy 4:2; II Timothy 2:25; Hebrews 6:3; 10:26; and I John 5:16.

41:38 *And Pharaoh said unto his servants, Can we find such a one as this is, a man in whom the Spirit of God is?*

Pharaoh recognized that God's Spirit had given Joseph marvelous wisdom and knowledge. (Cp. Deut. 34:9; Isa. 11:2;

and Dan. 5:11.) Note that the Spirit's indwelling enabled Joseph to maintain a good testimony in Egypt, even as slave and prisoner. Earlier, Potiphar had seen that "Jehovah was with him, and that Jehovah made all that he did to prosper in his hand" (Gen. 39:3, A.S.V.). Also, by His Spirit, "Jehovah was with Joseph, and showed kindness unto him, and gave him favor in the sight of the keeper of the prison" (Gen. 39:21, A.S.V.). The climax came when Joseph, by the Spirit's aid, interpreted Pharaoh's dreams and became thereby the saviour of Egypt and, primarily, his own father's household, from famine.

II. EXODUS—THREE REFERENCES

28:3   *And thou shalt speak unto all that are wise hearted, whom I have filled with the Spirit of wisdom, that they may make Aaron's garments to consecrate him, that he may minister unto me in the priest's office.*

31:3   *I have filled him with the Spirit of God, in wisdom, and in understanding, and in knowledge, and in all manner of workmanship.*

35:31   *And he hath filled him with the Spirit of God.*

While this first mention of the Spirit's filling does not answer for us the big question: How can I be filled? (which question will be answered eventually by Christ himself in John 7:37, 38), this context does provide an ideal background for the Spirit-filled life. Think back to those Exodus days. What a joy, what a privilege, what an honor to make those special garments for the priests, to build that magnificent Tabernacle, to gaze upon the brightness and the luster of those precious stones, to appreciate the value and the beauty of all that silver and gold. How satisfying the high artistic ability to magnify Christ typically. How fascinating to weave the wire of gold with "the blue, the purple, the scarlet, and the fine-twined linen."

Details in these Tabernacle accounts stand out like guide-posts. (Cp. I Cor. 10:11.) God used Bezaleel, Aholiab and others.

How can we get Him to use us? This story suggests how.

1. We must deeply desire God's complete will for our lives. As we read again what the record says in Exodus 31:1–6 we perceive why: "I have called," "I have filled," "I have given," "I have commanded." Thus we remember that "little is much" *only* when God is in it. God has a plan for our lives. Only that counts for eternity.

2. We must be wise-hearted. For God says, ". . . in the hearts of all that are wise hearted I have put wisdom." That is, we must use to the utmost the little that God gives us before He will give us more. "For whosoever hath, to him shall be given, and he shall have more abundance: but whosoever hath not. from him shall be taken even that he hath." This implies diligence. We must *apply* truth. We must use, for instance, such passages as Proverbs 2:1–5.

3. We must be filled with the Spirit. There was no other way then to magnify Christ in type, and there is no other way now to magnify Him in Person.

4. We must abide in Christ. Bezaleel's name suggests this condition. His name means *in* (the) *shadow* (i.e., protection) *of God*. All must dwell there for constant power. For "he that dwelleth in the secret place of the most High shall abide under the shadow of the Almighty" and, consequently, be able to say, "God is my refuge and my fortress."

Bezaleel and Aholiab lived under the Law as minors; they delighted in types, mere shadows. We in Christ today bask in the noontide of grace as adults; we glory in realities. Let's hasten on, therefore, to know Christ in the fulness of the Spirit.

III. NUMBERS—SEVEN REFERENCES

11:17 *I will take of the Spirit which is upon thee. and will put it upon them.*

11:25 *And the LORD came down in a cloud, and spake unto him, and took of the Spirit that was upon him, and gave it unto the seventy elders: and it came to pass. that, when the Spirit rested upon them. they prophesied. and did not cease.*

11:26 *But there remained two of the men in the camp, . . .
and the Spirit rested upon them, and they were of them
that were written, but went not out unto the tabernacle:
and they prophesied in the camp.*

11:29 *And Moses said . . . would to God that all the LORD'S
people were prophets, and that the LORD would put his
Spirit upon them!*

God took of the divine power and energy which rested
upon Moses and endowed the elders with a portion of the
same gifts, especially that of prophecy. "It" refers to the power,
not to the person, of the Spirit. Scripture rightly translated
never calls the Spirit "it." The Authorized Version is in error
in passages such as Romans 8:16. The seventy were empowered
in union with Moses as he was empowered in union with God:
There is *one* fellowship.

The Spirit is infinite and can't be diminished in a life,
except by sin; the more one shares His power with others.
the more abundantly he enjoys it. One fire in Moses started
seventy other fires. Here is a pattern for spreading divine fire.

In the expression "they prophesied" (vs. 26), we have the
first mention of this kind of prophesying. Such prophets became,
for the time being, mouthpieces for the audible utterance of
thoughts which were not theirs but the Spirit's.

Eldad and Medad, men who were enrolled as elders, didn't
go out to the tabernacle where the other elders prophesied.
We're not told why. Nevertheless, the Spirit came upon them
in the camp and they, too, prophesied. Joshua, jealous for
the honor and authority of Moses, protested. But Moses, the
meekest of men, was neither selfish nor sectarian. (Cp. Mark
9:38, 39.)

This incident reminds us of one among the early Moravians
at Herrnhut, Germany, August 13, 1727. "Zinzendorf, who
gives us the deepest and most vivid account of this wonderful
occurrence, says it was a sense of the nearness of Christ bestowed in a single moment, upon all the members that were
present; and it was so unanimous that two members at work

twenty miles away, unaware that the meeting was being held, became at the same time deeply conscious of the same blessing" (Greenfield).

24:2   *And Balaam lifted up his eyes, and he saw Israel abiding in his tents according to their tribes; and the Spirit of God came upon him.*

Here we have another instance of the gift of prophecy, and this time to an unconsecrated man whom the Spirit later deserted. (Cp. the use of the gift by the carnal Corinthians in I Cor. 14:29–33.) Eventually, Balaam became a "soothsayer" (Josh. 13:22), and today he is screaming with anguish in the prison of lost spirits. "God used his mouth but touched not his heart." The dangers of becoming disciples of Balaam are real. It will not do merely to know and to teach the Word of God. Be warned concerning those who forsake the right way and go astray—"having followed the way of Balaam the son of Beor, who loved the hire of wrong-doing" (II Pet. 2:15, A.S.V.).

27:18   *And the LORD said unto Moses, Take thee Joshua the son of Nun, a man in whom is the Spirit, and lay thine hand upon him.*

The indwelling Spirit's ability to quicken, shape and qualify Joshua to succeed Moses is clear evidence that He is a person. This reference should be studied in connection with Deuteronomy 34:9.

IV. DEUTERONOMY—ONE REFERENCE

34:9   *And Joshua the son of Nun was full of the Spirit of wisdom; for Moses had laid his hands upon him: and the children of Israel harkened unto him, and did as the LORD commanded Moses.*

This last mention of the Spirit in the Pentateuch sounds the keynote again, life at its Spirit-filled best. Joshua received, by the laying on of hands, the spiritual gift of wisdom for the leadership of Israel. Also. Moses publicly committed to Joshua his authority, not as a prophet, but as a leader.

Praise God, the very first section of the Bible teaches us that humble believers can be filled with the Spirit, that bramble bushes can blaze (Ex. 3:2).

2

The Spirit in the Books of History and Experience—Divine Fellowship

IN THESE BOOKS, as in the Pentateuch, the Spirit is seen rather as the divine Agent and Energy than as a distinct personality in the Godhead. He appears as God himself, active and energetic on man's behalf. The New Testament will show great progress beyond the Old concerning the doctrine of the Spirit; nevertheless, these passages thrill the soul. Men became mighty when the Spirit of the Lord came upon them. Some Old Testament saints reappear among the heroes of Hebrews 11.

Seven books in this section don't mention the Spirit: Joshua, Ruth, Ezra, Esther, Proverbs, Ecclesiastes, and Song of Solomon. The other ten contain thirty-three references: Judges, seven; I Samuel, seven; II Samuel, one; I Kings, two; II Kings, one; I Chronicles, two; II Chronicles, four; Nehemiah, two; Job, three; and Psalms, four.

I. JUDGES—SEVEN REFERENCES

3:10 *And the Spirit of the LORD came upon him [Othniel], and he judged Israel, and went out to war.*

Here the Spirit bestirs himself against apostasy: He uses men of faith to do something about it. Remember, a public official or soldier "is a minister of God" (Rom. 13:4), and that he, like Othniel, always needs supernatural help.

6:34 *But the Spirit of the LORD came upon Gideon.*

The Spirit "clothed himself with" Gideon (Heb.). (Compare the same idea in I Chron. 12:18, II Chron. 24:20.) The Spirit always stands ready to enable willing hearts to do the will of God. Dangers and difficulties never become too great for those who are filled with the Spirit, filled with supernatural courage and wisdom.

11:29   *Then the Spirit of the LORD came upon Jephthah.*

Hebrews 11:32 enrolls Jephthah among the Old Testament heroes of faith—this despite the fact that he was "the son of another woman" (Judg. 11:2). Faith received the Spirit's mighty aid, and after his noble words failed to avert war, the Spirit came upon him for waging war splendidly. God honors faith, let us note incidentally, even more than He honors consecration.

13:25   *The Spirit of the LORD began to move him [Samson]*
        at times in the camp of Dan.

From the very beginning the Spirit urged and impelled Samson to mighty acts, though by fits and starts, developing in him, not the gift of prophecy, but the spirit of patriotism.

14:6   *And the Spirit of the LORD came mightily upon him*
       [Samson], and he rent him [a young lion] as he would
       have rent a kid, and he had nothing in his hand.

Spirit-filled Samson killed a young lion with his bare hands. What dauntless courage, and what strength of body!

14:19   *And the Spirit of the LORD came upon him [Samson],*
        and he went down to Ashkelon, and slew thirty men of
        them, and took their spoil.

15:14   *And when he [Samson] came to Lehi, the Philistines*
        shouted against him: and the Spirit of the LORD came
        mightily upon him, and the cords that were upon his
        armor became as flax that was burnt with fire, and his
        bands loosed from off his hands.

Later, Samson slew a thousand men with "a new jawbone of an ass." Apparently, his consecration as a Nazarite was the condition of the Spirit's power in his life; because when he forfeited his Nazarite separation. "the LORD departed from him" (Judg. 16:20).

II. I AND II SAMUEL—EIGHT REFERENCES

10:6 *And the Spirit of the LORD will come upon thee [Saul], and thou shalt prophesy with them, and shalt be turned into another man.*

10:10 *And when they came thither to the hill, behold, a company of prophets met him; and the Spirit of God came upon him, and he prophesied among them.*

Saul received the power of the Spirit to prophesy in a condition of ecstatic inspiration. but he didn't receive the grace of the Spirit to change his heart. Also the Spirit of God came upon him as a seal and pledge of divine help for the ruler of God's people. That is, God suddenly endowed him with ability to act in a manner far superior to his previous character and habits. Saul the peasant became Saul the king.

11:6 *And the Spirit of God came upon Saul when he heard those tidings, and his anger was kindled greatly.*

(The American Standard Version adds "mightily" after "came.") In this case, then. empowering meant to Saul a flash of righteous anger. A horrible threat (v. 2) by Nahash the Ammonite "lay for a reproach upon all Israel." This fanned the fire of mighty wrath kindled by God's Spirit. So Saul stepped forth to fulfill his royal calling to deliver his people. God's Spirit will help our leaders today, too. Let us pray for them (I Tim. 2:1, 2).

16:13 *Then Samuel took the horn of oil, and anointed him in the midst of his brethren: and the Spirit of the LORD came upon David from that day forward.*

From that day David began to grow and develop marvelously, becoming "skilful in playing, and a mighty man of valor, and a man of war, and prudent in speech, and a comely person; and Jehovah was with him" (16:18).

16:14 *But the Spirit of the LORD departed from Saul, and an evil spirit from the LORD troubled him.*

How unspeakably sad! Note the unchangeable sequences: "And Saul was afraid of David because the LORD was with him, and was departed from Saul" (I Sam. 18:12); he said, "God is departed from me and answereth me no more, neither by prophets, nor by dreams" (I Sam. 28:15); "an evil spirit from God troubled him"—that is, God's judicial action sent a demon into his soul (I Sam. 16:14).

19:20 *The Spirit of God was upon the messengers of Saul, and they also prophesied.*

19:23 *And the Spirit of God was upon him also, and he went on, and prophesied.*

Saul sent three successive but unsuccessful posses to arrest David, and the spiritual power of Samuel's school of the prophets made temporary prophets of them, posse by posse. When Saul undertook to do the job personally, he himself was so empowered that he not only prophesied again, as he had done years before, but he even "stripped off his clothes also, and prophesied before Samuel in like manner, and lay down naked all day and all that night." He lay in his undergarment unconscious, so completely was he overcome by the ecstasy. In the New Testament days of fuller light, Paul explains, "the spirits of the prophets are subject to the prophets; for God is not a God of confusion, but of peace" (I Cor. 14:32, 33). Despite this final brief influence of the Spirit on Saul, he became guilty of suicide (I Sam. 31:4).

23:2 (II Sam.) *The Spirit of the Lord spake by me [David], and his word was in my tongue.*

Here we have a beautiful example of the "inspiration of God," in which "literature," the letter, becomes "Scripture," the letter in-breathed by God. David, the sweet psalmist of

Israel, affirms that his last psalm (II Sam. 23:2–4) "was not the product of his own mind, the invention of his own poetic genius, or the result of his own penetrating sagacity; it was the inhabitation of the divine Spirit. whose extraordinary influence had qualified him to be an inspired writer, supplying the matter and enabling him to select appropriate language, a fitting vehicle for the form of sacred song."

III. I AND II KINGS—THREE REFERENCES

18:12 *The Spirit of the LORD shall carry thee [Elijah] whither I know not.*

(Cp. II Kings 2:16 and Acts 8:39.) Obadiah evidently believed that, for the past three and one-half years. the Spirit had kept Elijah from arrest by Ahab's secret police. Meditate on this story in I Kings 18 and ask God to make you an Elijah rather than an Obadiah. The power of the Spirit will make the difference.

22:24 *Which way went the Spirit of the LORD from me to speak unto thee [Micaiah]?*

This question was asked of Micaiah, a true prophet of the Lord, by Zedekiah, a lying prophet of wicked King Ahab. Ahab's prophet claimed that he spoke by the Spirit of Jehovah, and when Micaiah contradicted him, he struck Micaiah on the cheek, saying, in effect, "How is it that the Spirit of God speaks one thing by me. another by you?"

2:16 (II Kings) *... let them go [Elisha], we pray thee, and seek thy master [Elijah]: lest peradventure the Spirit of the LORD hath taken him up, and cast him upon some mountain, or into some valley.*

The flesh vainly tries to help the Spirit. These unbelieving students reveal their ignorance of the ways of the Spirit. (Cp. Mark 12:24.)

IV. I AND II CHRONICLES—SIX REFERENCES

12:18 *Then the Spirit came upon Amasai, who was chief of the captains, and he said, Thine are we, David, and on thy side, thou son of Jesse: peace, peace be unto thee, and peace be on thy helper; for thy God helpeth thee. Then David received them, and made them captains of the band.*

The Spirit "clothed himself with" Amasai. (Cp. Judg. 6:34 and II Chron. 24:20.) Evidently David suspected the Benjamites until, by the secret impulse of the Spirit, Amasai convinced him to the contrary. The Spirit will show us today, also, on whose side to stand—who is being helped by God.

28:12 *Then David gave to Solomon ... the pattern of all that he had by the Spirit.*

The pattern of Solomon's temple came by the Spirit. Remember II Samuel 23:2 (already quoted); then ponder verse 19: "All this, said David, the Lord made me understand in writing by his hand upon me. even all the works of this pattern."

15:1 (II Chron.) *And the Spirit of God came upon Azariah the son of Obed.*

Azariah, controlled by the Spirit, warned and encouraged King Asa: "Be ye strong therefore. and let not your hands be weak: for your work shall be rewarded."

18:23 (Same as I Kings 22:24, which see.)

20:14 *Then upon Jahaziel ... came the Spirit of the LORD in the midst of the congregation.*

In answer to King Jehoshaphat's prayer for help in a great crisis, the Spirit used a prophet who is mentioned nowhere else in Scripture, to give peace and assurance of deliverance.

24:20 *And the Spirit of God came upon Zechariah.*

Here again, as in Judges 6:34 and I Chronicles 12:18, the Spirit "clothed himself with" a man. Thus empowered, Zechariah denounced the transgressions and apostasy of God's people, and paid with his life for the precious privilege of being the Spirit's mouthpiece: he was stoned "at the commandment of the king in the court of the house of the LORD" (v. 21). (See Matt. 23:35.)

V. NEHEMIAH—TWO REFERENCES

9:20 *Thou gavest thy good Spirit to instruct them.*

This is a reference to the distribution to the seventy elders of the spiritual gifts enjoyed by Moses (Num. 11). (To say that God's Spirit is "good" is to suggest that He is holy; however, the Old Testament never uses the phrase: "the Holy Spirit." The epithet "holy" in Ps. 51:11 and Isa. 63:10, 11 signifies "the Spirit of God's holiness.") Instruction by the Spirit is nowhere else distinctly mentioned in the Old Testament.

9:30 *Yet many years didst thou forbear them, and testifiedst against them by thy Spirit in thy prophets.*

God's faithful and patient Spirit warned the ten tribes, beginning with I Kings 14:15, for about 260 years and the remaining two tribes for 135 years longer. (Cp. II Kings 17:13 and II Chron. 36:15, 16). Nehemiah acknowledges that this enormous guilt of resisting the good Spirit of God was the reason for their captivities.

VI. JOB—THREE REFERENCES

26:13 *By his Spirit he hath garnished the heavens.*

God's Spirit sends both storm and calm; He has all power. God's method in the established order of nature is to do things *by His Spirit.* That gorgeous sunrise or sunset, those resplendently beautiful snowflakes, those majestic mountains, those glorious colors of the rainbow—all are beauties of our Lord Jesus applied by the Spirit's heavenly paintbrush. Len G. Broughton tells of a young woman whose life was changed by the realization that nature's beauty is but a reflection of Christ's beauty:

Some years ago we had in our church one of the loveliest young women I ever knew; well-educated, wonderfully attractive and beautiful. And, oh, how the devil did bid for that woman! She knew the devil was after her. He wanted to win her to the social life of the city; he wanted to get her in every card group possible and every other thing that would waste her time and her attractive personality; but there was something in her that pulled the other way. She saw how in service for God and humanity she might make her life count for more of good. It was to her a real pull, a struggle.

In the midst of all this pull and struggle she went to the country to spend a weekend with her mother. One afternoon she went down into the meadow, and as she returned along by the side of the fence she saw a beautiful flower, a dog fennel.

"What a pretty thing!" she said to herself.

She started to pluck it, but suddenly remembered the odor of it was bad. She sat down by the side of the road and looked at that flower as it waved in the breezes just enough to reveal its beauty. She decided to pluck it, odor or no odor. Then she pulled it apart, and at the base of the petals saw the beautiful blending of colors that distinguishes the blossom of a dog fennel.

While she looked at it, she declared she heard a voice speak sweetly, lovingly, "My child, Christ painted that flower; it is His; and if you will let Him, He will paint your heart and life with thoughts and deeds of beautiful service for earth and heaven."

She realized that this was the voice of the Spirit of Christ. Then, she got down on her knees by the roadside and got to know Christ in the power of the Spirit. She was brought by the Spirit to see the beauty and glory of Christ everywhere, even in a dog fennel.

27:3 *All the while my breath is in me, and the Spirit of God is in my nostrils.*

33:4 *The Spirit of God hath made me, and the breath of the Almighty hath given me life.*

Job claims to be in his right mind in spite of his sufferings. This is not a reference to the indwelling of the Holy Spirit, but rather to life itself—to the creative activity of the Spirit and to the "impersonal life-force from God in all men" (Wright). (Cp. Gen. 2:7.)

VII. PSALMS—FOUR REFERENCES

51:11 *Cast me not away from thy presence; and take not thy holy Spirit from me.*

Does David here recall that "the Spirit of the LORD departed from Saul"? (I Sam. 16:14). Anyway, he confesses his own transgressions, iniquities and sins; he begs God for forgiveness, cleansing and restoration. It's not a question of salvation, but of fellowship and service (II Sam. 12:13; Rom. 4:6–8). The presence of God by His Spirit means cleansing, restoration, joy and usefulness. David will then teach transgressors the ways of God and sinners will be converted unto Him.

104:30 *Thou sendest forth thy Spirit, they are created: and thou renewest the face of the earth.*

God, by His Spirit, not only created all life, but He thus also sustains it. By His Spirit He is immanent. "All existence derives—in the present tense—from Him. and exists in Him." Its life depends upon His life, moment by moment. This is true of physical life in unsaved people as well as saved people. All men are dependent upon God. by His Spirit. for every breath. J. Stafford Wright illustrates immanence:

> God, the Creator, is different from a human Creator. If I make a piece of furniture, its continued existence does not depend upon my own existence. When I die, the piece of furniture will still be here; my life is not in it. But, if the Bible is correct, the relation of God to the universe has in it something more. God Himself sustains

the universe in existence, so that if it were possible for God to die, at that moment the universe would fall into nothingness. . . . The universe is not in any sense necessary for the existence of God, but God is necessary for the continued existence of the universe.[1]

Compare Genesis 2:7; Acts 17:27, 28; Colossians 1:27; and Hebrews 1:3.

139:7 *Whither shall I go from thy Spirit? or whither shall I flee from thy presence?*

By His Spirit God, a spiritual Being, is present everywhere. This leaves no place for the sinner to hide (Amos 9:2; Jer. 23:24).

143:10 *Teach me to do thy will; for thou art my God: thy Spirit is good; lead me in the land of uprightness.*

"Let thy good Spirit lead me" (mgn., A.S.V.). Thus David prayed for the leadership of God's gracious and merciful Spirit in times of danger. (Cp. Neh. 9:20.) God's good Spirit is our only Guide into "the land of uprightness"—where we neither stumble nor are obstructed in our happy progress.

These thirty-three references in the books of history and experience have given us good illustrations of the Spirit's ability to bring men into fellowship with God, some into sweeter fellowship than others. They portray the Spirit wonderfully efficient, even in Old Testament days, in making God real in human experience. Since Pentecost the Spirit has, in a richer, fuller way, made believers flaming cressets in this dark world (Mt. 5:14-16; Lk. 12:35; Phil. 2:15).

3

The Spirit in the Prophetic Books— Divine Inspiration

ACCORDING TO THE PRINCIPLE of development in Scripture, the doctrine of the Spirit in the prophetic books, compared with the truth He reveals about himself in the previous books, makes marked progress. Up to this point we've seen Him primarily as the Author of divine power which comes on particular individuals for the performance of special duties. In the prophetic books we learn more of His work as Author of divine inspiration and revelation.

Progress is also made in relation to man's spiritual life— good or bad. Previously, the Spirit had to do mainly with the material universe and man's official duties. The Psalms introduced the moral aspects of the Spirit's relation to man; the prophets develop this idea. Watch also for the prophetic aspects of the Spirit's ministry in preparation for the Messiah, and the growing evidence that the Spirit is a distinct Person in the Godhead.

Nine of these books don't mention the Spirit—Jeremiah. Lamentations, Hosea, Amos, Obadiah, Jonah, Nahum, Habakkuk, and Zephaniah—but this does not mean that these prophets were less spiritual or less inspired than others. It is characteristic of the Spirit seldom to refer to himself. Inspiration is recognized by other standards. There are forty-four references to the Spirit in the other eight prophetic books: seventeen in Isaiah. fourteen in Ezekiel, five in Daniel, two in Joel, two in Micah, one in Haggai, two in Zechariah, and one in Malachi.

I. ISAIAH—SEVENTEEN REFERENCES

W. H. Griffith Thomas has pointed out that Isaiah reveals an almost complete doctrine of the Spirit.[1] The Spirit is a person· perfect, 11:2; omniscient, 40:13; equal with Christ, 48:16; Deity, 59:21. The Spirit works: giving guidance and victory, 30:1; 59:19; 63:14; restoring national Israel, 32:15, 44:3; exercising divine judgments, 34:16; empowering the Messiah, 42:1; 61:1; and delivering Israel from Egypt, 63:11.

11:2 *And the Spirit of the LORD shall rest upon him, the Spirit of wisdom and understanding, the Spirit of counsel and might, the Spirit of knowledge and of the fear of the LORD.*

Note the seven marks of perfection, and compare Isaiah 42:1 and 61:1 for the Spirit's empowering of Christ. The words "shall rest upon him" signified that the Spirit should abide permanently upon the Messiah. Provision was made at Calvary and Pentecost for the Spirit to rest likewise upon all who believe on Christ glorified, by virtue of their oneness and union with Him (John 7:38).

30:1 *Woe to the rebellious children, saith the LORD, that take counsel, but not of me; and that cover with a covering, but not of my Spirit, that they may add sin to sin.*

God's people always "add sin to sin" when they seek help from people rather than from their God. (See I Sam. 23:2-4 and II Sam. 5:19, 23.)

32:15 *Until the Spirit be poured upon us from on high, and the wilderness be a fruitful field, and the fruitful field be counted for a forest.*

This promise to Israel (and through her to the Gentiles) of future spiritual and material abundance is repeated in Isaiah 44:3, made everlasting in Isaiah 59:21, and reaffirmed in Eze-

kiel 39:29. Israel's realization awaits the Millennium; many will
be filled with the Spirit then. Doubtless Isaiah and Ezekiel knew
of Joel's fuller prophecy (2:28–30).

Pentecost was an earnest of this gracious promise; the full
accomplishment belongs to future Israel. F. C. Jennings points
out that this verse involves both Pentecost and Israel's blessings
after the rapture of the Church.

> As the land flourished under a twofold blessing of
> rain, the early and the latter, so there shall be a corres-
> ponding twofold pouring out of the Holy Spirit upon its
> people. The first, or the early, rain fell at Pentecost. . . .
> God, the Holy Spirit, came to this earth at Pentecost, nor
> has He ever returned to Heaven whence He came. . . .
> There *can* therefore be no second effusion during this
> dispensation, for He is already here. . . . When Israel is
> restored to her land, and her remnant to Jehovah, then
> there shall be a second effusion of the Spirit as here told,
> and the land shall bloom in accord with it.[2]

34:16 *Seek ye out of the book of the LORD, and read: no
one of these shall fail, none shall want her mate: for my
mouth hath commanded, and his Spirit hath gathered them.*

Not one jot or one tittle shall fail of all that the Spirit dic-
tates by the mouth of God's prophet.

40:13 *Who hath directed the Spirit of the LORD, or being his
counsellor hath taught him?*

The Spirit is omniscient; no one is qualified to teach Him.
He, not man, is the Counselor. That is, no man instructed the
Spirit in creation: man did not then exist.

42:1 *Behold, my servant, whom I uphold; mine elect, in
whom my soul delighteth; I have put my Spirit upon him;
he shall bring forth judgment to the Gentiles.*

Isaiah denounced Israel as a rebellious and faithless servant,
but called upon the whole world, both Jew and Gentile, to behold
God's true and perfect Servant who was utterly obedient (John

4:34; Heb. 3:2; 10:7). God put His Spirit on the Man Christ Jesus that He might provide redemption for all men (Matt. 3:16; Heb. 9:14; Luke 4:18, 19).

44:3	*For I will pour water upon him that is thirsty, and floods upon the dry ground: I will pour my Spirit upon thy seed, and my blessing upon thy offspring.*

Here the promise of Isaiah 32:15 is repeated and made more personal. As cold water slakes exhausting thirst, and refreshing rains reinvigorate dying vegetation, so does the empowering of the Spirit cause vitality and spiritual prosperity. Are you thirsty, really thirsty? This "water" is poured upon the thirsty *only* (John 7:37–39).

48:16	*And now the Lord GOD, and his Spirit, hath sent me.*

The American Standard Version reads: "And now the Lord Jehovah hath sent me, and his Spirit." The Father sent Christ to provide, and the Spirit to apply, redemption. Note the equality of the Spirit with Christ, and the distinct persons in the Godhead.

59:19	*When the enemy shall come in like a flood, the Spirit of the LORD shall lift up a standard against him.*

The Lord shall overcome Israel's enemies in the future, when Christ returns. And until that time, the Spirit, if depended upon, will give us victory, too. He will, for instance, suggest the very Scriptures necessary for us to quote to Satan in time of temptation (Matt. 4:4; Eph. 6:17). Note again, in the Isaiah verse, evidence of the Spirit's distinct personality.

59:21	*As for me, this is my covenant with them, saith the LORD; my Spirit that is upon thee, and my words which I have put in thy mouth, shall not depart out of thy mouth, nor out of the mouth of thy seed, nor out of the mouth of thy seed's seed, saith the LORD, from henceforth and for ever.*

Abundant spiritual blessings, especially the Scriptures, shall abide permanently for Christ, His seed, and His seed's seed, whether during the Church age or the Millennium. All of God's treasures for this world are hidden in Christ (Col. 2:3, 10). Note here evidence of the deity of the Spirit.

61:1 *The Spirit of the Lord GOD is upon me; because the LORD hath anointed me to preach good tidings unto the meek; he hath sent me to bind up the broken-hearted, to proclaim liberty to the captives, and the opening of the prison to them that are bound.*

The title, "the Spirit of the Lord GOD," indicates the Spirit's relationship to the Father—the Father anointed His righteous Servant, Christ, at His baptism (Matt. 3:16, 17; Acts 10:38. Cp. Isa. 11:2; 42:1; and 59:21). Note the clearest evidence yet that the Spirit is a distinct Person in the Triune Godhead.

63:10 *But they rebelled, and vexed his holy Spirit: therefore he was turned to be their enemy, and he fought against them.*

63:11 *Where is he that put his holy Spirit within him?*

63:14 *As a beast goeth down into the valley, the Spirit of the LORD caused him to rest: so didst thou lead thy people, to make thyself a glorious name.*

Israel's rebellions began in the wilderness and continued until God sent the divided nation into captivity (II Chron. 36:16). In captivity Israel remembered God's past blessings and longed for Him who had sent His holy Spirit among them, who had caused them to rest, as the cattle that go down into the valley (cp. A.S.V.).

The epithet "holy" represents God's Spirit of holiness. (Cp. Ps. 51:11.) F. C. Jennings suggests that "to the pious Jew the term 'Spirit' seems to have referred when thus used to the realized presence of God. . . . It is the felt, realized presence of God who is Spirit, and in our chapter is a parallel idea to 'the angel of His presence.'" [3]

Thus the activities of the Spirit reveal our God as a spiritual Being, an infinite, plural personality, who can fellowship with other persons. He created and prepared the earth to be inhabited by persons—by us. He intervenes in our affairs for our good. He has a great purpose of redemption, a Redeemer, and an Agent to apply that redemption. Bless the Lord, O our souls!

If some of the Spirit's activities seem to us abnormal, let's hasten to admit that it is only a "seeming." Let us always bear in mind that "the manifestation of the Spirit," whether it be in Old or New Testament times, is always given for the profit of all (I Cor. 12:7). Whatever the Spirit did then, is doing now, or shall ever do, is for the benefit of those concerned. He is all powerful; He is gracious and loving. Let Him have His way!

II. EZEKIEL—FOURTEEN REFERENCES

2:2 *And the Spirit entered into me when he spake unto me, and set me upon my feet, that I heard him that spake unto me.*

This citation and ten others concern Ezekiel personally. Three additional ones relate to Israel in the future. Here the Spirit enabled Ezekiel to stand up like a soldier and receive his commission. Ezekiel had been upon his face; the Spirit set him upon his feet. The attitude of awe and adoration was changed into that of expectant service and manifest courage.

3:12 *Then the Spirit took me up, and I heard behind me a voice of a great rushing, saying, Blessed be the glory of the LORD from his place.*

Apparently the Spirit actually lifted Ezekiel off the ground, and, as he turned his face toward Tel-abib, ready to warn the hard-headed captives, he heard "the voice of a great rushing"—evidently the noise of the wings of the Living Creatures, who were praising the glory of God. (Cp. Acts 2:2, where Spirit-filled witnesses magnified the Christ of God.)

3:14 *So the Spirit lifted me up, and took me away, and I went in bitterness, in the heat of my spirit; but the hand of the LORD was strong upon me.*

The Spirit transports Ezekiel to Tel-abib for a bitter task, but the hand of his covenant-keeping God sustains him and urges him forward. For other instances of men carried bodily by the Spirit, read I Kings 18:12; II Kings 2:16; Mark 1:12; and Acts 8:39.

3:24 *Then the Spirit entered into me, and set me upon my feet, and spake with me, and said unto me, Go, shut thyself within thy house.*

This is the second time the Spirit entered into Ezekiel (see 2:2). The first enabled the prophet to receive a commission to speak for God; this enables him to be silent for God.

8:3 *The Spirit lifted me up between the earth and the heaven, and brought me in the visions of God to Jerusalem.*

In this instance Ezekiel was not literally lifted up, as in Ezekiel 3:12, 14 and 11:1. For other such transportations, see Ezekiel 11:24; 37:1; and 43:5. Also compare II Corinthians 12:2; Revelation 4:2; 17:3; and 21:10.

11:1 *Moreover the Spirit lifted me up, and brought me unto the east gate of the LORD'S house.*

This again is literal. Solomon's temple was not destroyed until 586 B.C.; Ezekiel experienced this physical transportation before that date.

11:5 *And the Spirit of the LORD fell upon me, and said unto me, Speak: Thus saith the LORD.*

Righteous indignation was aroused in Ezekiel by the Spirit at the contempt of Jehovah, shown by the scorners. Also note that the Spirit, a person, is Author of divine revelation and inspiration.

11:24 *Afterwards the Spirit took me up, and brought me in a vision by the Spirit of God into Chaldea, to them of the captivity. So the vision that I had seen went up from me.*

For the stages of the departure of the Shekinah from Jerusalem, see Ezekiel 8:4; 9:3; 10:4, 18; and for the return to the Millennial temple, see 43:2–5.

36:27   *And I will put my Spirit within you, and cause you to walk in my statutes, and ye shall keep my judgments, and do them.*

That this verse refers to the Spirit's indwelling of Jewish believers during the Millennium is proved by verse 28. It can't be restricted to the Church.

37:1   *The hand of the LORD was upon me, and carried me out in the Spirit of the LORD, and set me down in the midst of the valley which was full of bones.*

The Spirit gives Ezekiel a glimpse of God's method of Israel's full restoration. Scofield gives the key to Ezekiel 37:

> Having announced (Ezekiel 36:24–38) the restoration of the nation, Jehovah now gives in vision and symbol the method of its accomplishment. Verse 11 gives the clue. The 'bones' are the whole house of Israel who shall then be living. The 'graves' are the nations where they dwell.[4]

37:14   *And shall put my Spirit in you, and ye shall live and I shall place you in your land: then shall ye know that I the LORD have spoken it, saith the LORD.*

For the Spirit's ministry to future Israel, see Isaiah 32:15; 44:3; Joel 2:28, 29; Zechariah 12:10; Acts 2:18, 19; and 15:13–18.

39:29   *Neither will I hide my face any more from them: for I have poured out my Spirit upon the house of Israel, saith the Lord God.*

Pentecost was an earnest of this—"the early rain"; whereas "the latter rain" is yet to come on Israel.

43:5 *So the Spirit took me up, and brought me into the inner court; and, behold, the glory of the LORD filled the house.*

God's presence in the cloud of glory fills the Millennial temple. (See remarks on Ezekiel 11:24.)

III. DANIEL—FIVE REFERENCES

4:8 *But at the last Daniel came in before me, whose name was Belteshazzar, according to the name of my god, and in whom is the Spirit of the holy gods: and before him I told the dream.*

Doubtless, Nebuchadnezzar had no correct idea of God's Spirit, but he did know that Daniel possessed a spirit different from that of his gods. We know who gave Daniel that wholesome spirit of supernatural wisdom, the Spirit of Jehovah. Consequently, we capitalize *spirit* in these instances.

4:9 *Because I know that the Spirit of the holy gods is in thee.*

Nebuchadnezzar, a heathen. believed in many gods, all of whom were unholy; they made "no pretension to purity, even in the opinion of their votaries." All he knew about Daniel's God was that His Spirit was different; in ignorance he spoke of "gods" in the *plural*. Or. some translate, "the Spirit of the holy God."

4:18 *Thou art able; for the Spirit of the holy gods is in thee.*

5:11 *There is a man in thy kingdom, in whom is the Spirit of the holy gods.*

5:14 *I have even heard of thee, that the Spirit of the gods is in thee, and that light and understanding and excellent wisdom is found in thee.*

Many in Babylon came under the power of Daniel's Spirit-filled testimony. We today, like Joseph and Daniel in those faraway days. can by the Spirit's mighty aid. maintain good testimonies despite the circumstances. Here's an opportunity for men and women away from home in the service of their country.

IV. JOEL—TWO REFERENCES

2:28, 29 *And it shall come to pass afterward, that I will pour out my Spirit upon all flesh; and your sons and your daughters shall prophesy, your old men shall dream dreams, your young men shall see visions:* (29) *And also upon the servants and upon the handmaids in those days will I pour out my Spirit.*

What a wonderful promise, found in the oldest of the writing prophets! It has a twofold fulfillment. In the sense of "the early rain," it was fulfilled on the day of Pentecost. In the sense of "the latter rain," it will be fulfilled at the time of Christ's second coming.

"All flesh" signifies that Gentiles as well as Jews shall enjoy this abundance of spiritual rain. (See comments on Isa. 32:15 and Ezek. 39:29.) "Peter saw in the events of his day an earnest that God would yet completely bring to pass all that Joel prophesied" (Charles L. Feinberg).

V. MICAH—TWO REFERENCES

2:7 *O thou that art named the house of Jacob, is the Spirit of the LORD straightened? are these his doings? do not my words do good to him that walketh uprightly?*

It's not the delight of the Spirit to threaten God's people with chastening and shame. Neither is He straightened that He cannot help them. Iniquity, evil and rebellion make rebuke and chastening necessary, and blessing impossible. Micah's Spirit-filled ministry, like Paul's, cuts both ways (II Cor. 2:16).

3:8 *But truly I am full of power by the Spirit of the LORD, and of judgment, and of might, to declare unto Jacob his transgression, and to Israel his sin.*

Fearless confession in the face of false prophets! The Spirit enabled Micah to exert a holy influence, and to pronounce impartial sentence upon God's enemies and on His backslidden people. with a courage that could not be bought off with a dainty meal. Such a ministry stood in glaring contrast to that of most of the prophets of Micah's day (Micah 3:5).

VI. HAGGAI—ONE REFERENCE

2:5   *According to the word that I covenanted with you when ye came out of Egypt, so my Spirit remaineth among you: fear ye not.*

God's Spirit ever remains with His people. even though they be a mere remnant. He may not work as He once did, but He will use all who are willing to be made useable. Such were Haggai and Zechariah, to whom God said. "Fear ye not." (He says "Fear not" or "Be not afraid" to us 125 times in Scripture!)

VII. ZECHARIAH—TWO REFERENCES

4:6   *Then he answered and spake unto me, saying, This is the word of the LORD unto Zerubbabel, saying, Not by might, nor by power, but by my Spirit, saith the LORD of hosts.*

This oft-quoted verse reveals God's secret of victory in any dispensation or situation. Study the context: (1) A testimony to the world can be sustained *not by human means* but only by God's Spirit. verses 1–6. (2) All obstacles disappear before faith exercised in the power of God's Spirit, verses 7–9. (3) Small things in man's eyes are often great things in God's sight. verse 10. (4) God supplies the Spirit through His "anointed ones." verses 11–14. (5) Christ is His "Anointed One" for us today (Acts 10:38).

7:12   *Yea, they made their hearts as an adamant stone, lest they should hear the law, and the words which the LORD of hosts hath sent in his Spirit by the former prophets: therefore came a great wrath from the LORD of hosts.*

God's Spirit had given inspired messages to the prophets. The former prophets—Samuel, Ahijah, Jehu, Hanani, Elijah, Elisha, Joel, Jonah, Hosea, Iddo, Shemiah, Micaiah, and even Huldah the prophetess—all had warned in the power of the Spirit. Notice, again, that the Spirit is the Agent of divine inspiration.

VIII. MALACHI—ONE REFERENCE

2:15 *And did not he make one? Yet had he the residue of the Spirit.*

God was not limited that He could not have created and blessed other nations by His Spirit, just as He did Israel. He had the rest of the Spirit's power which could have been used to choose other nations. Yet He made only one, Israel.

Thus, with a key reference, we close our study of God the Spirit in the Old Testament. From the time He stopped striving with the race as a whole (Gen. 6:3), He worked with one nation, Israel, only. He made Israel an inspired, supernatural people in order to produce through them the Messiah. God himself wrought *by His Spirit*.

To summarize: (1) We've seen God himself active in His creation by His Spirit, giving life to the natural order, the animate order, and the human order. (2) Likewise, we've beheld Him calling and training His chosen nation, Israel, particularly to produce through them the Messiah. He bestowed special powers on their leaders, inspired their prophets and blessed their worship—all by His Spirit and chiefly to give the world a Saviour.

Therefore, the doctrine of the Spirit in the Old Testament "is really the doctrine of a Divine immanence placed side by side with the predominate Old Testament thought of the Divine transcendence" (Thomas). Thus, we've been prepared for "the doctrine of Divine providence and the specific New Testament idea of the indwelling of the Spirit of God" on the basis of Christ's work at Calvary—God's full answer to man's infinite need.

Before passing on to the New Testament, however, we may say that no light on the subject of the Holy Spirit was given in the period between the Testaments. Only Scripture gives us light. and God gave no additional Scripture during this period.

In the OT Apocrypha and in Josephus the references to the Spirit are nearly always echoes of a long-past age when the Spirit was active among men. In no particular is the contrast between the canonical and non-canonical literature more striking than in the teaching as to the Spirit of God.[5]

4

The Spirit in the Synoptic Gospels—
Divine Presence

THE NEW TESTAMENT contains 284 direct references to the Spirit, as compared with 91 in the Old. Every New Testament book speaks of the Spirit, except three short and personal ones: Philemon, II and III John. This is true despite the fact that the Spirit never unnecessarily calls attention to himself. It's not the number of times we read of Him but the experience for which He stands that counts. He stands for Christ in experience, God active in redemption. So we enter the New Testament with more eagerness than we did the Old.

Although the record of the Holy Spirit in the Synoptic Gospels is given by men who wrote after the unique event of Pentecost, the view of Him is more like that in the Old Testament than the view in John's and Paul's epistles. According to the Synoptists, even Christ's teaching upon the subject goes but a little way beyond that of the Old Testament. Most of the references have to do with our Lord as the Messiah: His consecration, His testings and His ministry. Little is said in the Synoptics about the Spirit's ministry to believers.

It will be helpful in our later study of the problem of the transition period in The Acts, and also the question of miracles today, to notice, at this point, that the manifestation of God's supernatural power in human history is like the ocean tide: it ebbs and flows, waxes and wanes. Extraordinary power comes in "cycles" (Trench). This was true for Israel during Old Testament days; the spiritual tide came in and went out time and again. We see in the New Testament, however, the highest spiritual tide ever known. A special divine movement began at the time of our Lord's birth. This flood tide of the Spirit lasted some sixty years and' then began to recede. If we'll remember this important fact, it will give us comforting light on the problem of miracles then and now.

The Gospels of Matthew, Mark, and Luke mention the Holy Spirit thirty-five times. (The American Standard Version always translates the Greek word *pneuma* as Spirit, whereas the Authorized Version often translates *pneuma* as Ghost, a Middle English word.)

I. MATTHEW—TWELVE REFERENCES

God, by the virgin birth of Jesus Christ, identified Deity with humanity; Deity appeared on earth in permanent human form, making possible richer fellowship of God with men.

1:18 *She was found with child of the Holy Ghost.*

1:20 *That which is conceived in her is of the Holy Ghost.*

Reason or revelation—which shall reign here? Revelation must. We cannot, shall not, yield to intellectual pride. Consequently we take these inspired statements by simple faith. We believe the second Person of the Godhead was joined to humanity to make the Person of Christ. We humbly accept the inscrutable mystery: that Christ could be begotten by the Holy Spirit, the third Person, and yet become the Son of the Father, the first Person. We confidently reckon that Christ became a man by generation and the last Adam by creation. We see a miracle in Mary's becoming the mother of a holy and sinless Child, since she was born a sinner like the rest of us. We also understand that Christ possessed a human nature as well as a human body. (Cp. Luke 1:35.)

This is the historic position, as stated by stalwarts like William R. Newell and A. T. Robertson: "God by the Holy Spirit, and not a human father, communicated the life to the ovum in the womb of the virgin."

The Holy Ghost, not Joseph and not any man, was responsible for the pregnancy of Mary.... We see here God sending His Son into the world to be the world's Saviour and He gave Him a human mother, but not a human father so that Jesus Christ is both Son of God and Son of Man, the God Man (Robertson).

3:11 *He shall baptize you with the Holy Ghost and with fire.*

"He shall baptize you in the Holy Spirit and in fire" (A.S.V.). Just as John the Baptist baptized in water those who repented, so Christ should baptize in the Holy Spirit and fire those who should believe (Acts 1:5). You'll note that the preposition "with" (or "in") before the word "fire" is in italics; it is not in the Greek and was added by the translators. That is, "Spirit and fire are coupled with one preposition as a double baptism" (McNeile). Two things were to take place in connection with the baptism which Christ should administer. First, believers should be made members of His body (I Cor. 12:13); secondly, they should also be empowered for service (Acts 1:8). This wondrous baptism took place for the 120 on the day of Pentecost. On that memorable day Christ began to send His holy "fire on the earth" (Luke 12:49, 50). Aside from certain features connected with the beginning of the Christian era, that historic day of Pentecost holds up to view normal Christianity.

Beginning on that day of Pentecost, Christ's ministry, in the Person of the Spirit, has been mightier than John's. Also our ministries may now glow with holy fire (II Tim. 1:6). Full faith in the God-Man in glory gives us "the zeal of service, the flame of love, the fervor of prayer, the earnestness of testimony, the devotion of consecration, the sacrifice of worship, and the igniting power of influence" (T. E. Marsh) which characterize this baptism of fire.

The "unquenchable fire" mentioned in the next verse (Matt. 3:12) apparently refers to judgment at Christ's second coming. Isaiah speaks of a time "when the Lord shall have washed away the filth of the daughters of Zion, and shall have purged the blood of Jerusalem from the midst thereof, by the spirit of judgment and by the spirit of burning" (4:4). (See also Mal. 3:2.) Furthermore, this "fire" has to do with the eternal condition of all who enter hell. (Cp. Mark 9:43, 48.) Two kinds of fire, therefore, are represented in verses 11 and 12; all people must either enjoy the one or suffer the other for all eternity.

3:16 *He saw the Spirit of God descending like a dove, and lighting upon him.*

The three Persons of the Godhead share in this great moment of public dedication: the Son identifies himself with the sinful race for whom He is to be made sin; the Spirit descends "in a bodily form, as a dove, upon him" (Luke 3:22, A.S.V.); and the Father speaks out of the heavens, saying, "This is my beloved Son, in whom I am well pleased."

The scene testifies to the fact that the Holy Spirit will manifest the dove-like qualities of purity, innocence, meekness, and lowliness in Jesus throughout His earthly ministry.

4:1 *Then was Jesus led of the Spirit into the wilderness to be tempted of the devil.*

Only Spirit-filled people are equipped to win the battle "against principalities, against powers, against the rulers of the darkness of this world, against spiritual wickedness in high places" (Eph. 6:12). Compare Mark 1:12 and Luke 4:1 and note that the agency, the sphere and the influence of the Spirit, are all three implied in the three accounts.

10:20 *For it is not ye that speak, but the Spirit of your Father which speaketh in you.*

These humble Galilean believers are to be delivered up to councils, governors and kings for their testimony to Christ. How encouraging this promise! "But when they deliver you up, take no thought how or what ye shall speak: for it shall be given you in that same hour what ye shall speak." This does not mean that the Spirit will not speak to us before that hour—He may do so—but He certainly will speak in that hour, both to us and through us; He is the Spirit of inspiration. Neither does this make Bible study unnecessary. A. T. Robertson warns "stupid and lazy preachers" that "Christ is not talking about preparation of sermons!" This is "instruction to martyrs, not to preachers." (See remarks on Mark 13:11 and Luke 12:12.)

12:18   *Behold, my servant, whom I have chosen; my beloved, in whom my soul is well pleased: I will put my Spirit upon him, and he shall show judgment to the Gentiles.*

Matthew confirms that the prophecy in Isaiah 42:1–4 was fulfilled in Christ, the power of the Holy Spirit being the chief feature. (See comment on Isa. 42:1.)

12:28   *But if I cast out devils by the Spirit of God, then the kingdom of God is come unto you.*

Christ, the God-Man, humbled himself and served men. not in His own power, but in the power of the Spirit of God. Thus He preached, comforted, freed, healed, and cast out demons. But the Pharisees claimed He did all these things, not by the power of the Spirit, but by the power of Beelzebub, the prince of demons (Matt. 9:34; 12:24). Why? Either because they knew better and wanted to deceive the people, or because they were blind to spiritual things. If they were lying, they thereby were wilfully destroying their own sense of distinction between truth and error. If they were already so blinded by prejudice, envy and hatred that they could not recognize the Spirit in Christ's ministry, then they were too far gone ever to repent.

12:31, 32   *Wherefore I say unto you, all manner of sin and blasphemy shall be forgiven unto men: but the blasphemy against the Holy Ghost shall not be forgiven unto men. (32) And whosoever speaketh a word against the Son of man, it shall be forgiven him: but whosoever speaketh against the Holy Ghost, it shall not be forgiven him, neither in this world, neither in the world to come.*

The idea of "blasphemy" occurs many times in Scripture—both Old and New Testaments. It simply means *to vilify, to speak evil against, to abuse.* Here it means *to speak evil against the Holy Spirit.* The Pharisees had so abused the Holy Spirit that they had at last definitely. and officially—after often taking serious thought about the matter (Matt. 9:34; 11:18–24; 12:14)—ascribed to Satan the works of the Spirit. By so doing they had sealed their eternal doom (Matt. 12:22–37, 45; 13:13; 23:1–39).

Can men commit this sin today? Can they continue to call black white until they lose the ability to choose between the two? Can men become totally blind to the things of the Spirit? (See I Tim. 4:1. 2 and Heb. 6:3; also cp. Gen. 6:3.) As an instance in point, A. T. Robertson cites Nietzsche.[1] Although this blaspheming German philosopher, Friedrich Wilhelm Nietzsche (1844–1900). was born the son of a Lutheran minister and the grandson of two. he became militantly anti-Christian. What about professed Christians such as those described in II Timothy 3:1–5? What about the Communists? Can people deny the existence of God so long they really become convinced there is no God? Can they preach "abolish all private property" until they feel justified in killing millions of people—as in China—in order to do so? What about infidels who declare "that Fundamentalism shows demonic traits when it believes the Bible to be the Word of God and when it asserts that Christ was God"? What about Fundamentalists today who. like the Pharisees then. vilify the work of the Spirit in others? What about materialist psychologists who attempt to rationalize conversion?

Why should we seriously answer these questions? Because our Lord gave warning against the fatal sin of blasphemy. not for the sake of those who had already committed it. but for those who were in danger of doing so. Let us beware of vilifying God in the Person of the Holy Spirit. As Holy Spirit He would fellowship with us. We can experience God's grace in no other way. And. if you fear you have already committed this sin. be sure of this one thing: If you're the least bit interested in your own spiritual welfare, you've not blasphemed the Spirit. How may you know? By the very fact that He is still striving with you; otherwise you would not be interested. "And let him that is athirst come. And whosoever will, let him take the water of life freely."

22:43   *He saith unto them, How then doth David in the Spirit call him Lord?*

This verse affords another instance of divine inspiration. David's voice, pen and vocabulary were used; but the Spirit chose the right words from David's vocabulary and made them His. So we have David's pen and David's vocabulary but not David's words; they're God's words—the Bible is verbally inspired. (Cp. Mark 12:36.)

28:19   *Go ye therefore, and teach all nations, baptizing them in the name of the Father, and of the Son, and of the Holy Ghost.*

This familiar command of weighty import has suffered much at the hands of both friend and foe. Foes have objected that "this language in the mouth of Jesus is too theological and is not a genuine part of the Gospel of Matthew for the same reason." Sometimes friends place it in a dispensational pigeonhole. A. T. Robertson devoted to this subject a chapter in his *The Christ in the Logia* in which he proved these words to be genuine and relevant. In fact. this verse unites all the lines of Christ's earlier teaching and associates the three Persons of the Godhead in their unity with the work which His disciples were to do from that time forward.

Behold also a mystery which belongs to the divine life itself: God in relation to God. Joseph Cook gives a helpful statement of the facts:

> The Father with the Son and the Holy Spirit is God; the Father without the Son and the Holy Spirit would not be God. The Son with the Father and the Holy Spirit is God; the Son without the Father and the Holy Spirit would not be God. The Spirit with

the Father and the Son is God; but the Spirit without the Father and the Son would not be God. [2]

Consequently, we see that baptism in Matthew 28:19 is into the *name*, not names, of the Father and of the Son and of the Holy Spirit. This proves trinal baptism—baptism in the name of the Father, then of the Son, then of the Holy Spirit—to be unscriptural. It must be baptism into the name of the Triune God. Statements like those found in Acts 8:16 and 19:5 simply emphasize the fact that the name of Jesus is the essential part of baptism. Ironside explained it like this: "These men were baptized in the name of the Lord Jesus. that is by His authority which. of course. implies baptism unto the name of the Holy Trinity." [3]

II. MARK—SIX REFERENCES

1:8 *I indeed have baptized you with water: but he shall baptize you with the Holy Ghost.*

See explanation of Matthew 3:11.

1:10 *And straightway coming up out of the water, he saw the heavens opened, and the Spirit like a dove descending upon him.*

See remarks on Matthew 3:16.

1:12 *And immediately the Spirit driveth him into the wilderness.*

(See comment on Matt. 4:1.) The forty days in the wilderness were under the direct control of the Holy Spirit. The entire earthly life of Jesus, from His birth to His death and resurrection, was lived in the power of the Holy Spirit. Mark's word "driveth" is stronger, bolder, and more vivid than Matthew's "was led up" or Luke's "was led" (A. T. Robertson).

3:29 *But he that shall blaspheme against the Holy Ghost hath never forgiveness, but is in danger of eternal damnation.*

See discussion of Matthew 12:28, 31, 32.

12:36 *For David himself said by the Holy Ghost, the LORD said unto my Lord, Sit thou on my right hand, till I make thine enemies thy footstool.*

This Scripture illustrates both the human and the divine elements in inspiration. "David himself said"—this emphasizes the human element. David spake as he was moved by the Holy Spirit; thus, David's pen wrote God's words! "To say, therefore, as the 'higher' critics do, that this Scripture (Ps. 110:1) is not David's at all, is not only to make Christ himself a liar, but comes perilously near to blasphemy against the Holy Spirit" (A.T.R.). (Cp. Matt. 22:43 and II Sam. 23:2.)

13:11 *For it is not ye that speak, but the Holy Ghost.*

(Cp. Matt. 10:20 and Luke 12:12.) Illustrations of the Holy Spirit's speaking through a believer in times of peril and crisis may be found in Acts 4:8; 13:9 and II Corinthians 13:3.

III. LUKE—SEVENTEEN REFERENCES

1:15 *And he shall be filled with the Holy Ghost, even from his mother's womb.*

John the Baptist's attitude toward Christ set the standard for all future believers: "He must increase, but I must decrease." It's true, the more completely the hidden Spirit controls our lives, the more fully Christ is magnified in us.

1:35 *The Holy Ghost shall come upon thee, and the power of the Highest shall overshadow thee: therefore also that holy thing which shall be born of thee shall be called the Son of God.*

Thus Gabriel explained to Mary, a virgin, how she should become the mother of the Messiah. She should conceive in her womb by the direct action of God the Holy Spirit. The Holy Spirit, like the cloud of God's presence, would come upon and overshadow her, manifesting the power of the Most High. Mary's womb should be made productive apart from man, by the life-giving power of the Holy Spirit. This record bases the sonship and sinlessness of Christ, not on His pre-existence but on His conception by the Holy Spirit. (Cp. Matt. 1:18, 20.)

1:41   *Elizabeth was filled with the Holy Ghost.*

Thus, Elizabeth understood what had happened to Mary. "It is worthy of note that both of these women, filled with the divine and spiritual power, acknowledged the deity of Christ" (A.T.R.).

1:67   *And his father Zacharias was filled with the Holy Ghost and prophesied.*

Compare I Samuel 10:10; 19:23 and I Corinthians 12:10.

2:25–27   *And behold, there was a man in Jerusalem, whose name was Simeon, . . . and the Holy Ghost was upon him. (26) And it was revealed unto him by the Holy Ghost, that he should not see death until he had seen the Lord's Christ. (27) And he came by the Spirit into the temple. . . .*

Most of the people in Jerusalem knew nothing about the blessed Holy Spirit; but Simeon knew Him, for he lived under His control. He lived close enough to God to hear His still, small voice, and also doubtless studied the Word, being especially familiar with the prophecy in Daniel 9:25, 26.

3:16   *He shall baptize you with the Holy Ghost and with fire.*

See comment on Matthew 3:11.

3:22   *And the Holy Ghost descended in a bodily shape like a dove upon him.*

See discussion of Matthew 3:16.

4:1   *And Jesus being full of the Holy Ghost returned from Jordan, and was led by the Spirit into the wilderness.*

See remarks on Matthew 4:1.

4:14 *And Jesus returned in the power of the Spirit into Galilee: and there went out a fame of him through all the
region round about.*

Our word "dynamite" comes from the Greek word *dynamis*
here translated "power." Our Lord lived and ministered in
the power of the Spirit.

4:18 *The Spirit of the Lord is upon me, because he hath
anointed me to preach the gospel to the poor; he hath
sent me to heal the broken-hearted, to preach deliverance
to the captives, and recovering of sight to the blind, to
set at liberty them that are bruised.*

Isaiah (61:1, 2) had predicted the Messiah would exercise supernatural power on behalf of the poor in spirit, the
broken-hearted, the slaves to sin, the blind and the bruised.
To the amazement of His home town, Jesus here claims the
prediction is fulfilled in Him. He made this claim, for one
reason, because the Spirit of the transcendent God had come
upon Him at the time of His baptism. He stood before His
boyhood acquaintances as the Anointed One, the Christ. With
"gracious words" He amplified His claim, and with salty
words, He applied it. Disbelieving, they were "filled with
wrath, and rose up, and thrust him out of the city, and
led him unto the brow of the hill whereon their city was
built, that they might cast him down headlong." To use power costs the user. He who uses it is despised: for example,
George Fox, John Wesley, Bunyan. Christ died at Calvary.
Fifty million early Christians "followed in His train." And
many more millions in our day have done the same.

10:21 *In that hour Jesus rejoiced in the Spirit, and said, I
thank thee, O Father, Lord of heaven and earth, that
thou hast hid these things from the wise and prudent,
and hast revealed them unto babes, even so, Father; for
so it seemed good in thy sight.*

The American Standard Version reads, "He rejoiced in the Holy Spirit." A. T. Robertson explains: "This holy joy of Jesus was directly due to the Holy Spirit. It is joy in the work of His followers, their victories over Satan, and is akin to the joy felt by Jesus in John 4:32–38 when the vision of the harvest of the world stirred His heart."

11:13 *If ye then, being evil, know how to give good gifts unto your children: how much more shall your heavenly Father give the Holy Spirit to them that ask him?*

Absence of the article "the" before "Holy Spirit" in the Greek original may imply our Lord wasn't talking about receiving the Holy Spirit as a Person to indwell but about receiving His power and gifts. It's always in order to ask our Father to equip us for service. (Cp. Ps. 51:11 and Eph. 5:18.) God ever delights to give His presence and power to those who seek in prayer. (See exposition of Acts 8:15–19.)

12:10 *And whosoever shall speak a word against the Son of man, it shall be forgiven him: but unto him that blasphemeth against the Holy Ghost it shall not be forgiven.*

"Word" here means doctrine in expression. Christ was and is the Word, the doctrine of God in expression, even God himself made known in human form. When a soul becomes the human expression of abuse against the Holy Spirit, that soul is doomed eternally; he has committed the unpardonable sin. (Cp. Matt. 12:31, 32.)

12:12 *For the Holy Ghost shall teach you in the same hour what ye ought to say.*

See comments on Matthew 10:20 and Mark 13:11.

Before passing on, let's glance at Luke 24:49, for it prepares us for the climax. It connects the doctrine of the Spirit in the Old Testament and the Synoptic Gospels with John's Gospel, where Christ enlarges on "the promise," and Acts, where the promise is fulfilled. It reads: "And, behold. I send the promise of my Father upon you: but tarry ye in the city of Jerusalem. until ye be endued with power from on high." After Acts 2. the infinite love of God and His great salvation could be imparted. applied. and infused by the Spirit as He worked on the basis of Christ's redemption. Paul will explain the precious meaning and realization of this eternal redemption, which transforms human darkness into spiritual flambeaux (Eph. 5:8). No wonder the disciples were "continually in the temple, praising and blessing God" (Lk. 24:53).

The Spirit in the Fourth Gospel—
Divine Promises

HERE WE DISCOVER Christ's own summital teaching on this awakening theme. It's high truth. It concerns the most important Helper in all the world, and yet One who is the most neglected Person. When it comes to teaching heart-warming facts about the blessed Holy Spirit and the condition for enjoying His power, nobody goes beyond our Lord. Though John wrote his Gospel many years after Paul's doctrine of the Spirit had permeated the churches, he reveals that our Lord himself had already reached "the high-water mark of Christian thought on this subject." [1]

Accordingly, this Gospel, as compared with the Synoptics, shows distinct progress in the Spirit's revelation of himself. For instance, there's clear-cut, positive evidence that the Spirit is a person, and a divine Person. No other book in the Bible represents the Spirit as personal more definitively than this Gospel.

Furthermore, in this Gospel the Spirit is more closely associated at all points with redemption than in the Synoptics. John alone prepares us to understand Christ's presence in the person of the Paraclete. Yet, no one can question that the fourth Gospel represents the Spirit as "a self distinct from Christ." [2] In His office as Paraclete, moreover, the Spirit is described by our Lord as another Person like himself, another who is called to the believer's aid—One who stands ready and able to give all necessary help.

Only nineteen verses in the fourth Gospel mention the Spirit directly; yet they are exceedingly rich in meaning, with forty-four references, as compared with thirty-five in all three of the Synoptic Gospels.

1:32, 33 *And John bare record, saying, I saw the Spirit descending from heaven like a dove, and it abode upon him. (33) And I knew him not: but he that sent me to baptize with water, the same said unto me, Upon whom thou shalt see the Spirit descending, and remaining on him, the same is he which baptizeth with the Holy Ghost.*

The Spirit descending as a dove to abide upon Jesus was God's confirming sign to the Baptist that Jesus was the Messiah. Notice that it is Christ who is to do the baptizing; the Spirit is to be the *element* of baptism. "To come under the Spirit's power and influence, as every Christian does when he believes, is to have been baptized by that influence" (Chafer). (Cp. Matt. 3:16; Mark 1:8 and Luke 3:22.)

3:5 *Jesus answered, Verily, verily, I say unto thee, Except a man be born of water and of the Spirit, he cannot enter into the kingdom of God.*

The expression "born of water and the Spirit" (A.S.V.) refers to one twofold act: the Spirit's use of the Word in regeneration (Titus 3:5). This is characteristic of Christian experience: both the Agent and the instrument are always necessary. The Gospel is the "seed" and the Spirit is the life. (Cp. I Pet. 1:23–25.) The Spirit creates in the heart the conditions for the Word to germinate, sprout and grow. (Let those who imagine they find here a proof-text for baptismal regeneration explain why there is no "water" mentioned in verses 6 and 8.)

In view of the fact that Nicodemus was a ruler of the Jews, Bible students have asked the question whether renewal for Old Testament saints meant the same as regeneration for New Testament saints. Galatians 4:1–7 answers: Old Testament be-

lievers were children, having been born again just as truly as
New Testament believers; the difference was one of standing:
the former, that of minors; the latter, that of adult sons.

3:6 *That which is born of the flesh is flesh; and that which is
     born of the Spirit is spirit.*

The Greek has the perfect tense, "that which hath been born
of the flesh," signifying the *state* of the unsaved person; that
is, all people have been born into a depraved, sinful race; and,
consequently, live on a low, merely human plane. On the other
hand, "that which hath been born of the Spirit" refers to the
state of the saved person, that of heavenly, not earthly, origin
and manner. He has been born from above, and can, by the
power of the Spirit, live "in the heavenlies." Also note that *the
principle of life which the Spirit imparts* "is spirit." In fact,
every time God saves a man, He performs a miracle—similar
to putting a sheep's nature into a hog's body. The words "be
born" in verses 3, 4, 5, and 7, incidentally, are in the aorist
tense, marking the *fact* of birth (Vincent). All this describes
human spirits as dead toward God (Eph. 2:1) until they are
made alive by the Spirit's use of the Word (Eph. 2:5), by a
creative act of God the Holy Spirit.

3:8 *The wind bloweth where it listeth, and thou hearest the
     sound thereof, but canst not tell whence it cometh, and
     whither it goeth: so is every one that is born of the Spirit.*

Observe the sovereignty—the supreme and independent power—of the Spirit and, also, that born-again people have evidences
in their lives of the work of the invisible Spirit: "the wind
bloweth."

The margin of the American Standard Version suggests
"The Spirit breatheth" instead of "The wind bloweth." And,
indeed, the Spirit is the "Breath" of the transcendent God.
Wycliffe and other translators, moreover, retain "Spirit" here
and argue for it. In either case, the meaning seems to be:
the new birth is inexplicable, entirely independent of and
beyond man (John 1:13).

3:34 *For he whom God hath sent speaketh the words of God:*
for God giveth not the Spirit by measure unto him.

Why did God not measure the Spirit unto Christ, His sent
One? Because Christ was perfectly qualified for an unlimited
relationship with the Spirit. The "dove," consequently, was
never frightened away nor grieved by Him. It follows, therefore, that our relationship to and fellowship with Christ determine the measure of the Spirit's blessings in our lives (Eph.
6:10).

4:24 *God is Spirit: and they that worship him must worship*
him in spirit and in truth (A.S.V. mgn.).

Our Lord's conversation with the Samaritan woman clearly
characterizes New Testament worship as radically different from
Old Testament worship. Whereas believers under the Old Covenant worshiped in Jerusalem only (II Kings 18:22 and Deut.
12:13, 14), and by "carnal ordinances" (Heb. 9:10), believers
under the New Covenant worship in heaven (Heb. 4:14–16).
Thus we worship "in Spirit and in truth."

This is possible because "God is Spirit." He is Spirit, as
He is Light and Love; eternally existing in three Persons.
the Father, and the Son, and the Holy Spirit. In other words.
God, as such, does not have a physical, material body. He is
spiritual, not corporeal.

Accordingly, people must worship God in the commonwealth of, the fellowship created by. the Spirit, and hence in
reality. Spiritual believers do this. They enjoy this commonwealth of the Spirit on the basis of Christ's redemption and by
means of His High Priesthood. Accordingly, we include John
4:24 in our list of references to the Spirit.

6:63 *It is the Spirit that quickeneth; the flesh profiteth noth-*
ing: the words that I speak unto you, they are spirit, and
they are life.

Here also we must look behind the scene to discover the
hidden Spirit. But He is surely here. For He is the Breath of
God and the Life of God in the words of Jesus. He *must* be

present; otherwise there could be no quickening. He, the Agent, brings home to the heart the spirit of the Gospel. The result is new spiritual life. For the Spirit alone is the experiential life-giver. (This verse and I Cor. 15:45 formed the basis of the Nicene Creed's affirmation of faith in the Holy Spirit.)

7:39 *(But this spake he of the Spirit, which they that believe on him should receive: for the Holy Ghost was not yet given; because that Jesus was not yet glorified.)*

Connect this parenthetical verse with verses 37 and 38 and you have the most beautiful picture in the Bible of Spirit-filled living. We shall return to this pregnant portion in our last chapter, but let us notice, in passing, a few important details. The first clause, "But this spake he of the Spirit," introduces John's explanation of verses 37 and 38; otherwise, we might never know that in those verses our Lord was illustrating the nature of the Spirit's New Testament ministry. That is, it's a hidden ministry, magnifying Christ in believers until "rivers of living water" flow from within them.

Concerning the personality of the Spirit, A. T. Robertson points out that the Greek pronoun here translated "which" should be translated "whom," as in John 14:17, 26. "It is purely a grammatical gender which we do not have in English," he says.

The second clause informs us that those pre-Pentecostal believers were to become, on the day of Pentecost, beneficiaries of the New Testament ministry of the Spirit. For the statement "the Holy Ghost was not yet given" means His Church-age work had not yet begun. The reason: "Jesus was not yet glorified" and believers were not yet one organism in Him. That is, the Spirit's miracle of making believers "one body" (I Cor. 12:13) and one with a glorified Christ could not be performed before Christ had been glorified as a man.

Incidentally, on that great day of Pentecost the Spirit of God became known on earth as *the Spirit of a Man.* In the discerning words of Andrew Murray, the Spirit ". . . came as the Spirit of the glorified Jesus, the Spirit of the Incarnate, crucified, and exalted Christ, the bearer and communicator to us, not of the life of God as such, but that life as it had been interwoven into human nature in the person of Jesus Christ. ... His human nature constituted the receptacle and dispenser of the Divine Spirit." [3] Since Pentecost, therefore, the Spirit of God and the Spirit of Jesus, the God-Man, are one and the same.

John 14 through 16 gives us Christ's own mature doctrine of the Spirit. No matter what the manifestations, no one can ever rise higher in Christian experience than this promised fellowship, communion, and joint participation with the Father and the Son. Let's therefore study this portion carefully to get God's full answer to life's frustrating questions. Let's glance at the whole; let's also look at it verse by verse. An analysis of these three chapters reveals the mystical relationships of Christ and the Father, Christ and the Spirit, and the Triune God and believers—all realized and sublimated in the presence and the power of the Spirit.

1. Christ is the Way (on the basis of Calvary) to the Father's house.
2. Christ is the Truth (embodied in Scripture).
3. Christ is the Life (applied by the Spirit).
4. Christ (anointed by the Spirit) reveals the Father.
5. Christ is going away—and coming again in person at the end of the age.
6. He will come on the day of Pentecost, however, *in the person of the Spirit*, to empower believers.
7. The condition: "...ye believe in God, believe also in me."

14:16, 17 *And I will pray the Father, and he shall give you another Comforter, that he may abide with you for ever:*
(17) Even the Spirit of truth; whom the world cannot receive, because it seeth him not, neither knoweth him; but ye know him; for he dwelleth with you, and shall be in you.

Our Lord's public ministry is now over, and His disciples are deeply troubled when they learn He is going away to the cross and to heaven. What will become of their Messianic hopes and of them? Will they be left orphans? To comfort them Jesus promises to speak to the Father that He may give them another Person of the Godhead to abide with them for ever.

"He shall give you." Christ refers ultimately to the promise of Joel 2:28, 29: ". . . I will pour out my Spirit upon all flesh. . . ." He is speaking of its fulfillment—so far as the Church is concerned—on the day of Pentecost. The Spirit is to proceed, however, not only from the Father (14:16, 26), but also from the Son (15:26; 16:7).[4]

"Another Comforter." This new designation of the Spirit again unmistakably marks Him as a person. Although the word *Spirit* is in the neuter gender, Comforter (Gr., *Parakletos*) is masculine. We find here, moreover, the first use of pronouns referring to the Spirit, and they are all masculine. That the Spirit, besides, is a divine Person is implied by the things He does, for only Deity could do them.

Next, *Parakletos* (transliterated, Paraclete) literally means "one who is called to someone's aid." In this case the Holy Spirit was One called to the aid of the disciples, who otherwise could have been left "orphans" (A.S.V., mgn.). At the end of this section we shall return to this idea of Paraclete and amplify its meaning.

"Even the Spirit of truth." Whereas Christ is the truth, the Paraclete is "the Spirit of truth." Christ is the fire; the Paraclete is the heat and light of the fire. Christ is the balm; the Paraclete is the fragrance of the balm. Christ is God; the Paraclete is the presence of God—*"whom the world cannot receive."* The lost can't see, know or receive the Paraclete apart from Christ. *"But ye know him; for he dwelleth with you, and shall be in you."* The Spirit rested on Christ and Christ abode with the disciples; therefore, the Spirit, too, dwelt with them; and they were beginning to recognize His presence. (Note, in passing, the "hiddenness" of the Spirit, and also the fact that He makes believers Christ-conscious rather than Spirit-conscious.) The Spirit began to dwell *in* them on the day of Pentecost. Indeed, the idiom in verse 18, "I will come to you," implies that Christ

himself came (in the person of the Spirit) to indwell (cp. Gal. 2:20). This coming, of course, is not Christ's own second coming, as promised, for instance, in Acts 1:11: "... this same Jesus, which is taken up from you into heaven, shall so come in like manner as ye have seen him go into heaven." [5]

This key statement, "I will come to you," let me repeat, is our Lord's way of saying "I will be present with you in the person of the Spirit." Thus they were not left orphans. Instead, they experienced the fulfillment of His promises: "... because I live, ye shall live also"; "At that day ye shall know that I am in the Father, and ye in me, and I in you"; "... My Father will love him, and we will come unto him, and make our abode with him." All this was realized in the presence and power of the Spirit. Read the Book of Acts with this in mind!

14:26 *But the Comforter, who is the Holy Ghost, whom the Father will send in my name, he shall teach you all things, and bring all things to your remembrance, whatsoever I have said unto you.*

"In my name." "For the Spirit to be sent in the name of Jesus means he is sent as the representative of Jesus, as the one who is to carry on his work" (Conner). *"He shall teach you."* After Pentecost the Paraclete enabled the apostles rightly to interpret Christ, and brought to their remembrance the things they subsequently recorded in Scripture (cp. John 2:22).

15:26 *But when the Comforter is come, whom I will send unto you from the Father, even the Spirit of truth, which proceedeth from the Father, he shall testify of me.*

The nature of the Paraclete's ministry is revealed in the main part of this verse, "He shall testify of me." The next verse says, "And ye also shall bear witness." Thus this is a twofold witness, the Spirit speaking through us and to others (cp. 16:7). Indeed, without the internal witness of the Paraclete to others, our witness would be in vain. For He must unstop spiritual ears, open spiritual eyes and illumine darkened hearts before the lost can or will receive the Gospel (cp. Acts 5:32).

So He testifies by silently turning the spotlight on the Christ of God, glorified *as a man*. Here again we see that Christ alone is not "the answer." We must have the Spirit!

16:7, 8 *Nevertheless I tell you the truth; It is expedient for you that I go away: for if I go not away, the Comforter will not come unto you: but if I depart, I will send him unto you. (8) And when he is come, he will reprove the world of sin, and of righteousness, and of judgment.*

"*It is expedient for you*"—what a startling statement! Yet, as we know, our Lord had to go to heaven by way of the cross and the resurrection before His redemptive power could be released to the world. Indeed, otherwise "there would have been no redemptive power to release" (Conner). It was expedient, therefore, it was good, it was to their advantage that the historical Jesus go away, so His holy fire would be sent on earth (Luke 12:49–53). Thus His burning passion would spread, reveal, warn. In this manner His inextinguishable blaze would separate, purify, soften; would transform lives, even "turn the world upside down." Also it was expedient because His spiritual presence in the person of the Paraclete would dwell *in*, not merely *with*, them. "*Come unto you.*" The Paraclete would not deal directly with the lost, but through believers. Thomas states that "not a single passage can be discovered in the New Testament which refers to His direct action on the world." [6]

"*He will reprove.*" Moreover, this departure was profitable because the subsequent ministry of the Paraclete (toward the world) would necessarily be different from what Christ's earthly ministry had been. Christ had been humble, gracious, kind and merciful—constantly delivering from diseases, demons and sins. On the other hand, the Paraclete would be unbending, piercing, wrathful. Why? Because the world had rejected Christ. God had sent His Son, not to condemn the world, but that the world might be saved through Him, and the world had spurned God's love. Now our Lord would send the Paraclete to reprove, to convict, to convince the world of sin, and of righteousness, and of judgment. The world—urged on by "religion"—had rejected, denied, despised, spat upon and crucified the One who came to save them, God's only begotten Son! Wherefore the Paraclete would convict the world of the seriousness of all this (John 3: 18, 36). In other words, God's wrath, as well as His love, must now be revealed (Rom. 1:18).

This work of the Spirit toward the world would be three-fold. The coming of the Paraclete would prove: (1) the world was fatally wrong in refusing to believe on Christ; (2) Christ was divinely right in His claim to be the Son of God; and (3) Satan had lost the war with God; other skirmishes would be fought certainly, but Satan had been once for all defeated. After Pentecost, therefore, the work of the Spirit must be definitely different from what Christ's had been. Hence it was to the advantage of the disciples that Christ go away—for a time.

Notice in the Book of Acts instances of this differing ministry of the Spirit. Observe how He came upon the disciples and, through them, mightily convinced the lost of the wrath of God:

> Now when they heard this, they were pricked in their heart (2:37).

> But ye denied the Holy One and the just, and desired a murderer to be granted unto you; and killed the Prince of life, whom God hath raised from the dead; whereof we are witnesses (3:14, 15).

> ... and great fear came on all them that heard these things (5:5).

> And great fear came upon all the church, and upon as many as heard these things (5:11).

> When they heard that, they were cut to the heart... (5:33).

> And they were not able to resist the wisdom and the Spirit by which he spake (6:10).

> When they heard these things, they were cut to the heart, and they gnashed on him with their teeth (7:54).

Christ came to reveal the love of God. But when that love was despised, the Spirit came to convince of the wrath of God —in order that many might repent and be saved after all. "Where sin abounded, grace did much more abound."

16:13–15   *Howbeit when he, the Spirit of truth, is come, he will guide you into all truth: for he shall not speak of himself; but whatsoever he shall hear, that shall he speak: and he shall show you things to come. (14) He shall glorify me: for he shall receive of mine, and shall show it unto you. (15) All things that the Father hath are mine: therefore said I, that he shall take of mine, and shall show it unto you.*

"*He will guide you.*" The Paraclete enabled Matthew, Mark, Luke and John to record the historical facts of the Gospel, as set forth in the four Gospels. He guided Luke in his record in The Acts of the Apostles of the early propagation of the Gospel. Likewise too Paul was shown the meaning of the Gospel, which he later expounded in his epistles. So it was with all Scripture, including the General Epistles and The Revelation. And whereas in that day the Spirit completed the revelation, today He guides us into the right understanding and practice of all Scripture.

"*He shall not speak of himself.*" This doesn't mean the Spirit never speaks *about* himself, but rather that He doesn't speak from *himself* (cp. A.S.V.). He speaks from Christ; that is, with Christ's authority and power and blessing. In this way the Paraclete continues Christ's work on earth (see Acts 1:1); for "whatsoever he shall hear, that shall he speak." "The Spirit is like light. Light does not exist so much for its own sake, but rather that we may see other things through the medium of light. The Holy Spirit is not in the world to call attention of men to himself but rather to bear witness to Christ" (Conner).

"*He shall glorify me.*" Here Christ's doctrine of the Paraclete comes to a climax. This statement towers high. It's a "definite promise of the Spirit's guidance in interpreting Christ" (A.T.R.). We see, incidentally, that Christ is "the answer" *provided* He is rightly "interpreted." "Jesus makes God known by being the incarnation, the embodiment of the very life of God.... But an objective, historical revelation of God is not enough.... To make God ... real and living to men in their own experiences is the work of the Divine Spirit." [7]

"All things that the Father hath are mine." The Paraclete will also show us how to make God in Christ relevant in all conditions and situations, so we're in no sense left desolate. Wonderful anticipation! Wherefore we *must* have the Spirit in power. The need is absolute. For, our Lord said, "He shall receive of mine and show it unto you."

Eleven times in these three verses (16:13–15) we are informed that the Spirit is a person, yea, a Person in the Godhead; for only Deity could perform the things here promised. Think of it! A divine *Person* glorifies Christ in our character, walk and service by reporting, declaring and rehearsing to us the moral attributes and graces of God in Christ. Thus the Paraclete reproduces Christ and His things in our experience, even the fruit of the Spirit (Gal. 5:22, 23).

Now we must take a fuller look at this word Paraclete. So expect now your bosom to swell! Open up the joyful lacrimal glands and the tear ducts. For the blessed Paraclete is ready to mean to you everything Christ would if He were here in the body. If you can't weep in gratitude for this divine provision, weep because you cannot weep. How shall we begin to describe the Spirit? This new view of Him is so rich, so full. Translators stand amazed at the possibilities in *Paracletos*. Indeed, Phillips does not attempt to translate *paracletos* as a proper name; he simply says, "I shall ask the Father to give you someone else to stand by you, to be with you always." Strictly speaking, "the Holy Spirit does not really have a name" (A. W. Jackson). The King James rendering "Comforter" is precious but not adequate, as may be illustrated by the labors of the American Standard Version committee. A majority, but not two-thirds, of this committee voted for "Advocate" or "Helper" instead of "Comforter" in their translation of *Paracletos*. But when two-thirds did not vote for a change, they retained "Comforter" and put "Advocate" or "Helper" in the margin.[8]

In our effort to amplify *Paracletos*, we may speak of the Holy Spirit as the Alphabet of Christian experience. In fact, we can find one or more appellations for each letter of the alphabet, as, for example:

*A*gent, Advocate (Christ's with us), "Spirit of adoption"
*B*enefactor of the churches (I Cor. 12)
*C*omforter, Counselor, Christ's Spirit (Rom. 8:9)
*D*eputy, Defense Attorney
*E*nlightener, filling our bosoms with hope (Eph. 1)
*F*ire (Matt. 3:11)
*G*uide, God's Spirit, "Spirit of grace"
*H*elper—Another just like Jesus
*I*ntercessor (Rom. 8:26)
*J*esus' Spirit (Acts 16:7, A.S.V.; Phil. 1:19)
*K*eeper (see I Pet. 1:5)
*L*ife, Spirit of; Lord's Spirit (II Cor. 3:18)
*M*erciful Protector (Chinese trans., according to Don Hunter)
*N*ourisher (see Eph. 3:16–19)
"*O*pener" (He opens doors for us, Rev. 3:7)
*P*erfector, Preserver, power
*Q*uickener (see Eph. 6:10–18)
*R*evealer (Rev. 1:10), Restrainer (II Thess. 2:7)
*S*ilent Partner, Stand-by, Sanctifier
*T*eacher, Truth's Spirit (John 14:16)
"*U*ser" (He uses us)
*V*icar, "Vindicator"
*W*itness (John 14:26; I John 5:8); and
X, *Y* and *Z* may stand for characteristics unknown

How may we enter more fully into this unparalleled discourse of our Lord? (John 14—16). What's the condition? Is it necessary to go after "tongues" or some other questionable experience? Really now, on what condition does the Spirit take control of our lives? How can we get Him to use us? Read through these chapters again and underline the following: ". . . believe in God, believe also in me"; "Believe me . . . believe me"; "He that believeth on me, the works..."; "...ask in my name"; "...love me"; "Abide in me"; "...continue in my love"; "...love one another"; "..bear witness"; "...be of good cheer."

Note this condition our Lord made for power, fruitfulness and joy. We shall take up this all-important matter again in our last chapter. Suffice it to say now that we may know the Lord in any or all these blessed respects. We today may enter fully into what the disciples experienced on the day of Pentecost: "...joy...joy...joy...peace...good cheer" (16:16–33).

20:22 *And when he had said this, he breathed on them, and saith unto them, Receive ye the Holy Ghost.*

Certain expository details connect this verse with the Book of Acts. The Greek, for instance, indicates that this was a strong breathing, suggesting (1) the Old Testament Breath of God now revealed as the New Testament Breath of the Man Christ Jesus, and (2) the saying, "Receive ye the Holy Ghost," as prophetic of the "rushing mighty wind" of Pentecost. Also, the absence in the Greek (John 20:22) of the article "the" may imply that our Lord was talking about consciously receiving power rather than a Person (see Luke 24:49, Acts 1:8; 2:4). Anyway, this point of view fits the context of Acts. It explains how they would be able to witness effectively for Christ, to "reign in life" (Rom. 5:17), to "triumph in Christ" (II Cor. 2:14), to bear "the fruit of the Spirit" (Gal. 5:22), to live "in heavenly places in Christ" (Eph. 1:3), to "rejoice in the Lord alway" (Phil. 4:4), and to look "for that blessed hope" (Titus 2:13). Hence, in no way were they left orphans. And neither are true believers today left comfortless, desolate, forsaken, lonely, friendless, helpless, and liabilities to their communities. No! "The Comforter has come." He came on that day of Pentecost to inwell and to empower the Church. Consequently, He is present today to indwell and to empower all those who believe on the Man in the glory (7:37–39). God is our Helper, God expressed in the Spirit of a Man—God in fellowship with men.[9]

Fellow servants of Christ—pastors, evangelists, teachers,

missionaries—let's take courage! Our problem is simple: stay so close to the Man in the glory that His Breath will fall on us. Then His prosecuting Attorney can convict sinners, not merely of sins, but of the sin, the crime of the ages, believing not on the God-Man who died for them. Then He can make us, too, good witnesses. When we're confronted with failure, He can keep us off the shelf. When our churches go to sleep, He can wake them up. When we need power to reach that "uttermost part of the earth," He can give it. If the Christian movement in our part of the world is on the defensive, He can put it on the offensive. Our Lord promised, "I will not leave you comfortless: I will come to you." For the fulfillment of this promise, see the Book of Acts and behold how the God who is here can make us blazing flames of sacred love.

The Spirit in The Acts of the Apostles — Divine Power Demonstrated

WHAT'S THE LESSON OF LESSONS to be learned in the Book of Acts, and never for one moment to be forgotten? In the Old Testament, there was the lesson of divine immanence. In the Synoptic Gospels, we saw the Spirit resting upon the Messiah. In the Gospel of John, we heard Christ promise "another Comforter." What is the main thing in The Acts? Could it be a missing note in contemporary Christian testimony? Is it the reason for rethinking "the answer"? Yes, for the supreme thing in The Acts is the arrival of a Person *who had never been here before.* That is, the omnipresent Spirit became present in a different way and for a different purpose. He came, in fact, in the absence of Jesus and as Jesus' Agent, to take over as Lord on earth. Since Pentecost, therefore, everything pertaining to the will and work of God on earth has been in His hands. And yet He has kept himself hidden and managed all things so as always to exalt the Lord's Christ. For example, whereas there are fifty-eight references to the Spirit in this Book of Acts, Christ is mentioned over two hundred times.

Wherefore let's give due heed to the relationship and functions of Christ and the Spirit for this age. Let's remember that Christ in His own person is in heaven. And let's note the new things the Spirit does on earth. He empowers believers who now enjoy adult standing before God (see 1:8; 2:4; 4:8, 31;

69

6:3, 5, 8; 7:55; 8:17; 9:17; 10:45; 11:24; 13:9, 52; 19:6).
He enables men to preach Christ-magnifying sermons (e.g..
2:36; 3:14. 15; 4:11. 12; 5:31; 7:37; 8:35; 9:20; 10:36). He
disciplines the church (5:3). judges stubbornness (7:51). com-
forts (7:55; 9:31). counsels (8:29; 11:28), sends out missionaries (13:4). directs their labors (16:6. 7). gives victory over
Satan (13:9), preserves unity in the churches (15:28). and
makes men overseers of them (20:28). You see, Christ *in
absentia* continues on earth in the person of the Paraclete, and
only so. This basic fact must be remembered as we interpret
the rest of the New Testament: the Spirit of Jehovah now
operates on earth for the Godhead as the Spirit of the Man Christ
Jesus. We must cherish the Spirit therefore. just as did the
apostles. Manifestly Christ alone in heaven is not God's
answer. This is the leading lesson in The Acts. Indeed. "The
advent of the Holy Spirit is second in importance to nothing
but the first advent of Christ. God gave His Son that He
might also give the 'other comforter' " (Stifler).

The Spirit is called "Holy Ghost" (Middle English for
Holy Spirit) forty-two times and "Spirit" nine times in the
Authorized Version of Acts. The American Standard Version
capitalizes "spirit" in 6:10; 11:12. 28; and adds "Spirit" in
4:25. There are good reasons, moreover. for capitalization
in a few other instances, making fifty-eight direct references
in all.

1:2 *Until the day in which he was taken up, after that he
through the Holy Ghost had given commandments unto
the apostles whom he had chosen.*

In a former treatise to Theophilus (his Gospel). Luke had
testified to what "Jesus *began* both to do and to teach." Now
he traces for Theophilus what Jesus continues to do and to
teach—by His Spirit in His followers. He explains how He,
God's risen, glorified Christ, goes forward in the person of the
Spirit and in the message of the Gospel from Judaism to the
whole world.

During the forty days after His resurrection. our Lord

appeared ten times to His disciples. At least three times—
during His fifth, eighth, and tenth appearances—He gave them
the Great Commission. This He did "through the Holy Ghost."
You see, the risen God-Man would still operate on earth, but
now through Spirit-filled men. Consequently, by symbolism
and by commandment, He impressed upon the disciples their
need of power (John 20:22; Luke 24:49; Acts 1:4).

1:5   *For John truly baptized with water; but ye shall be
baptized with the Holy Ghost not many days hence.*

John's baptism symbolized repentance; in it the people
confessed their sins, implying their depravity and owning
oneness with a lost race. Christ's baptism was to make believers one with Him in His worldwide program of redemption.
This dynamic baptism was only a few days off. Christ did not
tell them how many days off, or that it would occur on the
day of Pentecost. Why? Because there was responsibility on
their part to be ready. as the first recipients, to receive the
full benefit.

1:8   *But ye shall receive power, after that the Holy Ghost is
come upon you: and ye shall be witnesses unto me both
in Jerusalem, and in all Judea, and in Samaria, and unto
the uttermost part of the earth.*

Before this. the apostles had repeatedly (see Greek) and
urgently asked, "Lord, wilt thou at this time restore again
the kingdom to Israel?" When He finally answered, notice
carefully that He didn't tell them there would never be a
restoration. If there is never to be a restoration. as some teach,
this pertinent question demanded an answer quite different
from the one our Lord gave. This was the very time to let
them know the truth about their nation's future. But, instead
of telling when the kingdom would be restored, He simply said
that the restoration was a private and personal matter with
the Father (Vincent). Then He proceeded to discuss a more
immediate matter.

The important thing. therefore, that Luke wanted Theophilus to see, that Christ wanted the apostles to see, and that God wants us to see, was and is that the empowering of the Holy Spirit would make witnesses to Christ out of them and us. That is, worldwide witnessing, not the restoration of the kingdom to Israel, came next on God's program.

The word "power" implies, first of all, our desire and ability to know and to do the will of God despite all opposition. Again, Len G. Broughton defined spiritual power as "the ability to bring things to pass by way of heaven." In other words, this power is the art of working with God in such a way that others will see only God at work. The expression "is come upon you" means the Holy Spirit so possesses us—you—that we spontaneously witness for Christ. The statement "Ye shall be my witnesses" implies the fact that we are to *be* something before we can *do* anything: the being precedes the doing. Let's also note carefully that our Lord said "both," not "either," in Jerusalem . . . Judea . . . Samaria . . . uttermost part. In short, empowered believers witness by life and lip everywhere.

1:16 *Men and brethren, this scripture must needs have been fulfilled, which the Holy Ghost by the mouth of David spoke before concerning Judas, which was guide to them that took Jesus.*

Here is another instance of divine inspiration. David, being a prophet (Acts 2:30), was a spokesman or mouthpiece of the inspiring Spirit.

2:4 *And they were all filled with the Holy Ghost, and began to speak with other tongues, as the Spirit gave them utterance.*

As this particular day of Pentecost was being observed, the apostles and disciples, about 120 in all, including the women and Mary, "were all with one accord in one place." Christ in glory was the object of their faith. The fresh memory of His death, burial and resurrection filled their hearts and minds as did His promise of the Paraclete. They were not doing something to be blessed; they were *believing on* Someone

(John 7:37–39)! Such a spiritual atmosphere created a like-mindedness. Continued prayer and supplication prepared them to receive God's great Gift.

"And suddenly there came a sound from heaven as of a rushing mighty wind, and it filled all the house where they were sitting" (v. 2). A heavenly tornado swept into the house, filling it "as a bath is filled with water, that the disciples might be baptized with the Holy Ghost, in fulfillment of Acts 1:5" (A. T. Robertson). Baptism in the Holy Spirit is not specifically stated, but we know from Acts 11:16 that it took place at this instant. Accordingly verse 3 speaks of the emblem of power: "There appeared to them also tongues like flames that were distributed and that settled on each one of them" (Berkeley Version). (Cp. Ex. 3:2ff.; Luke 3:16; 12:49.) *"And they were all filled with the Holy Ghost"*—baptized *and* filled in the same moment. Baptism was in the subconscious; filling was the conscious faith-experience. This sets the standard: normal fellowship with Christ is an experience of power *consciously* received and enjoyed by faith, a conscious supply of conscious need. Salvation is by blood and by consciously received power. In other words, we're intuitively sensitive to Christ's Spirit as He applies the value and power of Christ's shed blood. The only way to experience Christ, therefore, is in the power of His Spirit.

Here's the fundamental difference between merely knowing Christ mentally and really knowing Him spiritually. Compare the disciples before and after Pentecost, for instance. Before Pentecost the apostles had many advantages: they had spent three years with Jesus; they had witnessed and performed miracles; they knew the facts of the Gospel; Christ had opened up to them the prophetic Scriptures; they enjoyed a gracious spirit of prayer and supplication; they were in one accord; and "they were continually in the temple, praising and blessing God" (Luke 24:53). But they had no New Testament power! For they had not been made one with Christ in His finished work. On Pentecost, however, they were united with the Man in the glory (I Cor. 12:13); they could now draw upon Him and be filled with His power. So, they consciously underwent a radical change of attitude toward Christ; they came to possess a new, revolutionary faith in and love for Him. All this was enjoyed in the power of the Holy Spirit as God's second Gift, involving the impartation and application of full salvation. They were sensitively raised by faith from the dull level of man's things into the heavenly radiance of the things of the Spirit. Throughout this Book of Acts this is typical of normal Christians.

Thus filled, they "began to speak with other tongues, as the Spirit gave them utterance"—"clear, loud continued utterance under miraculous impulse" (Vincent). In supernatural ecstasy the apostles used the various languages of the Jews and proselytes present to speak "the wonderful works of God," because the Spirit had come that all nations might hear the complete Gospel: the Jews first (2:14ff.), the Samaritans (8:17), the Gentiles (10:44), and those of John's baptism (19:6). Evidently this is the reason God gave. in each instance, the unusual evidence. Luke wanted Theophilus to see this: God wants us to see this.

2:17, 18   *And it shall come to pass in the last days, saith*
           God, I will pour out of my Spirit upon all flesh: and your
           sons and your daughters shall prophesy, and your young
           men shall see visions, and your old men shall dream
           dreams: (18) And on my servants and on my handmaidens
           I will pour out in those days of my Spirit and they shall
           prophesy.

We believe this quotation from the prophet Joel has a twofold fulfillment. Those features not fulfilled in the "last days" of the Church age will be fulfilled in the "last days" of the Kingdom age. (See remarks on Joel 2:28, 29.) F. F. Bruce comments as follows on "upon all flesh," the prominent feature of this passage:

> Luke probably sees in these words an adumbration
> of the worldwide Gentile mission, even if Peter himself

did not realize their full impact when he quoted them on the day of Pentecost. Certainly the outpouring of the Spirit on a hundred and twenty Jews could not in itself fulfil the prediction of such outpouring 'upon all flesh'; but it was the beginning of the fulfillment.[1]

2:33 *Therefore being by the right hand of God exalted, and having received of the Father the promise of the Holy Ghost, he hath shed forth this, which ye now see and hear.*

Thus Peter climaxes his first Spirit-filled sermon, the sermon that won three thousand souls. Every preacher should carefully study its structure—introduction, three main points, and conclusion—its spontaneity. psychology, quotations, and courage—everything about it. It is a masterpiece preached by a common fisherman! Hear him: "There is a Man in the glory. This Man whom you crucified, God has exalted. Proof? His prosecuting Attorney is here; all of us are conscious of His presence. Jesus is in heaven and has done what He promised to do when He got there: '... shed forth this, which ye now see and hear.... Therefore let all the house of Israel know assuredly, that God hath made that same Jesus. whom ye crucified, both Lord and Christ.' " With such ministry by Peter, the Paraclete had no trouble convincing his hearers. (Cp. John 16:7–11.)

2:38 *Then Peter said unto them, Repent, and be baptized every one of you in the name of Jesus Christ for the remission of sins, and ye shall receive the gift of the Holy Ghost.*

Repentance is an unqualified and permanent change of attitude and inner disposition toward God the Father. toward Christ, and toward self. Hence Peter exhorted his Jewish audience to change their attitude toward God's Son, whom they had crucified, and whose prosecuting Attorney was among them. "Remission" was the *basis* or *ground* of baptism. not the *aim* or *purpose* (A. T. Robertson). That is, penitents were to be baptized on the basis of remission of sins. The phrase "gift of the Holy Ghost" implies the Spirit's personal and permanent indwelling, and that as the Spirit of God's Son, the Man Christ Jesus. This fact makes possible our position in God's family, not as minors, but as adults (Gal. 4:6). Thus God's second Gift, the Spirit, enables us to appropriate the fulness of His first Gift, the Son. Notice in passing that, although these 3,000 converts received the Spirit just as did the 120, they did not hear a heavenly tornado, see tongues of fire, or speak in other tongues. Why? The Church as an organism had already been formed earlier that day. But we know they received power because the three thousand soon became five thousand (4:4).

4:8 *Then Peter, filled with the Holy Ghost, said unto them, Ye rulers of the people, and elders of Israel....*

This scene occurred before the assembled Sanhedrin, doubtless in the Hall of Hewn Stone. It was awesome. Peter needed courage, and apparently he had it. Perhaps he recalled the Lord's previous instruction for a crisis like this: "Settle it therefore in your hearts, not to meditate before what ye shall answer: for I will give you a mouth and wisdom, which all your adversaries shall not be able to gainsay nor resist" (Luke 21:14, 15). In any case, he was consciously filled with the Spirit by faith. Incidentally, we should distinguish, perhaps, between the use of the aorist passive, "filled," as in this verse, and the use of the adjective "full." Some think the one denotes a special moment of inspiration, and the other the abiding character of a Spirit-filled man (as Stephen in Acts 6:5).

4:25 *Who by the Holy Spirit, by the mouth of thy servant David didst say, Why did the Gentiles rage, and the peoples imagine vain things?* (A.S.V.)

The Authorized Version has no reference to the Spirit in this verse; but many others do, including American Standard, Rotherham, Weymouth, Moffatt, the Amplified and Berkeley. It is divine inspiration again. (Cp. Acts 1:16; Matt. 22:43.)

4:31   *And when they had prayed, the place was shaken*
        where they were assembled together; and they were all
        filled with the Holy Ghost, and they spake the word of
        God with boldness.

Prayer often but not always precedes filling (Luke 3:21;
Acts 1:14; 4:8; 9:17; 13:9). Note here too, that prayer strengthens faith (Mark 9:29). God gives special fillings for crises,
for extra hard jobs, for bringing about the right attitude; in
this case, for "boldness." Luke explained this earth-shaking
event to Theophilus as a fresh filling, an experience which
they consciously enjoyed by faith.

5:3   *But Peter said, Ananias, why hath Satan filled thine*
        heart to lie to the Holy Ghost, and to keep back part of
        the price of the land?

The prominent person of the Godhead in this situation
was the Holy Ghost, working behind the scene. He is, after
all, God's adequate provision for the churches. And witness
again that, although unseen, the Paraclete must be recognized.
If Ananias had honored Him, he would not have acted a lie
toward God (v. 4).

Eventually, every heart becomes Satan-filled or Spirit-filled.
You and I, therefore, have the grave responsibility of protecting
our hearts. Consider how easy, and yet how serious, it is to
lie to the Holy Spirit. For it's a terribly black sin which can
be committed in the brightest fellowship. Essentially it consists
in caring more about what people think of us than we do
about what God thinks of us; man can make a god out of
man's opinion. Now look at the various aspects of this fatal
sin. Avoid them. Instead of humility and sincerity, Ananias
and Sapphira chose hypocrisy. Instead of liberality, greed filled
their hearts. In a fellowship of growing faith and increasing
joy, they nourished doubt and fear. While openly pretending
loyalty to the Son of God, they secretly practiced conspiracy
and deception. How sad. They defiled an atmosphere of rev-
erence toward God with acts of idolatry, ingratitude and

profanity. Dishonor toward God brought dishonesty before men. The desire for the praise of men and popularity brought forth the condemnation of men and of death. Ananias and Sapphira belied their profession of faith in Christ, and by doing so, insulted God the Spirit. Tragic.

Note the many ways to commit this fearful sin: by keeping our names on the church roll when we know we are not saved, by professing to be fully yielded to God when secretly we are not, by making public dedications of our lives when we do not wholeheartedly intend to live up to them, by leaving the impression that we are giving sacrificially when we are not, and by singing lies to God just in order to feign worship. You'll agree that due recognition of Christ's Spirit in our churches today would make such sins impossible.

5:9   *Then Peter said unto her, How is it that ye have agreed together to tempt the Spirit of the Lord? behold, the feet of them which have buried thy husband are at the door, and shall carry thee out.*

Observe that New Testament titles of the Spirit imply His deity: "Spirit of the Lord," "Spirit of Christ," "Spirit of his Son," "Spirit of God," "Spirit of the living God," "Spirit of truth," "Spirit of life in Christ Jesus," "Spirit of your Father," "Spirit of adoption," "Spirit of promise," "the eternal Spirit," "Spirit of grace," "Spirit of glory" and "Spirit of Jesus" (Acts 16:7, A.S.V.; Scofield mgn.). When Ananias and Sapphira tempted "the Spirit of the Lord." they tried the patience of Deity—a terrible affront!

5:32 *And we are his witnesses of these things; and so also is the Holy Ghost, whom God hath given to them that obey him.*

"Obey" here can't be the obedience of legalism; God's curse is upon that (Gal. 1:8, 9). We can't buy, work for, or merit God's power (Acts 8:18–24). The condition of all spiritual blessings, however, is "obedience of faith"; that is, obedience issuing from faith (Rom. 1:5; Gal. 3:5). Our Lord spoke in John 14:21, 23 of this deliberate, habitual, loving obedience of faith:

> He that hath my commandments, and keepeth them, he it is that loveth me: and he that loveth me shall be loved of my Father, and I will love him, and will manifest myself unto him. . . . If a man love me, he will keep my words: and my Father will love him, and we will come unto him, and make our abode with him.

Complete submission to God as sole authority in spiritual matters (Acts 5:29) constitutes one of the chief ingredients of faith for power. You'll find it implied in the condition for "rivers of living water": "He that believeth *on* me" (John 7:38).

6:3 *Wherefore, brethren, look ye out among you seven men of honest report, full of the Holy Ghost and wisdom, whom we may appoint over this business.*

6:5 *They chose Stephen, a man full of faith and of the Holy Ghost.*

Stephen was a Spirit-filled man; that was his abiding character. Perhaps Luke hoped Theophilus would emulate him. (There's no record that these men spoke with other tongues. Indeed, there's no record that the apostles ever did again after the one demonstration on the day of Pentecost.)

6:10 *And they were not able to resist the wisdom and the Spirit by which he spake.*

First, we confront here a problem in our study of the Spirit. It's this: the difficulty in distinguishing personalities in the intimate communion between the regenerated human spirit and the Paraclete. That is, which was Luke thinking of here, Stephen's spirit or God's Spirit? The Authorized translators evidently thought he had Stephen's spirit in mind, for they did not capitalize the "s" in spirit. (They couldn't consult the Greek, of course, because it never capitalizes the "s" for Spirit.) So, our problem here becomes one of interpretation as well as of explanation. This is the case, moreover, many times from here throughout the New Testament: for example, Acts 19:21; 20:22; Romans 1:4; 7:6; 8:6; 12:11; I Corinthians 14:2; II Corinthians 3:6, 8; Ephesians 1:17; and II Timothy 1:7.

Note the various interpretations, then, of Acts 6:10. Phillips says "spiritual force" and the New English Bible puts "inspired wisdom." The Scofield margin has "Holy Spirit" and most other translators capitalize the "s": as American Standard and Berkeley, Weymouth, Moffatt, Newberry, Rotherham and Amplified. I suggest that doubtless Luke meant Stephen's spirit empowered by the Holy Spirit. For is it not a case of the Paraclete coming unto a believer to convict the lost? (John 16: 7–11). Certainly it was not Stephen's unaided spirit, for those religious leaders could have withstood that. So we see in this verse the intimacy between Stephen's spirit and the Holy Spirit and, therefore, may capitalize the "s."

Let's look a little more closely, in the second place, at the Paraclete's conviction of the unsaved. For there can be no repentance apart from conviction and there can be no saving faith apart from repentance.

7:51   *Ye stiffnecked and uncircumcised in heart and ears, ye do always resist the Holy Ghost: as your fathers did, so do ye.*

For generations most of Israel's leaders had strongly challenged the Holy Spirit and His words in their prophets; some of their prophets they had put to death. Now Stephen gives, at least by implication, the threefold message designed for conviction: you're wrong for not believing on Jesus, the "Just One"; He was right in claiming to be the Son of God; wherefore you're guilty, because you stand with the prince of this world who "hath been judged." Consequently, the council ensconced in Herod's Temple with its gleaming white marble and heavy plates of gold, exploded in fury. If the many were not convicted, how about Saul of Tarsus?

7:55   *But he [Stephen], being full of the Holy Ghost, looked up steadfastly into heaven, and saw the glory of God, and Jesus standing on the right hand of God.*

Thirdly, this story of the first Christian martyr should inspire us to "follow in his train." Millions did in those first generations of Christianity and other millions have done so in our generation. How? By staying "full of the Holy Ghost." They weren't content to live on the plane of *average* Christians; they paid the price for *normal* fellowship "with the Father and with His Son Jesus Christ." Moreover, let's pray earnestly for this kind of testimony around the world in this evil day.

8:15–19   *Who, when they were come down, prayed for them, that they might receive the Holy Ghost:* (16) (*For as yet he had fallen upon none of them: only they were baptized in the name of the Lord Jesus.*) (17) *Then laid they their hands upon them, and they received the Holy Ghost.* (18) *And when Simon saw that through laying on of the apostles' hands the Holy Ghost was given, he offered them money,* (19) *saying, Give me also this power, that on whomsoever I lay hands, he may receive the Holy Ghost.*

We take the position that these Samaritans were truly saved before Peter and John arrived (v. 12). According to the pattern of experience from Pentecost on, they received the Spirit as a Person to indwell them when they believed the Gospel. Compare the experience of the three thousand of Acts 2, the multitudes of Acts 4:4 and 5:14, and the "great company of the priests" of Acts 6:7. The Man in the glory was the object of their faith; when they believed on Him, the Spirit, without calling attention to himself, quietly entered their hearts and gave joint-witness with their spirits that they were now redeemed. Nothing is said about their recognition of the Spirit; apparently that was normal experience for all believers in Jerusalem. They all knew about Pentecost.

Believing, therefore, that the faith of these Samaritans was genuine, Peter and John prayed for them that they might consciously receive by faith the filling of the Spirit. Consequently, power fell upon them; already hidden in their hearts, the Paraclete made them aware of His presence. This was evidence to all that the Samaritans, who were regarded by the Jews as racial and religious half-breeds, also had received the New Testament ministry of the Spirit. The faith of all was thus confirmed.

Thus we believe that Peter and John prayed that the Samaritan believers might receive the *filling* rather than the *person* of the Spirit. Absence of the article "the" in the Greek in verse 17 implies this meaning; that is, they definitely received by faith spiritual power. (Cp. Luke 11:13.) This essentially is the view of many expositors, including Whedon, Erdman, Hackett, F. F. Bruce, and A. T. Robertson.

The laying on of hands made the sanction of Peter and John more impressive; the once despised Samaritans were now fully identified with the Jewish believers in Jerusalem. God had poured out His Spirit on the Samaritans, too; "all flesh" was included in His redemption.

What about Simon? Evidently he didn't really believe the "things concerning the kingdom of God, and the name of Jesus Christ" as did the other Samaritans. For when he saw the others consciously receive power, his reaction showed his faith was not genuine. In other words, "he didn't know what it was all about." (See vv. 18–23.)

What is the lesson for us today? This: The Book of Acts is not a book of doctrine, but rather of the practice of doctrine; and the doctrine practiced here—aside from dispensational truth—is the fact that the distinguishing mark of normal Christianity is spiritual awareness by faith of Christ's presence in the Spirit. Power at the beginning of Christian experience is the normal thing (II Tim. 1:7). This implies that every new believer today should be taught immediately to recognize and cherish the Paraclete—His person, His presence, and His power; that He dwells in the heart to magnify Christ in the body. Thus he will be both born of the Spirit and filled with the Spirit, truly and fully saved. This is the foremost lesson in Acts, amplified. (Question: How can we get the Spirit to fill us today? John 7:37–39 and Ephesians 3:16–19 give the answer: believe deeply and fully on Christ Jesus.)

8:29 *And the Spirit said unto Philip, Go near, and join thyself to this chariot.*

God uses various means of guidance: in verse 26 it's "the angel of the Lord" who speaks to Philip; here it's the Spirit. This could be because Philip constantly. voluntarily and actively "walked in the Spirit."

8:39 *And when they were come up out of the water, the Spirit of the Lord caught away Philip, that the eunuch saw him no more: and he went on his way rejoicing.*

"Suddenly and miraculously caught away" is the comment by Robertson and Vincent here. For other instances of physical transportation. see Genesis 5:24 with Hebrews 11:5; I Kings 18:12; Ezekiel 3:12. 14; 11:1; II Corinthians 12:2; and I Thessalonians 4:17.

9:17 *And Ananias went his way, and entered into the house; and putting his hands on him said, Brother Saul, the Lord, even Jesus, that appeared unto thee in the way as thou camest, hath sent me, that thou mightest receive thy sight, and be filled with the Holy Ghost.*

Here is an instance of a believer being perceptibly filled with power under the ministry. not of an apostle, but of an obscure Christian. Truly the "wind bloweth where it listeth. and thou hearest the sound thereof. but canst not tell whence it cometh, and whither it goeth." In Acts 8:38 a "deacon" baptizes (without the authority of a local church) the treasurer of the Ethiopian court. and here a simple disciple is used to commission Christ's most illustrious apostle! (Would not some consider this very "irregular"?)

Saul must have been a saved man when Ananias came to minister to him, because Ananias addressed him as "Brother Saul." When Saul received the Spirit to indwell his heart. we're not told. Evidently he had not been conscious of the Spirit's quiet entrance; all his attention had been centered on Jesus whom he had been persecuting. But, under the ministry of Ananias, he became aware of the Spirit's filling. Also, "he received sight"; he saw that the Jesus of Nazareth, whose disciples he had been ravaging. was not only the Messiah of Israel but also the Lord of glory.

Consequently, Saul became intelligently obedient: he "arose, and was baptized." His subsequent ministry demonstrated his desire and ability to know and to do the will of God at all costs. But the chief evidence of this filling was that Jesus became precious to him. There was a radical change of attitude, a revolutionary faith in and love for the Man he had previously hated. Thus he became our example, a normal, Spirit-filled believer (I Cor. 4:16; 11:1; Phil. 3:17; I Thess. 1:6).

Paul's conscious experience of the Paraclete as the Spirit or Breath of Jesus again illustrates the main lesson in Acts: No matter how definite our conversion experience, we need to be faith-filled with the Spirit.

9:31 *Then had the churches rest throughout all Judea and Galilee and Samaria, and were edified; and walking in the fear of the Lord, and in the comfort of the Holy Ghost, were multiplied.*

The way to multiply believers and edify our churches: be alive, by faith, to God in the person of the Holy Spirit.

10:19 *While Peter thought on the vision, the Spirit said unto him, Behold, three men seek thee.*

Cornelius received instruction from without, by "an angel of God" (v. 3); Peter received it from within, by the Spirit. Both men were alive to impressions from God.

10:38 *How God anointed Jesus of Nazareth with the Holy Ghost and with power: who went about doing good, and healing all that were oppressed with the devil; for God was with him.*

God empowered Jesus for His work as Messiah. This "power" is defined by what follows as *power* to perform miracles; and Christ's miracles, especially His power over demons, were proof of His Messiahship.

God "anointed" Jesus, and we, too, may be empowered, not in some experience apart from Christ, but in faith-identification and union with Him (Eph. 6:10). As Christ recognized and honored the Spirit, so should we. Thus, and only thus, is God with us, too.

10:44–47 *While Peter yet spake these words, the Holy Ghost fell on all them which heard the word. (45) And they of the circumcision which believed were astonished, as many as came with Peter, because that on the Gentiles also was poured out the gift of the Holy Ghost. (46) For they heard them speak with tongues, and magnify God. Then answered Peter, (47) Can any man forbid water, that these should not be baptized, which have received the Holy Ghost as well as we?*

Note carefully that this is not another Pentecost; it's not a new beginning, say of a Gentile church. (There is only *one* Church, and it began as a spiritual organism at Pentecost in Jerusalem.) It is, however, a breaking down of "the middle wall of partition" (Eph. 2:14) between Jew and Gentile, for God had said through Joel, "I will pour out my Spirit upon *all* flesh" (Acts 2:17). Here in the case of Cornelius He pours out His Spirit on Gentile flesh. Luke wants Theophilus to understand the universal character of Christianity, that it's not a development from Judaism but a new movement of God on earth. It seems that he takes special pains to show Theophilus that "all flesh"—Jewish (2:4), Samaritan (8:17), Gentile (10:44)—was to benefit by this marvelous, new, life-giving ministry of the Holy Spirit.

Cornelius and his friends were not thinking about an outpouring of the Spirit but about salvation (Acts 11:14). Yet, as Peter witnessed to the universal Lordship of Jesus Christ (vv. 34, 36, 43), His death and resurrection (vv. 39–41), and His ordination as Judge of all (v. 42), suddenly, and to the amazement of Peter's six Jewish companions (v. 45), "the Holy Ghost fell on all them which heard the word." In one moment they, by faith, received the person and enjoyed the power of the Spirit; they had an experience similar to that of the 120 Jews on the day of Pentecost (Acts 11:16). They

answered quickly to the presence and power of Christ's Spirit—
normal Christian experience. Aside from the dispensational
"scaffolding," this incident emphasizes still again the chief
lesson in Acts.

11:12   *And the Spirit bade me go with them, nothing doubt-*
        ing. Moreover these six brethren accompanied me, and
        we entered into the man's house.

Contention with Peter arose among the Jewish believers
in Jerusalem concerning Peter's ministry to the Gentiles as
such; he had not required the Gentiles to enter through the
Jewish gate, so to speak. In God-given wisdom, however,
he had taken to Cornelius' house six witnesses, and had them
with him in Jerusalem. When, in their presence, he declared
that "the Spirit bade me," and that "God gave them the like
gift" (of the Spirit) as He had given on the day of Pentecost, "they held their peace, and glorified God, saying, Then
hath God also to the Gentiles granted repentance unto life."
The lesson of lessons again: awareness of the Paraclete's control.

11:15, 16   *And as I began to speak, the Holy Ghost fell on*
           them as on us at the beginning. (16) Then remembered I
           the word of the Lord, how that he said, John indeed bap-
           tized with water; but ye shall be baptized with the Holy
           Ghost.

In response to faith in the preached Gospel—". . . while
Peter yet spake *these words*"—the Paraclete straightway performed His manifold work as at Pentecost. Consequently, Peter
was reminded of what the Lord had said about this higher
baptism, this baptism in the Holy Spirit (Acts 1:5).

This is further evidence of common New Testament experience: the baptism and the filling normally occurred at
the same time, at the moment of conversion. This fact is
stated doctrinally in I Corinthians 12:13: "For in one Spirit
were we all baptized into one body, whether Jews or Greeks,
whether bond or free; and were all made to drink of one
Spirit" (A.S.V.). E. P. Gould in *An American Commentary*

on the New Testament remarks as follows on the verb "drink": "The tense of the verb. necessarily denoting the past, and naturally a definite past, makes it probable that the statement refers to the first reception of the Spirit, not to continued nourishment by him." [2] That is, believers were impressively filled with the Spirit by faith at the moment of conversion.

11:24 *For he was a good man, and full of the Holy Ghost and of faith: and much people was added unto the Lord.*

The Paraclete. in response to faith, made Barnabas "a good man." "His benevolence effectually prevented his censuring anything that might be new or strange in these preachers to the Gentiles, and caused him to rejoice in their success" (Vincent). Also he was full of divine power and spiritual gifts, especially faith. Consequently. he was able to give the new church great help. so that the number of converts increased rapidly.

11:28 *And there stood up one of them named Agabus, and signified by the Spirit that there should be great dearth throughout all the world: which came to pass in the days of Claudius Ceasar.*

Agabus possessed the Spirit's gift of prophecy in the primary sense (cf. 21:10). Should we expect ministers today to have the same gift? This question will be discussed in connection with I Corinthians 12–14.

Luke's story now broadens. He consequently begins the second section of this treatise to Theophilus (Acts 13–28) with Antioch, and no longer Jerusalem, as the center of operations. Before he closes the record. the center is Rome: Christ is for *all* nations. "Jehovah. the God of the Hebrews," is now made known as Jesus. the Lord and Saviour of the whole world, operating on earth through His Spirit, the Paraclete. (Did this testimony to Theophilus win him to this Christ? We fully expect to meet Theophilus in heaven.)

13:2 *As they ministered to the Lord, and fasted, the Holy*
      Ghost said, Separate me Barnabas and Saul for the work
      whereunto I have called them.

Barnabas had previously enlisted Saul to help him at
Antioch. "And it came to pass, that a whole year they assembled themselves with the church, and taught much people. And the disciples were called Christians first in Antioch"
(11:26). Thus, gifted leaders, "prophets and teachers," were
developed. Now it was time to do something with this scriptural
knowledge.: They waited, therefore, on the Lord to find out
what to do. Who was in charge? "The Holy Ghost said, Separate *Me . . . I* have called." Christ's Vicar told them to send
out Barnabas and Saul in obedience to the Great Commission.
Accordingly, after prayer with voluntary fasting, in order
to be specially sensitive to the Spirit's communications, the
other leaders laid their hands on Barnabas and Saul and sent
them on their first missionary journey.

13:4 *So they, being sent forth by the Holy Ghost, departed*
      unto Seleucia; and from thence they sailed to Cyprus.

It is God's purpose for churches today to be just as conscious of the Spirit's presence and just as obedient to His control as were these early saints. Remember, we have no more
right to neglect the Paraclete than we have to neglect Christ.
We should, in fact, live close enough for Him to breathe
upon us, too (John 20:22).

13:9 *Then Saul, (who is also called Paul,) filled with the*
      Holy Ghost, set his eyes on him.

Saul, entrusted with the application of the Gospel to all
nations (Gal. 2:7), soon took the lead, yet in genuine humility,
and became known as Paul. At this juncture, Christ's Agent
on earth gave him "a special influx of power to meet this
emergency" (A.T.R.). No Christian, it follows, can "stand
against the wiles of the devil" without this "power from on
high" received by faith (Eph. 6:10, 11).

13:52   *And the disciples were filled with joy, and with the Holy Ghost.*

Paul and Barnabas left the new converts in Antioch (of Pisidia) consciously filled with the Spirit's gifts, especially that of joy.

15:8   *And God, who knoweth the hearts, bare them witness, giving them the Holy Ghost, even as he did unto us.*

Note here three things: (1) God gave the Paraclete as a Person to indwell those who believed (10:44). (2) He had done the same for the 120 at Pentecost (2:4). (3) He cleansed their hearts in connection with this second gift of salvation. the Paraclete (15:9). (See comment on 11:15, 16.)

15:28   *For it seemed good to the Holy Ghost, and to us, to lay upon you no greater burden than these necessary things.*

God's Spirit, now manifested as the Breath of Christ, so guided, inspired. and empowered the leaders and speakers— Paul and Barnabas. Peter and James. and doubtless others —that the satanic, divisive and accursed issue of legalism was defeated. preserving Gospel liberty and spiritual unity in the churches (16:4, 5).

This very important event affords a pertinent illustration of the church's part in the Kingdom of God on earth: to serve as the vehicle or instrument of the Spirit. Notice that the church was so conscious of being possessed and controlled by the Spirit "that He [the Spirit] was given prior mention as chief author of their decision" (Bruce). (Cp. John 16:13.)

16:6, 7   *Now when they had gone throughout Phrygia and the region of Galatia, and were forbidden of the Holy Ghost to preach the word in Asia, (7) after they were come to Mysia, they assayed to go into Bithynia: but the Spirit suffered them not.*

One great secret of Paul's success was his awareness of the Paraclete's help. His missionary journeys, therefore. "exhibit an extraordinary combination of strategic planning and keen sensitiveness to the guidance of the Spirit of God. whether that guidance took the form of inward prompting or the overruling of external circumstances" (Bruce).

Let us today joyfully and diligently look for and obey the Spirit's openings and closings. His leadings and guidings. for all things are subject to His will: missionary work, as well as our own private affairs. and vice versa. Let us deliberately by faith bring all things under the constant control of "the Spirit of Jesus" (16:7. A.S.V.; also Scofield mgn.).[3]

19:2 *He said unto them, Have ye received the Holy Ghost since ye believed? And they said unto him, We have not so much as heard whether there be any Holy Ghost.*

First, let's look at the context of this difficult yet very important passage. Luke is describing to Theophilus a cross-section of early Christianity. In previous chapters he has traced the break between Christianity and Judaism; here he shows that Christianity transcends and supersedes the teaching of John the Baptist.

The ministry of Apollos at Ephesus affords a good illustration of the extent of John's influence (18:24–28). For Apollos knew "only the baptism of John." Whereas Apollos was mighty in the Old Testament Scriptures. he knew nothing of Christ's redeeming work and the coming of the Spirit on the day of Pentecost. Yet he had "taught accurately the things concerning Jesus" as far as John had taught. But John. who had been beheaded months before Christ had accomplished redemption. had not experienced the great Pentecost. He had indeed foretold the baptism in the Spirit and the new dispensation. but he had not entered into it. His message of the "baptism of repentance." nevertheless. had spread far and wide.

Now these "disciples" whom Paul found in Ephesus, about twelve men, knew only "John's baptism" (19:3). Historically, they lived in the dispensation of the Spirit, yet practically,

in that before Pentecost. They weren't enjoying the full
Christian position as members of the body of Christ (I Cor.
12:13), as adult sons (Gal. 4:6). and as indwelt by the Paraclete. They had no New Testament fellowship with God; they
didn't know how to "draw nigh" (Heb. 7:19; 10:22). Thus
they didn't share the common experience of God's grace, "the
love of God ... shed abroad in our hearts by the Holy Ghost
which is given unto us.". If they were indeed born again, yet
they weren't filled with the Spirit.

Paul consequently asked them. "Did ye receive the Holy
Spirit when ye believed?" (A.S.V.), implying it was normal
experience to be consciously filled with the Spirit at the time
of conversion. When they answered, "Nay, we did not so much
as hear whether the Holy Spirit was given," he instructed
them accordingly; he led them to believe for power. Then they
were re-baptized "in the name of the Lord Jesus."

19:6   *And when Paul had laid his hands upon them, the
       Holy Ghost came on them; and they spake with tongues,
       and prophesied.*

Christianity is here taking another step of progress: the
Gospel prevails in all directions. Dispensational things shouldn't
be permitted to obscure the essential lesson: that there is no
application of Christ's great salvation apart from the obvious
ministry of the Spirit. Dispensationally, however, God uses
Paul to make it clear to all concerned that these newly baptized
disciples have been brought right into the Body of Christ, with
those gathered at Pentecost, in Samaria, in the house of
Cornelius, and wherever the Word has been preached and
believed. Paul, in a special way, lays his hands upon them
and they consciously receive two of the extraordinary gifts
of the Spirit.

Don't miss the thrust of this pivotal passage. Sincere
belief of doctrine, mere orthodoxy (James 2), is not enough;
there must be conscious contact with Christ in the Spirit.
"Loyalty" to our respective churches and denominational programs *without the New Testament ministry of the Spirit*

will get us no further than John's disciples were. Every new convert should be led into the full ministry of the Paraclete. Early leaders weren't satisfied until their converts were empowered, until they had a revolutionary love for Christ. Accordingly, may God be pleased to raise up today tens of thousands of teachers and preachers who know and practice this all-important lesson: the Spirit still comes experientially upon those who believe deeply and fully on Christ Jesus (John 7:37–39; Eph. 3:16–19)![4]

19:21 *After these things were ended, Paul purposed in the Spirit when he had passed through Macedonia and Achaia, to go to Jerusalem, saying. After I have been there, I must also see Rome.*

This verse reveals Paul's plan for the near future, and we believe it was also the Holy Spirit's plan; therefore we include 19:21 and 20:22 in our list. We do so for four reasons: (1) Several versions and translations capitalize the "s" in *spirit*, including Berkeley, Amplified. Weymouth. and Moffatt. (2) Paul must certainly have sought the Spirit's guidance in this far-reaching endeavor. as was his custom in all matters. (3) Paul's aim in life was. not to be "successful," but to suffer with Christ (Phil. 3:10). (4) Our risen Lord eventually put His stamp of approval on this journey (Acts 23:11).

20:22, 23 *And now, behold, I go bound in the Spirit unto Jerusalem, not knowing the things that shall befall me there: (23) save that the Holy Ghost witnesseth in every city, saying that bonds and afflictions abide me.*

See some of the later translations of "bound in the spirit": Worrell and Berkeley. "bound by the Spirit"; Phillips. "compelled by the Spirit"; New English Bible and Weymouth. "under constraint of the Spirit"; and Moffatt, "under the binding force of the Spirit." Also see remarks on 21:11.

20:28 *Take heed therefore unto yourselves, and to all the flock, over which the Holy Ghost hath made you over-*

seers, to feed the church of God, which he hath purchased with his own blood.

The Holy Spirit, in whose hands is the power of the Godhead on earth, calls and appoints ministers of the churches; both churches and ministers have the solemn responsibility of cooperating with Him, who is the presence of Christ.

21:4   *And finding disciples, we tarried there several days: who said to Paul through the Spirit, that he should not go up to Jerusalem.*

See remarks on 21:11.

21:11   *And when he was come unto us, he took Paul's girdle, and bound his own hands and feet, and said, Thus saith the Holy Ghost, So shall the Jews at Jerusalem bind the man that owneth this girdle, and shall deliver him into the hands of the Gentiles.*

The Holy Spirit, not by mere internal intimations but by a clear, full testimony in prophetic declarations "in every city," warned Paul of danger in Jerusalem (Vincent). Those Christians said "through the Spirit" that Paul "should not go up to Jerusalem." Note, however, that Agabus, speaking by the same Spirit, didn't tell him not to go but what awaited him there.[5]

28:25   *And when they agreed not among themselves, they departed, after that Paul had spoken one word, Well spake the Holy Ghost by Esaias the prophet unto the fathers.*

This quotation (Acts 28:26, 27) from Isaiah 6:9, 10 clearly implies the deity of the Spirit; for in Isaiah it's the "Lord" who speaks, and here it's the Spirit, another Person of the same Godhead.

Thus the Book of Acts clearly demonstrates our theme: Christ alone is not "the answer" but Christ *in the Spirit* is. For remember, let me repeat, Christ himself said of the Para-

clete, "He shall glorify me." And observe, according to The
Acts, the Spirit's tremendous success in magnifying Christ.
Ponder what He did for Christianity in those thirty years,
years of Roman rule over the earth. He demonstrated the
relevant, historical nature of Christianity, its vital connection
with the people and events of the day. Yet His very presence
made Christianity also spiritual: Christ's disciples were inspired,
they were empowered and they enjoyed victory. Muse over this.
Again, Christianity was ethical: it was primarily interested in
the good and the bad, in motives, in character, in the way of
eternal life. Still again, the Spirit made the fundamental difference between two directions for Christianity: a revival
of earthly and apostate Judaism, or good news for all nations.
That is, the Spirit revealed a universal Christ, not one just
for Israel. Weigh this. Thus God's risen, glorified Christ went
forward in the person of the Spirit and in the message of
the Gospel from Judaism to the whole world. And thus Luke
brought Theophilus up to date on the ministry of Christ, both
what He began in His own person (the Gospel of Luke) and
what He continued in the person of the Paraclete "to do and
teach" (Acts 1:1): Christ in His Spirit-filled servants "turned
the world upside down" (Acts 17:6).

Wherefore let us beware lest a solution of the so-called
"problem of the transition in Acts" downgrades the Spirit.
Our understanding of this transition from law to grace, from
the kingdom of Israel to the Kingdom of God may prove
difficult and even divisive, but solutions which tend to make
Christianity less supernatural and relevant are dangerous. In
seeking the right solution, let's note three important aspects
of the change. First, a change from emphasis on earthly things.
The kingdom of Israel and earthly things are prominent in
the Synoptics, but the churches and heavenly things come
to the front in The Acts and the Epistles. The kingdom of
Israel is mentioned only once in Acts, whereas the churches
are referred to twenty-two times.

Next, there's a change from the dispensation of law to the
era of grace: Samaritans are formally recognized; Gentiles, as

such, are saved, filled with the Spirit and baptized; disciples are called Christians; the council at Jerusalem recognizes and affirms that God is no longer dealing with believers on the principle of law but now solely on the principle of grace; Jews generally reject the Gospel while Gentiles in great numbers receive it; and national Israel's (temporary) rejection is confirmed, Israel having been set aside years earlier by our Lord himself (Matt. 23:38).

Finally, it should be observed that the change itself really takes place between Matthew 23:38 and Acts 2:1, and that only *adjustments* are made thereafter. For example, adjustment in worship is very slow, for the Christian Jews in Jerusalem are still worshipping in the Old Testament way many years after Pentecost (Acts 21:20ff.).

Now for the crucial question: Did these adjustments make Christianity less supernatural or less relevant? Did God withdraw certain "gifts" from His churches while leaving Satan and his demons just as powerful as ever? Some believe He did. Others say no. I simply ask more questions: Do not the tides of spiritual power ebb and flow? What if *organized* Christianity has only a "little strength"? (Rev. 3:8). What if Christendom does go into apostasy? Does not God still have a great future for His Church as an *organism?* (Eph. 4:13–16). Is Satan stronger than Christ? Isn't it both reasonable and scriptural to believe that God stands ready to exercise through us today all the supernatural power we need to cope with Satan and sin? Can't God defeat Satan in one time and place just as easily as in another? Isn't the Gospel still "the power of God unto salvation"? Whose fault is it that so many churches are dying today? Is it the Paraclete's? Is He not just as able today? [6]

While we insist that Christianity is still supernatural, we can't, however, expect the river to rise higher than its source; neither should we contend that the spiritual tide will rise as high in our day as it did in Peter's or Paul's. Men today aren't going to write other books of Scripture, or prophesy in the primary sense. But we may be sure that there is still a tide, that it could be higher in our day than it is. Indeed, this tide has risen considerably in some parts of our world.[7]

Evangelist Billy Graham saw physical as well as spiritual miracles in Korea. He testified over the radio from Seoul on March 4, 1956, that the Korean Christians were witnessing New Testament signs and wonders, and were exercising all the gifts: blind were seeing, and other unusual things were taking place.

I myself witnessed a physical miracle on Sunday, May 24, 1942, which tremendously strengthened my faith in spiritual miracles. I was then pastor of the Cherrydale Baptist Church, Arlington, Virginia. It came about like this. Our church fellowship had been deeply exercised about revival and spiritual awakening, and God brought us to believe in miracles today.

At that very time, as though God would test our new step of faith, one of our shut-ins, whom I affectionately called "Mother D——," asked me to use James 5:14, 15 in her behalf. She was seventy-seven years of age, had been critically ill for months; and several doctors, including her own son, had given her up to die.

But let it be said that the fifteen or twenty of us who remained after the morning service for this special ministry— she had been carried to the church building, having requested that the anointing and prayer take place there—obeyed every known condition of prayer and oneness of mind. And we were conscious of the need of a miracle equivalent to the resurrection of the dead. Accordingly, we cried to the God "who giveth life to the dead, and calleth the things that are not, as though they were." Again we had a sense of God's sovereignty in seeing fit to recover one person at the instance of His people's prayers while He may see fit to withhold recovery from another. There was in our hearts this difference between believing for *physical* healing and believing for *spiritual* healing: Spiritual healing always takes place immediately upon the condition of genuine faith because provision is made for the instantaneous salvation of soul and spirit. It's always God's will to save immediately any who believe the Gospel. But physical healing has to do with the body which is not yet redeemed (Rom. 8:10). It's not always God's will to heal the body here and now.

Our sister, however, had faith that God would heal her body, provided she comply with James 5:14, 15. We considered it, therefore, our duty and privilege to join her in "the prayer of faith." And God saw fit to heal her miraculously, for which we praised Him from the depths of our hearts.

There was marked consecration on her part for the rest of her life, some three or four years. (I left that pastorate December 31, 1943.) The Wednesday following her healing, she walked several blocks to the prayer meeting to give a glowing testimony. She was regular at all the services thereafter, and possessed a growing spirit of intercession and a deepening compassion for the lost.[5] Not only was my own faith greatly strengthened by this miracle in the physical realm, but Cherrydale Baptist Church came to life; and it has continued to make healthy, spiritual progress ever since.

So, what shall we conclude about the "transition"? Shall we agree with William R. Newell?

> Let us not dare to claim that the Holy Ghost is no longer willing to work in power amongst us. Because, for Him to do so is *God's plan.* Indeed, He is so working where not hindered. Let us confess the truth. Our powerlessness is because of unbelief—the inheritance of the sins of our fathers, the inheritance of a grieved Spirit. It may be true that He does not work as He once did; but let us admit two things: we dare not say, He is not willing so to work; and, we dare not say, It is God's plan that He does not! We can only say, *We have sinned!* So did Daniel (Dan. 9). So did Ezra (Ezra 9). So did they of Nehemiah's day (Neh. 9). Our days are days of failure, just like those. Nor will it do (as with so many enlightened saints) merely to 'see and judge the failure of the professed Church' and gather in the name of the Lord, and remember His death in the breaking of

bread every Lord's day. All this is good. But we must judge ourselves if we do not have real power amongst us. And the power of the Spirit. in a day of apostasy like this will bring us into a *deep burden over the state of things, and into prayer*, such as the great men of God made in the three chapters to which we have just referred! [9]

Of course we agree. Accordingly, the supreme feature of Paul's epistles, next in our study, is how to enter into the blessings of Acts 2:4—how to blaze with Pentecostal fire.

A THOUSAND YEARS HAVE COME

A thousand years have come and gone,
    And near a thousand more,
Since happier light from heaven shone
    Than ever shone before.
And in the hearts of old and young
    A joy most joyful stirred,
That sent such news from tongue to tongue
    As ears had never heard.

And we are glad, and we will sing,
    As in the days of yore;
Come all, and hearts made ready bring,
    To welcome back once more
The day when first on wintry earth
    A summer breeze began,
And, dawning in a lowly birth,
    Uprose the Light of man.

—Thomas T. Lynch

7

The Spirit in the Pauline Epistles—
Divine Power Experienced

WHEREAS JOHN'S GOSPEL reaches the high-water level of divine revelation concerning the Spirit, and The Acts pictures not only the high tide but even the spring tide of spiritual manifestation, Paul's epistles concern "the work of the Holy Spirit in the individual man, His methods and processes in the training of each soul for God." [1]

Accordingly Paul's epistles outline the place of the Spirit in the individual believer, in the organic church and in local churches. For the individual believer, Christ lives in him by means of the Paraclete. When looked at chronologically, the first six of Paul's epistles—Galatians, I and II Thessalonians, I and II Corinthians, and Romans—deal primarily with the Spirit's ministry to the individual. Ephesians, Colossians, and Philippians portray the Church as manifested in the local churches, where—according to I Timothy, Titus, and II Timothy—the Spirit presides.

In other words, Christ in heaven, through the Spirit on earth, supplies every need of every believer—every need of yours and every need of mine. Indeed, just as the Spirit moved upon the original chaos to bring order. fruitfulness, and beauty; so He does in the chaos of our sinful souls. If you and I will only let Him have His way—that is, neither resist. grieve, nor quench Him—He will make His contact with us, as regenerated human spirits, a blessed experience; He will purify, control, guide. assure, and conform us to the image of God's Son.

And all ye philosophers. psychologists, and psychiatrists. who seek a remedy for man's divided, frustrated, helpless state. you can surely find it in Paul's Gospel. In the realm of God's grace, ministered by God's Spirit, men lose their fears, resolve their doubts, get rid of their hesitation, unify their personalities, and achieve the good they desire. When we make much of the Holy Spirit in our experience it's impossible to be pessimistic and divided. Let us discover. therefore, more than anything else, and exercise ourselves in, the willingness of the Holy Spirit to take care of us, of every need, of every weakness, of every problem. "For God hath not given us the spirit of fear; but of power, and of love. and of a sound mind" (II Tim. 1:7).

We revert for a moment to the lesson of lessons in The Acts before we begin our study of the Spirit in the Epistles: we must remember that the early Christians knew the Paraclete from the beginning of their experience of grace; they recognized and honored Him as Christ's presence and power. In fact. the Corinthians magnified certain gifts of the Spirit to the neglect of Christ and the Paraclete's relation to Him. This is not true with many professing Christians today; they know nothing about the New Testament ministry of the Spirit; they are like the disciples of John at Ephesus. We must not forget, therefore, that both the Pauline and General Epistles imply a knowledge of the Paraclete on the part of those to whom they were addressed—indeed, to be filled with the Spirit was then normal Christian experience. Consequently. we shouldn't expect these epistles to tell their readers how to be filled initially. but rather how to maintain and enlarge that filling. Consider the following passages in this connection: Romans 12:1, 2; II Corinthians 3:18; Galatians 3:5 (cp. Conybeare and Howson's translation: "Whence. I say, are the gifts of Him who furnishes you with the fulness of the Spirit. and works in you the power of miracles?"); Ephesians 3:14–19; 5:18 ("be being filled") with 6:10 (Gr. *be empowered* in the

Lord). So, let's remember this about the Book of Acts: the grace of God, as early Christians well knew and many sincere believers today don't know, is enjoyed only by the ministry of "the Spirit of grace." We repeat. not the Christ of history merely is the answer, but the Christ of glory, now consciously present in the hearts of His people in the person and power of the Paraclete.

Now we move forward to watch the Book of Romans trace the mid-stream current of Christianity's supernaturalism: believers are taught how to reign as spiritual kings (5:21) in the "good. and acceptable, and perfect, will of God" (12:1, 2). Thirty-one citations are found. as follows: 1:4; 5:5; 7:6; 8:2, 4, 5 (twice), 6, 9 (thrice). 10. 11 (twice), 13, 14, 15, 16, 23, 26 thrice). 27 (twice); 9:1; 12:11; 14:17; 15:13, 16, 19, 20.[2]

These suggest eighteen phases of the Paraclete's work in us as individuals, all designed to conform us to the image of God's Son (8:28. 29): (1) On the basis of the primary meaning of the Cross (consummated in resurrection, 1:4), the Spirit pours out in our hearts the love of God, 5:5. (2) On the basis of the deeper meaning of the Cross (resulting in our deliverance from Law. 7:6). He sets us free from sin's bondage, 8:1–3. (3) He fulfills the righteous requirement of the Law (which is love) in our daily walk. 8:4. (4) He creates the right purpose in life. 8:5–8. (5) He enthrones Christ in our hearts, 8:9. (6) He makes Christ our life, 8:10, 11. (7) He gives us victory over sinful habits. 8:12. 13. (8) He creates in us the joy of adult sonship. 8:14. (9) He gives us courage, 8:15. (10) He assures us of security, 8:16, 17. (11) He encourages us, 8:18–25. (12) He inspires, guides, and strengthens our life of prayer. 8:26. 27. (13) He continues to pour out the Father's love in our hearts, 8:31–33. (14) And He pours out the Son's love in our hearts, too, 8:34–39. (15) He mediates righteousness, peace, and joy, 14:17. (16) He makes us abound in hope. 15:13. (17) He makes it possible, during this Church era, for Gentiles to come to God direct, through the shed blood of Christ, without being subordinated to the priestly nation of Israel, or of course, any earthly priest, 15:16. (18) He himself loves us, 15:30.

1:4   *And declared to be the Son of God with power, accord-*
     ing to the Spirit of holiness, by the resurrection from the
     dead.

This is a reference, doubtless, to Christ's own spirit, as contrasted with "the flesh." Nevertheless, it's Christ's spirit empowered by the Holy Spirit and, therefore, we count it, as do others, such as Phillips, New English Bible, The Berkeley Version, Rotherham, Weymouth, Moffatt, Amplified, Worrell and Newberry. The *Wycliffe Bible Commentary* says, "The resurrection from the dead was a fact proclaimed by Christians. But the powerful declaration of Jesus as Son of God by his resurrection was the work of the Holy Spirit in illuminating the full meaning of the historical fact." [3]

5:5   *And hope maketh not ashamed; because the love of God*
     is shed abroad in our hearts by the Holy Ghost which
     is given unto us.

What a "gusher"—this second reference to the blessed Comforter in the "chief book of the New Testament" (Luther), "the profoundest book in existence" (Coleridge), and "the cathedral of Christian faith" (Godet)! It implies so many new and comforting things—things that belong to all the saved. Avoid Melanchton's pitfall, the idea that believers receive the Spirit in a work of grace subsequent to conversion. For the pronoun "us" shows that the Spirit is given to *all* the justified at the moment of justification. In the power of the Holy Spirit, God comes into instantaneous personal contact with each and every true believer and floods his heart with the consciousness of His love. "O love of God, how rich and pure, how measure-less and strong!"

It is now possible to rejoice in these facts: sin has been put away, our "old man" has been crucified, all believers have been baptized into one body, we're indwelt by the Spirit, we're "new creatures in Christ Jesus," we've been "sealed with the Holy Spirit of promise," and we may now enter "into the holiest of all" (Heb. 9:8; 10:19–22). None of these great certainties could have been true of us or experienced by us before Pentecost.

This inspiring verse, however, aptly reminds us that God gave us not only His Son, but also His Spirit, and that one of the chief ministries of His Spirit is to encourage us in time of persecution and need. The Paraclete does this by making us conscious, in a direct personal way, of God's unspeakable love for us. Indeed, for the first time in the Bible the divine attribute of love is in Romans 5:5 immediately connected with the Spirit. So let's trust God in Christ! With all our thinking, feeling and willing ability, let the entire attitude of our soul toward God be that of TRUST. Then the Comforter can and will work.

Chapters 5–8 expound the doctrine of the Paraclete's operation on the principle of grace. And, of course, if we would have Him minister to us in a rich, full, deep, and fruitful way, we must understand this principle and how it works. Let it be admitted, that many earnest souls have enjoyed this principle to some degree without knowing the doctrine, yet knowledge of the doctrine helps much. It may be outlined as follows: the four justifying facts of the Gospel—Christ died, was buried, raised, seen—connote four sanctifying facts: (1) Christ died to deliver us from the power as well as the penalty of sin, (2) His burial symbolized the end of our history in Adam, (3) we share the likeness of His resurrection, and (4) we share His resurrection life. The Spirit works as we reckon on these facts. In other words, Paul's "doctrine of the Spirit is the necessary, vital, and essential complement of his doctrine of justification." [4] We must, therefore, study the Spirit in Romans 8 in the light of the preceding chapters 5–7. For, whereas Romans 3:21—5:21 expounds Christ our Righteousness reckoned to us in the righteousness of God the Father, Romans 6–8 explains Christ our Righteousness realized by us in the power of God the Spirit. The filling of the Spirit is implied from The Acts in order for us to enjoy the deeper meaning of the Gospel set forth here. So the work of the Spirit is not incidental in Romans 6, 7; it's fundamental.

The chief thing to learn in Romans 5 is the fact that God's grace abounded at Calvary much more than our sin abounded. Five times God tells us that His provision for us is "much more" abundant than the guilt and power of our sin. By His matchless, marvelous, infinite Spirit of GRACE, therefore, we can reign as kings through righteousness—that provided at Calvary—unto eternal life through Jesus Christ our Lord (v. 21).

Romans 6:1–14 fills our souls with heavenly light as it expounds to us this deeper meaning. That is, believers are absolutely one with Christ in His redemptive work, identified with Him. We don't have to wish or try, fast or pray, or do anything in order to be made one with Him; it's already a fact. We need only to know it and reckon on it in the power of the Spirit in order to experience it.

Consider the gist of Romans 6:2–5: "We who died to sin, how shall we any longer live therein?" When did we die to sin? We died to sin at the Cross (Gal. 2:20). When did we begin to experience this death? When we believed and the Spirit applied the Gospel. At that moment we were judicially associated by God with Christ; also we were baptized by the Holy Spirit into Christ's death, burial, resurrection, and life. Our water baptism witnessed to this oneness, which had both negative and positive effects. Negatively, our history as sinners ended; positively, we were placed on resurrection ground, "in newness of life." "For if we have been united with him in the likeness of his death, we shall be also in the likeness of his resurrection." That is, we have been planted together with, or grafted into, Christ—a work of the Spirit—and are now raised with Him to share His risen life.

Romans 6:6 states the fact that "our old man was crucified with Christ." In other words, we died, in the federal headship of Christ, with Him. Our history in the first Adam ended at Calvary. We're no longer in Adam's race; we're no longer akin to him; our former relationship to the world and to the old creation has been severed! "Our old man" re-

fers to our old selves, all that we were as a result of our natural relationship to the sin of Adam, our bond relating us
to Adam and all his depravity. For the truth is, in Adam we
were so incorrigibly wicked that we had to be crucified. But
since "our old man" was crucified with Christ, we're no longer connected with Adam and his race. We've "put off" the old
man with his desires, lusts, ambitions, hopes, judgments, and
doings (Col. 3:9). (Ephesians 4:22 exhorts us to make this
fact of position a practice of experience.) No more does "our
old man" have authority over us to make our bodies instruments of sin, that we should become servants of evil. Neither
are we longer responsible to provide a righteousness satis-
factory to God; Christ is that! Both positively and negatively,
Christ (in His Spirit) is all we need. *In Him* sin has no more
power over us than it would have over a man dead and buried.
In Him (formed by the Spirit) we are a new creation; the
things of Adam are passed away; behold, the things of Christ
are ours (II Cor. 5:17). Consequently, the body as an instrument of sin is now done away with; we are no longer in bondage to sin. The Spirit frees us (Rom. 8:2).

Romans 6:7 unlocks the emancipating meaning of this
whole section of the epistle, chapters 5–8: "For he that hath
died is justified from sin." That is, we're justified from indwelling sin. O struggling Christian, this key truth should
thrill your soul. Believe it! You have been justified, declared
righteous, by a holy God, not only from sins committed (3:24).
but also from the sin that dwells within you. For Christ was
our sin offering (Lev. 4) as well as our trespass offering (Lev.
5). You have been potentially released, made free, from the
slavery of sin. Let not Satan tell you otherwise. The Spirit
makes this actual (8:2).

See how the positive truth glistens against the background
of the negative: "But if we died with Christ, we believe that
we shall also live with him; knowing that Christ being raised
from the dead dieth no more; death no more hath dominion
over him" (6:8, 9, A.S.V.). All our features inherited from
sinful Adam died, positionally, with Christ; all spiritual rela-

tionship with Adam's race ended at the Cross. We're no longer
of the same nature as natural man; we're not of his kind at
all. We have no kinship with Adam and his descendants; we
in Christ are no longer possessed of a merely "natural" mind.
This means that we have, among many other blessed things,
a way of escape from our ugly selves and ways. For "death no
more hath dominion over him" or those who are empowered
by the Spirit! (8:10, 11).

Now look at this marvelous statement (6:10) about the
death with which you and I are identified: "For in that death
that he died, he died unto sin once for all; but in that life
that he liveth, he liveth unto God" (A.S.V. mgn.). You see,
we've been made one with Christ who lives unto God; that
is, we have the same relationship to God that He has. Indeed,
God sees us only in Him, and we, too, should see and reckon
ourselves only in Him before God. Christ (in the Paraclete)
was, and is, and ever shall be all we need. And we now are
free to share the risen life and power of Christ. Because, let
me repeat, not only has God declared us righteous concerning
what we have done, but He has also declared us righteous
concerning what we were, and, as to the flesh, still are. God
has identified us with the living Christ who died to *sin* as well
as to *sins*.

Romans 6:11, consequently, exhorts us to take up and
maintain the Gospel attitude. For, in fact, this makes the
practical difference between Christian position and Christian
experience: "Even so reckon ye also yourselves to be dead
unto sin, but alive unto God in Christ Jesus." Our victory over
the power of indwelling sin depends upon our reckoning;
for then the Spirit frees us (8:2). This deeper meaning is to
be known and counted on by faith. We should take up and
maintain, despite appearances, feelings, and all opposition, this
Gospel attitude: I died with Christ to sin; I live with Christ
to God; I count it true; I believe it for victory. All this is
realized in the power of the Spirit (8:13).

With such an attitude we refuse to let sin reign in our
bodies, making us obey their passions (6:12). Neither do we

keep on yielding the members of our bodies to sin as weapons of unrighteousness; but we present ourselves once for all unto God, not as members of Adam's race, but as alive from the dead. By faith we stand on resurrection ground with Christ, and once for all present our members as weapons of righteousness unto God (6:13). This attitude makes it possible for the Spirit to work (8:4); consequently, sin doesn't have dominion over us: for we're not under the authority of and liable to the penalties of law, but we're under the authority and power of *grace* (6:14).

Let us summarize: Our attitude is to be one of victory, that of spiritual kings reigning over sin that dwells within us. It is an attitude based on "knowing" the deeper meaning of the Cross, that we are one with Christ in His victory. We are to "know," "reckon," and "yield" so the Paraclete can make us "more than conquerors." This, by the way, makes the difference between being merely "religious," and living Christ. Many earnest believers try ever so hard to live Christ and yet they fail. It's because they're ignorant of God's provision.[5]

If we let the Spirit work on the principle of grace, "the sin that doth so easily beset us" will not defeat us: neither the "inferiority complex," nor self-pity, self-consciousness, discouragement, pride, hurt feelings, grudges. We shall, moreover, never be disappointed in ourselves, for we shall put no confidence in ourselves in the first place. We shall never struggle and hope to become better; because we reckon we died, and "it is no longer I that live, but Christ liveth in me." We shall never live "under the circumstances," but, in Christ, above them. Christ in the Spirit makes us overcomers.

Victor Hugo said, "No army can withstand the strength of an idea whose time has come." The time for a fresh realization of justification came in Martin Luther's day. Oh, that the time for a recognition and realization of identification—the blood-bought indentification of the saved sinner with Christ—might come in our day! God mightily enabled the Reformers to preach the Gospel for the sinner, but they never made clear the Gospel for the saint generally.[6]

Returning to our verse-by-verse exposition, we're warned in Romans 6:15–23 by a gospel red light: God exhorts all professing Christians to present the members of their bodies as servants to righteousness unto holiness—so Christ in the Spirit can deliver. The only other course possible to creatures depraved by sin is slavery to uncleanness and iniquity, with consequent eternal death. Those of us who have really repented and believed have a new nature (inspired by the Spirit) which gives us a hunger for sanctification, and leads us on into full enjoyment of that eternal life which we already possess. This is the line of thought here. The warning might be restated thus: If you continue to practice sin, you have never repented; if you have never repented, you have never been convicted of sin; if you manage to escape conviction of sin, and thus miss personal faith in the Crucified One, you will go to hell forever. "For the wages of sin is death; but the free gift of God [applied by the Spirit] is eternal life in Christ Jesus our Lord."

7:6 *But now we are delivered from the law, having died to that wherein we were held; that we should serve in newness of the Spirit, and not in oldness of the letter.*

This verse emphasizes the clear-cut contrast between the system of Law and the economy of Grace and leads us to a brief examination of the chapter.

Romans 7 expounds the fact that the saved person is not related to God on the principle of law; indeed, it shows that a person who attempts fellowship with Him by grace and law at the same time is guilty of spiritual adultery. The result is measureless sin and wretchedness. In verses 1–3 Paul illustrates the seriousness of trying both at the same time. But how can one who is in law-covenant with God—a Jew, for example—accept grace? The answer is good news: he can do it by faith in Christ who died and lives again. For Christ died to discharge him from the law; He lives again to give him newness of life (7:4). We're not only made dead to *sin* but we also are "made dead to the *law* through the body of Christ." Consequently, we can "bring forth fruit unto God," because we "serve in newness of the Spirit." We now have a new relationship to God, a new attitude toward His work, a new power to do it, and a new love to motivate us. It's somewhat like the case of an office secretary who marries her employer; her relationship to him is changed. She has a higher calling. She leaves his office for his home, where she lives by marriage principles instead of office rules. Or this changed status may be thought of as the difference between one's relationship to a judge and to a father. A believer, you know, is related to God primarily as a son to a father, not as a criminal to a judge. That is, he has been taken out of God's court and placed in His family.

Paul explains, furthermore, how law works. The principle of law is not the sin principle, but it does arouse sin in human hearts (Rom. 7:7, 8). For instance, when Paul himself attempted to fellowship with God under law, the result was: "Sin revived, and I died." [7] Dormant sin became alive in Paul: his fellowship was broken, and he became spiritually dormant (7:9). That is, the Spirit could not work. Law not only frustrates grace (Gal. 2:21); it also stirs up sin. That is, sin works through the law, "that which is good," to magnify itself in our experience (7:12, 13). The covenant of law, given to Israel (for one thing) to regulate and preserve human life on earth, Paul found to be unto "death" when placed in competition with God's covenant of grace (7:10).

Consequently, we dare not expect God to bless us on the basis, for instance, of our "religious" works. Because we're "carnal, sold under sin" (7:14). Our bodies are not yet redeemed (8:10), and, even as regenerated spirits, we have absolutely no strength apart from Christ's Spirit. Every so-called good thing we do apart from the Spirit is sin. We indeed possess new desires in our quickened spirits, but our flesh, our mere human nature, is weak and can't do that which is good (7:18). In addition, sin "dwelleth in" us, "evil is present." Grace doesn't change sinful human nature; rather it counts it crucified (Gal. 5:24). So. when we practice legalism, we find ourselves weak in that which is good and strong in that which is bad (7:19–23).

Let's beware. therefore. of the way we try to control self. For our intellects. tastes. feelings. emotions, imaginations and all our faculties, both of mind and of sensibility, are depraved. Consequently. every thought. word, and deed that doesn't originate from the Spirit comes from the "flesh" and manifests itself as "a work of the flesh." Indeed. we're hopelessly bad, all bad. in the flesh. Fallen human nature. let us be convinced. is an impure fountain. and all its streams are polluting. It can't send forth ought that is pure, holy, or good (cf. Lev. 15: "unclean ... unclean ... unclean," sixteen times). Only the Spirit can control it (8:14). Only grace can bring good out of it. Then how foolish to try to control ourselves by the wrong principle. or by two mutually exclusive principles (see Rom. 11:6). Those of us who. like Paul. have been beguiled. and have tried to use both methods at the same time must regretfully testify to the same experience: "O wretched man that I am! who shall deliver me from the body of this death?" Let's not despair, however. for. thank God. there's deliverance through Jesus Christ our Lord; there is "the law of the Spirit of life in Christ Jesus."

Thus we arrive at Romans 8. with twenty-two references to the Spirit. Here. in the light of Romans 6 and 7. and for the first time in Scripture, we're told why and how the Spirit can free believers from the power of indwelling sin: He works on the basis of Christ's shed blood. "There is therefore now *no* condemnation," either on account of sins committed (3:21—5:21) or on account of sin that dwells in us (6:1—8:39). Why? Because the Spirit helps us to quit practicing sin; the Spirit makes Christ "the answer." Since this point is so vital. and yet so neglected, let's linger awhile in this section of Scripture. One wishes he could discuss it with Paul himself! If one could. the dialogue might go something like this: "Paul, would you call this eighth chapter of Romans your Pentecost?"

"No, but chapters six through eight explain the way to benefit from the one and only Pentecost."

"What is this way, Paul? What is the condition?"

"Know and reckon on Gospel facts, that's all. The Spirit will do the rest."

"And what are the Gospel facts? Tell me again, Paul."

"There in brief are the *justifying* facts: declared righteous, forgiven, severed from Adam and put into Christ glorified, the gift of the Holy Spirit to indwell."

"That's wonderful! Are there other facts, too?"

"Yes, there are *sanctifying* facts also: you *in Christ* died to sin, were buried, raised and are now alive unto God; you also were discharged from law; but you *in yourself* are still a wretched sinner."

"In other words, Paul, I can choose to live in Romans 8 instead of Romans 7? I can choose, step by step, and Christ in His Spirit will deliver me continually from wretchedness. from sin?"

"Yes, indeed. That's what He did for me."

"Thank you, Paul. Thank you so much!"

I. The Spirit Frees Us from Sin and Death (8:1–11).

Our Lord promised this blessed freedom from sinful habits. you remember, in John 8:32: "And ye shall know the truth. and the truth shall make you free." Now Romans 8:2 tells us how; it's by "the Spirit of life in Christ Jesus." That is, according to Calvin: "The Holy Spirit is the bond by which Christ efficaciously unites us to Himself."

Here again we wish we could talk with Paul. For this remarkable concept of being "in Christ" truly dominated all his thought. You recall he spoke in 6:5 of the believer's being grafted into Christ. Would the conversation run somewhat like this? "Paul, what does this oft-used phrase mean?"

"It means the believer is identified and united with Christ

112 / FIRE, RADIANCE, AND LOVE

in glory, a supremely intimate relation and communion. It also points to Christ as the source. cause and power of the Christian's life."

"Does 'in Christ' sometimes refer to the believer's place in the organic Church, the Church which is His Body, Paul?"

"Yes, all this and more. Indeed. my expression 'in Christ' signifies the central aspect of salvation which is better experienced than explained." [8]

8:2 *For the law of the Spirit of life in Christ Jesus made me free from the law of sin and of death* (A.S.V.).

Thus Paul testified. The operation of the Spirit. mediating to him the life in Christ Jesus. made him free from the operation of indwelling sin and its result. death. This the law-principle could not do. because it had to work through sinful human nature. But by "sending his own Son in the likeness of sinful flesh and for sin." God "condemned sin the flesh" (v. 3). That is, Christ's work at Calvary made it possible for God, the Righteous Judge. not only to declare Paul righteous concerning sins committed (3:24) and his sinful nature (6:7). but also, by His Spirit. to condemn and nullify the power of sin in him, so that Paul ceased practicing sin.

A. *The Spirit Fulfills the Law* (8:3. 4). This is the first thing He does in setting us free.

8:4 *That the righteousness of the law might be fulfilled in us, who walk not after the flesh, but after the Spirit.*

The righteous requirement of the law is love (Matt. 22:37–40; Rom. 13:8–10) produced by the Spirit (Gal. 5:16–25). And the Spirit fulfills this requirement as we refuse to make our choices according to the standard of the flesh and make them according to His standard of Christ. In other words, the less we "organize life around the idea of the gratification of the physical senses" (Wright) and the more fully we reckon on oneness and union with Christ in glory. the more fruit of the Spirit we bear. Our walk. you see. determines not our security but our fruitfulness (John 15:5).

"Walk" means choice, step by step. That is, our part is not doing the best we can, struggling, fasting, praying, fighting; it's not eradication of the old nature, suppression, or imitation; it's the responsibility of choice, based upon the deeper meaning of the Gospel (Rom. 5:12—7:25). When we make the right choice, the Spirit does the fighting for us (Gal. 5:17); He counteracts sin; He makes us free. The expression "walk not after the flesh, but after the Spirit," let us emphasize, implies right choices both negatively and positively. Right choices turn on the power, so to speak. Then the Paraclete can make us free from every sinful habit: bitterness, criticism, jealousy, enmity, envy, strife, division—sins of the spirit; also sins of the flesh: impure thoughts and acts, drunkenness, doping, profanity, all questionable habits.

Some men were constructing a bridge across the mouth of a river flowing into the ocean. It developed that a certain pier could not be placed at the right spot because of an old, unused water main. After much consideration the foreman decided to change the location of the pier rather than try to remove the huge pipe from the bottom of the river.

However, a young engineer just out of college had a different idea and dared to speak to the boss about it. Reluctantly, the foreman gave the young man permission to try his plan.

While the tide was out, the novice had logs floated to the right spot, bound into a raft and secured to the old water main with strong chains. Then the young boss sat down and the old boss wanted to know why he was quitting.

He confidently replied, "Sir, just wait until the tide comes in."

And, sure enough, when God's irresistible tide came in, it jerked the obstructing pipe out of the way of the pier.

Likewise, in Christian experience we must despair of all that is merely human and rely wholly upon the supernatural, the Holy Spirit. There's absolutely no strength for deliverance in ourselves; human nature is "weak." "The Son of man can do nothing of himself." "I can of mine own self do nothing." "The Father that dwelleth in me, he doeth the works." Think of it! Even Jesus, the God-Man, accomplished the will of God not in His own strength. but "through the eternal Spirit."

So, grace enables us to get rid of self in order that God may work through us—by His Spirit. Many have been the struggles of souls ignorant of the deeper meaning of the Gospel to put out of the way the wisdom and power of man in the things of God. There was Saint Simon Stylites who lived on a pillar in Italy for over thirty years, trying to be holy. Yet he was probably the most self-righteous man in his generation. Then there was Thomas a' Kempis. ever striving to furnish a righteousness which God had already furnished in Christ. Pastor Monod preached in Paris a century ago on the text "when I am weak. then I am strong":

> This wretched strength of our own, this talent of our own, forms in us as it were a little cherished sanctuary, which our jealous pride keeps closed against the strength of God, in order to reserve for itself a last retreat. But if we could finally become weak, in good earnest, and despair absolutely of ourselves, the strength of God, diffusing itself throughout our entire inward man, and penetrating into the most secret folds. would fill us with all the fulness of God.

William R. Newell once said to D. E. Hoste of the China Inland Mission, "Pray for me that I may be nothing." Mr. Hoste replied. "No use to pray about that! You are nothing. Brother Newell; just take it by faith." Yes, one is set free. lifted right out of himself into Christ Jesus. in actual experience. Thus, one comes to know "the irresistible might of weakness." We choose; the Paraclete works!

But let us consider a bit further the implications of Romans 8:4 and its context. For instance. weakness lets grace work. That is, one of the greatest lessons a Christian or a church can learn is the inability of the flesh to help and its ability to hinder the Spirit. When a church has enough living faith to beg God for revival these days, there's usually so much human wisdom, eloquence. talent and energy of the flesh (not to speak of the enmity of the flesh) in the way that the Spirit can't guide the leaders into awakening. All dependence upon human ability, all walking after the flesh, must be eliminated before God's grace and power can operate fully. Sober reckoning upon our weakness will make many changes in our methods and messages. It will humble us, constrain us to pray, stop man-pleasing by the choir and the pulpit, and make a real prayer meeting out of the mid-week service. It will separate us from the things of the flesh which hinder the Paraclete.

Someone has said, "The 'death' and the 'life' are inseparably connected in the economy of grace. But, be it observed, *the life comes after the death*." Christ said, "Except a grain of wheat fall into the ground and die, it abideth alone." Truly, "The key to life is death." And Romans 8:4 gives the clue to victory: "Walk not after the flesh, but after the Spirit." For this death can be experienced only in the power of the Gospel; it's not by our struggling and "devotion," but wholly by grace through faith, according to Romans 6–8. By the Paraclete's help, a believer's human will can so concur with God's will that grace is virtually the sole principle at work in our hearts and service (I Cor. 15:10). Luther's prayer that shook the world is a striking example of the choice involved in Romans 8:4:

> . . . How weak the flesh, and Satan how strong! If it is only in the strength of this world that I must put my trust, all is over. . . . This is not my work but Thine. I have nothing to do here. Nothing to contend for with these great ones of the world. . . . The cause is Thine, O Lord, help me! Faithful and unchangeable God, in no man do I put my trust. It would be vain. All that is of man is uncertain; all that cometh of man fails. . . .

We deliberately give much attention to the supernaturalism of Romans 6–8. There may be room for difference of opinion about the supernatural manifestations in The Acts and I Corinthians, but one can't be hesitant here. Rather, let us demonstrate to the world today this normal supernaturalism, this genuineness of New Testament Christianity. And every person who has had a normal experience of grace possesses a deep desire to do this very thing. He longs that others may enjoy God's grace, too.

B. *Next, the Spirit Creates the Right Purpose in Life—To Please God* (8:5-8). These verses discuss the radical change of purpose involved in this miraculous experience, and contrast the evidences of the two standards of life, the flesh and the Spirit.

8:5, 6   *For they that are after the flesh mind the things of the flesh; but they that are after the Spirit the things of the Spirit. (6) For the mind of the flesh is death; but the mind of the Spirit is life and peace* (A.S.V.).

On this passage, I would feign ask Paul for more explanation.

"Paul, it's hard for me to get at what you are saying here. Maybe it would help for you to indicate the emphatic words."

"Emphasize the word *are* both times: '... they that *are* after the flesh ... and they that *are* after the Spirit.' I'm contrasting the difference between being dominated by the flesh and controlled by the Spirit. People dominated by the self-life purpose to do the things of the self-life; but they that are controlled by the Spirit purpose to do the things of the Spirit."

"Another detail, Paul, please—does the word *mind* in verse 5 mean the same as it does in verse 6?"

"*Mind* is a verb in verse 5 and a noun in verse 6. Read verse 6 like this: 'For the purpose of the flesh is death; but the purpose of the Spirit is life and peace.' "

"The only safe thing to do, then, Paul, is to cooperate with the Spirit for the right purpose in life?"

"True."

All depends on being in Christ Jesus and walking in the power of His Spirit. Otherwise, people are dominated by the flesh. Sin has dominion over them; consequently, they purpose

to do the things of the flesh. But on the other hand. real
Christians who are walking after the Spirit purpose to do
the things of the Spirit; they cherish salvation. magnify the
person of Christ. fellowship with the saints, study the Word
of God, pray. praise. walk in the light of prophecy and as
Jesus walked before men. According to verse 6. moreover, the
purpose of depraved human nature is to lead to eternal death;
but the purpose of the Spirit is to give eternal life and Christ's
peace. Verses 7 and 8 go on to explain that the purpose of
fallen human nature is enmity against God (James 4:4);
for it is not subject to the will of God, neither indeed can
be made subject. Indeed. human spirits imprisoned in the flesh
can't possibly please God.

C. *Again. the Spirit Enthrones Christ in Our Hearts* (8:9).

8:9   *But ye are not in the flesh, but in the Spirit, if so be that
the Spirit of God dwell in you. Now if any man have not
the Spirit of Christ, he is none of his.*

Note three steps to this enthronement—and heed the fearful
warning. First. you, a redeemed human spirit, are not imprisoned in the flesh. Next. you. a redeemed human spirit. are enshrined in God's Holy Spirit. He is the element in which you
live. like the fish in water. or the bird in air, vital. supplying.
protecting. Thus. in the third place, the Spirit of Christ, whom
Christ promised and whom Christ sent, enthrones Christ in
your heart according to Ephesians 3:16–19. Needless to say.
this means power. power. power!

The fearful warning: one who doesn't have the Spirit of
Christ and thus Christ himself, is not saved.

D. *Still Again, the Spirit Makes Christ Our Life* (8:10. 11).

8:10, 11   *And if Christ be in you, the body is dead because of
sin; but the Spirit is life because of righteousness. (11) But
if the Spirit of him that raised up Jesus from the dead dwell
in you. he that raised up Christ from the dead shall also*

quicken your mortal bodies by his Spirit that dwelleth
in you.

The Spirit makes Christ our life both now (v. 10) and
at the resurrection (v. 11). That is, our bodies are not yet
redeemed (cf. Rom. 7:24); therefore, they're dead so far as
fellowship with God is concerned. This is so because sin
dwells in them. Nevertheless, the indwelling Spirit keeps
mediating Christ's life to our redeemed spirits. "Though our
outward man perish, yet the inward man is renewed day
by day." And the Paraclete's ministry assures us of the resurrection of our bodies at the return of Christ (John 5:21).
Once He takes over in our hearts, He never stops until we
inhabit our glorified bodies (Phil. 3:20, 21). Thus He frees us
from the practice of sin and consequent eternal death.

II. *The Spirit Helps Us Live "in the Heavenlies"* (8:12–25).

8:13 *For if ye live after the flesh, ye shall die; but if ye*
through the Spirit do mortify the deeds of the body, ye
shall live.

Again God faithfully counsels us not to practice sin. Let's
always remember that even the heathen are "without excuse"
for practicing sin (Rom. 1:20). Let us learn well, therefore,
that justification connotes sanctification: ". . . the foundation
of God standeth sure, having this seal, The Lord knoweth
them that are his. And, Let every one that nameth the name
of Christ depart from iniquity." For indeed, as the eminent
French preacher Godet said somewhere, "Justification is the
strait gate leading to the narrow path of sanctification." So verses 12 and 13 are somewhat parenthetical. After them we begin
to see what it means to live in "the heavenlies":

A. *Where We Realize Our Adult Sonship* (8:14).

8:14 *For as many as are led by the Spirit of God, they are*
the sons of God.

This verse isn't talking about guidance. Guidance by the Spirit is indeed a blessed possibility, but that subject is discussed in other contexts. The context here is rather to be found in passages like Galatians 5:16–26, where we find the same verb "led." This phase of the Spirit's ministry penetrates our personality and works in us a consciousness of our position as adults in God's family. That we're "led" also means that we're borne along through life, as a ship is borne by trade winds across the ocean. We are taken hold of and accompanied by the Spirit all the way from earth to glory. We may, alas, lose our bearings at times but the Spirit overrules and keeps us headed in the right direction. This marks us as adult children in God's family.

B. *Where We Receive Courage* (8:15).

8:15 *For ye have not received the spirit of bondage again to fear; but ye have received the Spirit of adoption, whereby we cry, Abba, Father.*

The Spirit so illumines, persuades and empowers us to "act our age" that we call God "Father" in the most intimate and meaningful way. Thus He removes from our hearts "the spirit of bondage" and substitutes "the spirit of adoption." [9] "Servile fear becomes a filial fear proceeding from love." Our spirit becomes brave. courageous. dauntless.

C. *Where We Enjoy Assurance* (8:16, 17).

8:16 *The Spirit himslf beareth witness with our spirit, that we are the children of God* (A.S.V.).

Christians who live "after the Spirit" have two witnesses to the fact that they're God's children. One witness is their regenerated spirit; the other is the Holy Spirit who uses the Gospel to set them free (vv. 2–4), to create the right purpose in life (vv. 5–8). to enthrone Christ in their hearts (v. 9), and to make Christ their life (vv. 10. 11). Such believers cherish an inner assurance of their right relationship to God in the present and of their inheritance of glory in the future.

D. *Where Hope Grows Strong* (8:18–25).

8:23   *And not only they, but ourselves also, which have the
firstfruits of the Spirit, even we ourselves groan within
ourselves, waiting for the adoption, to wit, the redemption
of our body.*

Since the ministry of the Paraclete is only the firstfruits
of redemption, just think of what the future holds in store
for us—glorified bodies, reunion with loved ones, life in the
city foursquare, all our hopes in Christ realized! Meanwhile,
the Spirit enables us to fulfill another phase of our responsibility:
to be patient and hopeful until our Lord returns. As we choose
to be patient, the Spirit burnishes our hope. Thus we live "in
the heavenlies."

III. The Spirit Intercedes for Us (8:26, 27).

8:26, 27   *And in like manner the Spirit also **helpeth our
infirmity**: for we know not how to pray as we ought, but
the Spirit himself maketh intercession for us with groanings which cannot be uttered; (27) and he that searcheth
the hearts knoweth what is the mind of the Spirit, because
he maketh intercession for the saints according to the
will of God* (A.S.V.).

The believer, then, is responsible for "putting to death the
deeds of the body" (8:13), for patience (8:22–25), and for
intercession—his highest responsibility (8:26, 27). God will
not make the choices for us concerning these eternally vital
matters. But the Paraclete helps us all the way; He helps our
"weakness." First, He lays hold along with us to remove the
hindrances due to our weakness: unconfessed sins, past due
debts, offenses to and by others, grudges, envy, prejudice,
pride, lack of yieldedness to God, impatience, unbelief—any
and every iniquity "regarded" in the heart (Ps. 66:18). Also
He helps us to overcome our ignorance in spiritual things, and
so to prevail in prayer; for we know not how to prevail in
prayer as we ought.

The Paraclete helps by giving us a gracious spirit of intercession, even unto "groanings." He shows us that we have
not because we ask not; for example, that conditions in our
churches are largely what they are because we've failed in
our responsibility of intercession. Therefore, we "groan within
ourselves." The sense of our Christian duty to ascertain God's
will about conditions and souls, and to choose and pray that
God's will shall be done despite all opposition, brings deep
concern and sometimes tears. It is then, of all times, that
the Paraclete "super-intercedes" for us: He makes known
to the Father, who searches our hearts, His purpose in our
unuttered petitions and groanings; and thus He enables us
to prevail. The truth of this passage has made a great army
of prayer-warriors: Noah, Job (Ezek. 14:14), Abraham, Moses,
Samuel, Elijah, Daniel, Paul. "Praying" Hyde, E. M. Bounds,
David Brainerd, John Knox, John Welch, George Mueller,
Hudson Taylor—to mention only a few. Let's follow in their
train! This is a far cry from the praying of Pharisees, the
counting of beads, or the turning of a prayer wheel.

Without any doubt this doctrine of the Spirit in Romans 8
presents the main thrust of Christianity, its normal and most
essential supernaturalism. The widespread preaching of Christ
and His Spirit according to Romans would bring about the
revival we need. How to enjoy this power—the fulness of the
Spirit—may be summed up as follows: (1) Believe that there
is full victory in Christ for you, Romans 5. (2) Take up and
maintain the right attitude, Romans 6. (3) Depend upon the
right power, Christ in the Spirit, Romans 7. (4) Make the
right choices, Romans 8. This is living faith!

9:1   *I say the truth in Christ, I lie not, my conscience also
      bearing me witness in the Holy Ghost.*

Paul's love for Israel, like that of Moses (Ex. 32:32, 33),
was so great that it's not easy for us to estimate; we're tempted
to tone it down. Therefore, Paul called upon his Spirit-taught
and Spirit-empowered conscience to bear witness with him to

the amazing declaration that he could. "if it were right. go the length of being lost if Israel could be saved."

12:11 *In diligence not slothful; fervent in the Spirit; serving the Lord.*

Only the Spirit can keep us from being over-dignified. cold and unemotional on the one hand; or crestfallen. over-zealous and maudlin on the other. We. therefore, include this reference. Some translations capitalize the "s"; *The Wycliffe Bible Commentary*, for example. says. "They are not to be indolent. They are to be *aglow* (RSV). literally. *boiling*, with the Spirit." [10]

14:17 *For the kingdom of God is not meat and drink; but righteousness, and peace, and joy in the Holy Ghost.*

Paul is here discussing the exercise of Christian liberty in the church: that "the church has no authority to decide questions of personal liberty in things not expressly forbidden in Scripture." When God rules in the hearts of individuals. the Paraclete will cleanse of legalism and create righteousness, peace. and joy in the whole fellowship.

15:13 *Now the God of hope fill you with all joy and peace in believing, that ye may abound in hope, through the power of the Holy Ghost.*

Believe the facts of the Gospel (Rom. 3:21—11:36) until your heart becomes filled with joy and peace. but don't stop there; continue to appropriate the power of the Paraclete until you abound in hope for the future, here and hereafter. This verse marks "the highest development of Christian experience revealed in this great. fundamental Epistle of Romans." This is God's will for all of us. the normal state of everyone who is in Christ Jesus. Let's not be dejected. depressed, and discouraged! Rather, pray and work that your church may reach and maintain this high level of fellowship with God.

15:16 *That I should be the minister of Jesus Christ to the Gentiles, ministering the gospel of God, that the offering up of the Gentiles might be acceptable, being sanctified by the Holy Ghost.*

As Moses was God's minister to Israel, Paul was His minister to the Gentiles. Moses ministered the Law; Paul ministered the Gospel, now Israel's only hope. Israel was sanctified by Old Testament ordinances; believers today are sanctified by the Paraclete. In Old Testament times Gentiles were acceptable only as they approached God through the religion of Israel. That is, only Israel had the "blood that covers, the blood that hides." Now, of course, sin is not *covered*, but *put away* (John 1:29; Heb. 9:26). The Spirit's application of Christ's finished work at Calvary makes the amazing difference. Of this, Newell writes:

> Words fail us to express the glory of the privilege that today prevails in the humblest gospel meeting as a means of access to God, with an amazing free gospel-welcome to God *direct*, through the shed blood of Christ, that will cease instantly upon the rapture of the Church, when the Gentiles will no longer be under the astonishing blessing which has been theirs during the present gospel dispensation through the apostle Paul.[11]

15:19 *Through mighty signs and wonders, by the power of the Spirit of God; so that from Jerusalem, and round about unto Illyricum, I have fully preached the gospel of Christ.*

As the context implies, Paul's task and responsibility were unique. Yet he did God's will for him just as you and I must do God's will for us, "in Christ" (Phil. 4:13). And the manifestation of power was unique. He performed "special miracles" (Acts 19:11); he was robed with unique authority (I Cor. 4:18–21). God will give the power needed to make any ministry profitable (I Cor. 12:7). He is no respecter of persons.

15:30   *Now I beseech you, brethren, for the Lord Jesus Christ's sake, and for the love of the Spirit, that ye strive together with me in your prayers to God for me.*

A great verse with which to conclude our study of the Paraclete in Romans! All three persons of the Trinity are mentioned; the Spirit pours out God's love in our hearts (5:5) for the Lord Jesus Christ's sake. This loving work of the Comforter encourages us to strive in prayer for others, that, for Christ's sake, they may know and do the will of our Father. Our Triune God's love constrains us: in love the Father provided redemption, in love the Son procured redemption, and in love the Paraclete applies redemption. Paul begs—for Christ's sake and because of this love—for the earnest, prevailing prayers of the saints at Rome, that he may be able to visit them.

In conclusion, let's note that discussion of the Spirit in Romans implies previous knowledge and experience of the Paraclete on the part of the readers. Paul tells them, consequently, not how to receive the Spirit, but how to maintain and enlarge their experience of God's grace by His ministry. They doubtless were already Spirit-filled believers; already their "faith was proclaimed throughout the whole world" (1:8); "rivers of living water" were already flowing from within them.

Also note that Christ was indeed "the answer"—but Christ in the person and power of His Spirit. Truly, Christianity wouldn't be Christianity without the blessed Holy Spirit to give hope, fellowship with God and victory over indwelling sin.

So we pass from Romans to Corinthians with a fresh baptism of divine love. We have glimpsed God's perfect provision for our freedom from the slavery of sin; may our appropriation come nearer to perfection every day. We've learned the marks of a true Christian, and how to enjoy more fully Christ's life and peace. Also we've acknowledged our responsibility as mature sons of God, who expectantly look forward to the full realization of our inheritance in Christ Jesus. Until that glad time of universal, glorious liberty, we would be always Spirit-filled.

The Spirit in I and II Corinthians—
Divine Power Misused

A STUDY OF THE SPIRIT in the Corinthian Letters is next in importance to that in Romans. For "Paul here solves the problem of preserving and restoring the purity of the Church as a body consecrated to God in Christ" (Lange).

Conditions in Corinth were abnormal: the church faced grave dangers within and without. Within, intellectual conceit brought forth party strife; carnality spawned immorality. lawsuits, compromise with idolatry. abuse of the Lord's Supper. and misuse of spiritual gifts; lack of proper leadership resulted in doctrinal as well as moral perversion. Without, a fanatical and vicious heathen priesthood and its votaries—setting the example of religious worship for the whole Greek nation— spoke in "tongues" and manifested other spiritual "gifts." Much luxury and licentiousness corrupted the half million citizens of Corinth.

At the time Paul wrote to Corinth, he was laboring in Ephesus, where he "fought with beasts" (I Cor. 15:32) and spoke of the "distress that is upon us" (I Cor. 7:26, A.S.V.). Christianity was hated not only by the heathen religionists but also by the leaders of Judaism, who. having failed to recognize "the time of their visitation" (Luke 19:44). ceased not to cause confusion and to give opposition. It was a critical time for Christ's cause in Corinth, and elsewhere.

Seven new phases of the Paraclete's work appear in these

epistles: (1) He reveals to us the deep things of God (I Cor. 2:6–16). (2) He indwells the local church (3:16). (3) He imparts spiritual gifts for service (chaps. 12–14). (4) He promotes loyalty to Christ (12:3). (5) He forms the Church (12:13). (6) He serves as "earnest" (II Cor. 1:22, 5:5). (7) He transforms us into the image of Christ (3:17, 18). All these blessed ministries are implied in thirty-six references: I Corinthians 2:4. 10 (twice), 11, 12, 13, 14; 3:16; 6:11, 19 (twice); 7:40; 12:3 (twice), 4, 7, 8 (twice), 9 (twice), 11, 13 (twice); 14:2; II Corinthians 1:22; 3:3, 6 (twice), 8, 17 (twice). 18; 5:5; 6:6; 12:18; and 13:14.

I. I CORINTHIANS—TWENTY-FOUR REFERENCES

2:4 *And my speech and my preaching was not with enticing words of man's wisdom, but in demonstration of the Spirit and of power.*

Paul established the church in Corinth by preaching the simple, primary meaning of the Cross according to the dictate of the Paraclete. He feared and trembled lest human wisdom hinder his efforts. Consequently, he addressed men, not on the level of things temporal, finite and earthly; but on the level of things eternal. infinite and heavenly. Thus he preached in the "power" of the Spirit; that is, the Spirit witnessed in the hearts of his hearers to the truth which he preached.

The "demonstration of the Spirit" to which he refers evidently consisted in the miracles which were wrought (see Gal. 3:5; Acts 19:11; Rom. 15:19; I Thess. 1:5) and the spiritual gifts which were imparted (see I Cor. 1:4–8; I Thess. 5:19, 20) as a result of his preaching. The power of the Gospel was confirmed by the power of the Paraclete. Hopeless sinners of all classes. ages. and conditions were saved. The *Gospel* applied by the Spirit made the drunkard sober, the immoral moral, the thief honest. the profane reverent, the selfish unselfish (6:9–11). and also imparted to them various gifts for service (12:7).

2:10–13 *But God hath revealed them unto us by his Spirit:
for the Spirit searcheth all things, yea, the deep things
of God. (11) For what man knoweth the things of a man,
save the spirit of man which is in him? (12) Now we have
received, not the spirit of the world, but the Spirit which
is of God; that we might know the things that are freely
given to us of God. (13) Which things also we speak,
not in the words which man's wisdom teacheth, but which
the Holy Ghost teacheth; comparing spiritual things with
spiritual.*

Tremendous passage, this! First, the great doctrines of
grace can't be discovered by human logic, but are a divine
revelation unto saved and empowered men (vv. 10–12).
Secondly, these doctrines are received and transmitted in Spirit-
chosen words (v. 13). Only the Spirit of God could and
did search out the deep things of God and reveal them unto
us. We list nine of these great doctrines which God revealed
by the Paraclete: (1) Christ on the Cross—despised by proud,
unsaved men—brought Satan to nought, put our sins away,
bore the curse of the Law, severed us from our "old man,"
became sin on our behalf, ended our history in Adam, and
became our standing before God (I Cor. 1:18). (2) Perfect,
infinite, eternal righteousness is now available on the free-gift
principle, absolutely apart from all human effort (Rom. 3:21–
26). (3) Christ's death fully and eternally satisfied God's holy
nature for man's sin (Rom. 3:25). (4) Christ's death removed
the sin-barrier between God and men (II Cor. 5:19). (5) God
can now righteously forgive and eternally redeem all who
believe on Christ (Col. 1:12–14). (6) Believers are now made
one with Christ in the benefits, power, and glory of His death,
burial, and resurrection (Rom. 6). (7) All believers since
Pentecost become new creatures in Christ Jesus (II Cor. 5:17)
and are formed into one spiritual organism (I Cor. 12:12, 13).
(8) The Body of Christ as well as each member individually
is indwelt by the third Person of the Trinity, the Paraclete
himself, and we're built together as the great temple of God

(Eph. 2:22). (9) Through the Church, God makes known the various and manifold beauties of His *grace* (Eph. 2:7; 3:10).

The Paraclete also taught Paul which words in his own vocabulary to use in setting forth these deep things of God; how he could combine spiritual things with spiritual words and thus explain spiritual things to spiritual men. We thank God for the Holy Spirit and His infinite knowledge of the deep, secret things of Deity, and for His revelation of them to us in words we can understand; otherwise, we could never enjoy Christ and His great salvation. Christ couldn't be "the answer."

2:14 *But the natural man receiveth not the things of the Spirit of God: for they are foolishness unto him: neither can he know them, because they are spiritually discerned.*

Man, governed and influenced by proud, natural instincts instead of the Paraclete, cannot and does not accept and welcome into his heart these doctrines of grace. He can't know them in experience until he repents. But he can know them intellectually. For example, a person can know the plan of salvation, and an unorthodox theologian can memorize and mouth the fundamentals of orthodoxy. But the internal work of the Paraclete is necessary to overcome his sinful pride and to persuade him to accept Christ and to fellowship with Him. Humility and yieldedness to God the Holy Spirit is essential to an experiential knowledge of "the deep things of God." Otherwise, the precious doctrines of the true Gospel seem "foolish." Only "the Spirit of grace" can enable us to receive and appreciate grace! In other words, the "natural man" can know with the mind how to be saved without actually receiving salvation. That is, the experience of salvation is spiritually discerned. There must be illumination before there can be realization. Likewise, the unorthodox theologian, let me repeat, can know orthodoxy on the human plane but he can't be sure of it and experience its power without the Spirit's testimony to him personally. Indeed, apart from the internal witness of the Paraclete we may see and hear with the senses, we may see and hear with the mind, but we can't see and hear with the spirit. The natural man must have his spiritual eyes opened, his spiritual ears unstopped, and his spiritual darkness dissipated before he can be changed by grace (see Luke 24:31, 32, 45).

3:16 *Know ye not that ye are the temple of God, and that the Spirit of God dwelleth in you?*

Let us look at this verse in the light of its context. The Corinthian Christians presumed their extraordinary gifts were proof of their spirituality. Yet they weren't Spirit-filled; they were still carnal. They were still living on the creaturely, finite, temporal plane (3:1ff.). Consequently, Paul had been unable to teach them "the deep things of God" (2:10–13): Spirit-filled believers can go on to maturity; carnal believers cannot.

Neither were they properly aware of the nature and quality of the Church: of the fact that their local church was a manifestation of God's temple indwelt by His Spirit. They were in danger, therefore, of violating the seat of God's operations on earth, the place of His special Presence. So Paul warned them: "If any man by his doctrines and precepts shall pursue such a course as *tends* to destroy the church. God shall severely punish him." [1]

6:11 *And such were some of you: but ye are washed, but ye are sanctified, but ye are justified in the name of the Lord Jesus, and by the Spirit of our God.*

Paul mentions three phases of their salvation (not in logical order) experienced in the name of the Lord Jesus and in fellowship of the Paraclete (cp. Barnes and Ellicott).

6:19 *What? know ye not that your body is the temple of the Holy Ghost which is in you, which ye have of God, and ye are not your own?*

Our bodies are temples of the Paraclete. This, of course, does not mean that we've become Deity, but that the cleansing and enabling power and influence of Deity dwells in our bodies in a peculiar and unlimited way and measure. It also signifies our responsibility for making and keeping our bodies fit shrines for the indwelling of Deity.

Normal Christians know the Paraclete, and that He dwells in their bodies (see chapter on Acts). Professing Christians who are ignorant of this fundamental fact should by all means be taught, no matter how gifted they appear to be. For we should recognize and honor the person, presence and power of the Paraclete today just as did the early Christians. Harold Wildish of Jamaica tells how Captain Lou Zamperini did this very thing.[2] In Billy Graham's Los Angeles Crusade, Mr. Zamperini had a remarkable experience of saving grace. The Lord Jesus had done for him what the doctors and psychiatrists couldn't do—He had saved him from a nervous and mental collapse. The peace and sweetness of God's forgiveness in Christ had enabled him to forgive the Japanese prison-camp guards for two and a half years of torture, ridicule, and even unmentionable treatment. He had become a soul-winning Christian, having gone to the extent of returning to Japan to witness to his former abusers. All this, and yet he'd not known the Paraclete personally. Here is his testimony to Mr. Wildish:

> Do you know, Mr. Wildish, it was only a few weeks ago that I picked up a book by Dr. Torrey on *The Person and Work of the Holy Spirit of God*. As I read it, I suddenly realized that the Holy Spirit of God was a Person and that He actually lived in my body. I have been a forgiven sinner for two years, and I didn't know this. But as it burst upon my soul, tears came to my eyes; I put down the book and knelt down and spoke to the Holy Spirit and asked Him to forgive me for my rudeness, for my neglect.

7:40   *But she is happier if she so abide, after my judgment: and I think also that I have the Spirit of God.*

The fact that this judgment has been preserved in Scripture proved Paul was right, that he had the Spirit's approval.

12:3 *Wherefore I give you to understand that no man speaking by the Spirit of God calleth Jesus accursed: and that no man can say that Jesus is Lord, but by the Holy Ghost.*

Chapters 12–14 instruct us about "spirituals": the gifts of the Paraclete (chap. 12) are declared to be unprofitable when exercised without love (chap. 13); and prophecy exercised in love is shown to be superior to tongues, which are forbidden in the assembly, except when interpreted (chap. 14).

Spiritual warfare raged in Corinth: there were many demons against one Holy Spirit. How could the young believers— only recently "carried away," as in a flood of waters, by demon powers—distinguish the true from the false? The basic, all-inclusive test was that of *loyalty to Jesus Christ.* The battle cry of the spirits of error was, "Jesus is accursed"; that of the Paraclete, "Jesus is Lord."

12:4–6 *Now there are diversities of gifts, but the same Spirit. (5) And there are differences of administrations, but the same Lord. (6) And there are diversities of operations, but the same God who worketh all in all.*

Paul's solution is good for similar conditions today: the Spirit of Christ promotes loyalty to Christ by distributing appropriate gifts to each and every true believer, gifts to be used for and in and through the local churches. Christ, as Lord in heaven, in turn, directs us in the use of these gifts (I Cor. 4:1; 8:6; Rom. 12:11); God, in various ways, makes the gifts effective. Thus the Triune God maintains *unity in variety* in the Body of Christ as represented in the churches.

12:7–11 *But the manifestation of the Spirit is given to every man to profit withal. (8) For to one is given by the Spirit the word of wisdom; to another the word of knowledge by the same Spirit; (9) to another faith by the same Spirit; to another the gifts of healing by the same Spirit; (10) to another the working of miracles; to another discerning of spirits; to another divers kinds of tongues; to another the interpretation of tongues: (11) but all these worketh that one and the selfsame Spirit, dividing to every man severally as he will.*

Nine Miraculous Gifts. There is much difference of opinion about these gifts, as to whether God meant them for the primitive churches only or also for churches of our day. All agree there are other gifts for Christians today, such as those listed in Romans 12:6–8; but there's marked disagreement about these miraculous gifts. Of course, in a sense all gifts are miraculous—they are not natural, inherent talents or abilities—but Bible students divide them into the ordinary and the extraordinary.

Points of Exposition. Verse 7 offers us the key to this perplexing passage: the Spirit shows His power in our lives primarily for the purpose of edifying our local church, and not for our own personal good. That is, "To each is granted the evidence of the Spirit for the common welfare" (Berkeley V.). Paul emphasizes this point in 14:12: ". . . even so ye, forasmuch as ye are zealous of spiritual gifts; seek that ye may excell to the edifying of the church."

Let's examine these gifts briefly. Wisdom and knowledge come first. Some believers had the ability now and then, because of supernatural insight, to speak a "word of wisdom"; others, because of supernatural perception, a "word of knowledge." But mark this: their wisdom and knowledge were limited and imperfect (13:9); were on a low plane; they had to go to Paul for a solution to the problems which were destroying their testimony and blighting their service (7:1; 8:1; 12:1).

Wonder-Working Faith. Some at times had faith to heal and to perform other miracles. But observe that this extraordinary faith apparently was occasional. Even Paul could not heal and perform miracles at will. He could do nothing about his "thorn in the flesh." He did not heal Epaphroditus (Phil. 2:27), and he left Trophimus at Miletus sick (II Tim. 4:20). Fausset well says: "The Apostles had not the permanent gift of miracles any more than inspiration; both were vouchsafed only for each occasion, as the Spirit saw fit" (J. F. B. Com.).

What about the rising interest today in divine healing movements? We give you William R. Newell's answer: "Healing movements force some Scriptures, ignore others, and in my judgment grossly misinterpret and misapply others; and their results bring sadness to many intelligent and devoted Christians." [3] We add that God's primary purpose for this age isn't to heal our bodies but to conform our spirits to the image of His Son (Rom. 8:28, 29). This is the time of "groaning" (Rom. 8:23): our bodies are not yet redeemed (Rom. 8:11). Emphasis now is on spiritual transformation (II Cor. 3:18), and we all know that many times God can better change our lives while we suffer. We believe that churches generally, however, should develop faith to obey James 5:14–18. Ironside relates a remarkable instance of the practice of this injunction:

> In the early days of what is now generally known as 'the Brethren Movement,' Mr. J. N. Darby and Mr. J. G. Bellett were called in to many sick rooms in Dublin, where they acted literally upon the directions given here. Many remarkable healings were vouchsafed in answer to the prayer of faith; so much so that attention began to be centered upon these two brethren as special instruments used of God, in a way that troubled them, and they felt it wise to desist from going, but prayed together, or separately for the afflicted in a more private way, acting rather on verse 16 than on verse 14 and 15; God answered in the same grace as when the formal service was carried out.[4]

Christian history witnesses to miracle-working faith time and again down through the years. Raymond J. Davis, for example, tells of miracles in Ethiopia during the Italian occupation, 1935–1940:

> As in other eras of church history, God used miracles and other uncommon phenomena as a witness and sign to the people who did not have access to the written Word of God and His revelation in the Scriptures. At least three blind men were miraculously healed. Some

crippled ones were made well and some barren women bore children. These miracles according to the elders were used as signs and many people turned to the Lord because of them.[5]

Prophetic Insight. Prophecy and discerning of spirits were common in churches other than Corinth, and also in the Old Testament. In addition to the writing prophets there were Samuel's school of the prophets, King Saul, Miriam, Eldad, Medad, Deborah, Ahijah, Micaiah, Huldah, and many others. The major prophets in New Testament days were Christ and the apostles; but there were also Simeon and Anna (Luke 2:25–38), Agabus (Acts 11:28; 21:10), Judas and Silas (Acts 15:32), Paul's new converts at Ephesus (Acts 19:6), Philip's four daughters (Acts 21:9), and others. Instructions concerning prophecy included: "Let us prophesy according to the proportion of faith" (Rom. 12:6); "Despise not prophesyings" (I Thess. 5:20); and "Follow after love, and desire spiritual gifts, but rather that ye may prophesy" (I Cor. 14:1).

Obviously, this prophetic gift varied greatly in value from age to age and from person to person. The gift at Corinth was such that those who possessed it couldn't set the church in order; Paul had to do that. We believe that prophecy in the primary sense ceased with the writing of the last book of the Bible (cf. Rev. 22:18). Indeed (the Roman Church not withstanding), we've had no inspired Scripture since. The gift of "discerning of spirits," closely associated with prophecy, was exercised by Peter (Acts 5:1–11), Paul (Acts 13:10), and believers generally (I John 4:1–6); it was necessary because of false prophets, and appeared to be miraculous in some cases.

Before we briefly consider the question of tongues, we must glance at Paul's solution to the whole problem of "spirituals."

12:13 *For by one Spirit are we all baptized into one body, whether we be Jews or Gentiles, whether we be bond or free; and have been all made to drink into one Spirit.*

This verse refers to the most remarkable and significant, the most essential and vital, the richest and most influential "incorporation" on earth—the Church manifested in the churches. It explains how this unique organism came into being and was filled with the Spirit. "In one Spirit were we all baptized into one body, whether Jews or Greeks, whether bond or free; and were all made to drink of one Spirit" (A.S.V.). That is, in the power of one personality, the Paraclete, early believers, though differing in race and rank, were actually and consciously made one in Christ, and one Spirit flooded their souls with the love and joy of a common faith in Christ. At conversion, notice, they were both baptized in the Spirit and consciously "made to drink" of His fulness. Thus in one Spirit they became one body, were united, blended into a heavenly, Spirit-filled incorporation on earth. Let's remember, therefore, that "spirituals" are granted, not for private pleasure, but for corporate good.

14:2 *For he that speaketh in an unknown tongue speaketh not unto men, but unto God: for no man understandeth him; howbeit in the Spirit he speaketh mysteries.*

The "s" in "spirit" should be capitalized in this verse. For no man in spiritual ecstasy could utter secret matters unto God apart from the inspiration of the Holy Spirit. Consequently we count this as another reference to the Spirit; so do Moffatt, Weymouth, Berkeley and others.

Unkonwn Tongues at Corinth. To many at Corinth (but not to all) were given "kinds of tongues." Paul himself exercised this gift but preferred not to do so in public worship (14:18, 19). This was the most showy gift, and it gratified only the individual himself. Neither was the church edified by it when there was no interpreter (14:28). It was associated, moreover, particularly with emotions. Its overemphasis led to the neglect of those gifts associated with the intellect and the will. The carnal use of the gift was childish (14:20); and brought disunity. indecency. and disorder (14:10). When Paul wrote to more normal Christians, those in Rome, he didn't even mention tongues.[6]

Unknown Tongues Down Through the Years. A pertinent question to begin with is: How do the tongues of history and of today compare with those in New Testament times? The answer is: we just can't be sure. Even John Chrysostom (347?–407), who lived sixteen centuries closer to Paul's Corinth than we do, confessed ignorance of the facts. He consequently strongly protested the tongues in Constantinople in his day. Neither can we be sure of the degree of similarity between New Testament tongues and those of the ancient Greek religion, nor of the many Asian and African religions today which afford examples of the practice.[7]

Certainly one wonders when he reads of the variety of manifestations in the day of Irenaeus, the Montanists (second century), Origen (third century), Francis Xavier (thirteenth century) and the French Huguenots. In 1688, for example, there sprang up in France a sect called the Camisards who claimed to have all the gifts. We're told that fierce pressure of persecution developed an intensified religious experience. Protestants went into ecstasies. hearing supernatural voices and speaking with tongues; children were subjects of extraordinary manifestations. and uneducated persons prophesied in purest French.

Others also have claimed extraordinary gifts: Convulsionists (1730). Shakers (1747). Jumpers and Barkers (1760). Edward Irving, London, a brilliant and spiritual Presbyterian minister (1792–1834), sought to restore the apostolic gifts, but ended in disaster.[8]

Unknown Tongues Today. Some 2,000 Episcopalians are said to be speaking in tongues in Southern California, and 600 folk at the First Presbyterian Church of Hollywood. The movement is now snowballing worldwide. Adherents total in the millions, and many claim a "new Pentecost." Federal funds even support a special psychological and linguistic study, and many churches capitalize on the trend. For example, an ad in a Lansing. Michigan, paper reads: "Glossolalia: 70 received this experience [Holy Spirit] in a recent Flint, Michigan, revival now coming to Lansing."

Right Attitude Toward Unknown Tongues. Maynard James (to whom Martin Lloyd-Jones says, "I think the way you have handled the question of 'tongues' is quite perfect"), writes:

> We are glad that certain Pentecostal leaders have had both discernment and courage to acknowledge that a person can be filled with the Holy Spirit without speaking in tongues. Among them were the late T. B. Barratt and George Jeffreys. Even more authoritative is the statement by the European Pentecostal Conference held in Stockholm in the early summer of 1939. It admitted that tongues might occur apart from the Spirit's action; and that a Christian could be filled with the Spirit without the sign of tongues.[9]

Then this author states the position held for some sixty years by the Christian and Missionary Alliance: "Seek not, forbid not."

Add to this wisdom the following tests for all gifts: Do they magnify our Lord? Do they edify our church? Are they exercised in love? Are they used decently and in order? In case of tongues spoken by men in the assembly, is there an interpreter?

A comparison at this point of the supernaturalism of Corinthians with that of Romans proves very helpful: the miracles prominent in Corinthians are abnormal and on a lower spiritual plane than the miracle-life pictured in Romans 8. There's no doubt about that. In fact, the supernaturalism of Corinthians *without* that of Romans is unfruitful (I Cor. 13). Romans, it's easy to see, is basic and reveals the main thrust of Biblical Christianity.

When Do These Gifts Cease? Love never fails to be profitable, even after we get to heaven; but the gifts used to make known God's presence among us on earth (14:25) will not be needed in heaven. "When that which is perfect is come [the perfect state of all things, to be ushered in by the return of

Christ from heaven (Thayer)], then that which is in part shall be done away." [10]

The Expositors' Greek Testament states: "... 'that which is perfect' comes with the Lord from heaven." C. J. Ellicott: "*That which is perfect*: This verse shows, by the emphatic 'then,' that the time when the gifts shall cease is the end of this dispensation. The imperfect shall not cease until the perfect is brought in."

In verses 13:11, 12 Paul illustrates and applies this point. There will be use and development of some of the gifts—as a child's gifts of speech, reasoning, and understanding—throughout the earthly sojourn of the Church, ending only when we shall see "face to face." The graces of faith, hope, and love abide forever. Faith and hope here have the same permanent character as love. Faith is the everlasting foundation of the state of blessedness, the trustful apprehending, the fast-holding of Christ, the sole ground of salvation for time and eternity. Hope is the perpetual expectation of ever new and delightful manifestations of God's glory (Lange).[11]

Christian Supernaturalism. The unique character of the apostolic age would account for more signs and wonders then than now. Besides, miracles come in "cycles." (See introduction to Chapter Four.) But to take the attitude that Christianity is less supernatural today than it was in the first century because God has withdrawn certain Church-age gifts seems to us to lay the blame on God for present conditions in the churches. Surely God is just as ready to give *profitable* manifestations of the Spirit today as ever.

Bear in mind, however, that even apostolic miracles were always secondary and incidental: the *Gospel* was the power of God unto salvation. The apostles didn't hanker after miracles, and neither did the other Spirit-filled believers. For miracles didn't affirm the truth, and could be counterfeited to a certain degree (Ex. 4:11; John 10:21). But they did confirm the truth (Mark 16:20; Heb. 2:3, 4). We must be guided, therefore, by truth, not by miracles. Not all of God's Spirit-filled men performed miracles. "John the Baptist did no miracle" (John

10:41); neither did many other truly great men of God. Millions of martyrs died without performing miracles to save themselves. So, while we insist on the possibility of miracles today, let's not make more of them than God does. Rather, "By this shall all men know that ye are my disciples, if ye have love one to another." Love is primary; miracles are secondary. Miracles without love are worthless, and, if they are of Satan, dangerous. Our Lord said, "By their fruits [not by their miracles] ye shall know them." The world-changing supernaturalism of early Christianity wasn't the gifts, but the graces. For example, when mockers of Peter's and Jude's days denied the second coming on the basis of no supernatural happenings (II Pet. 3), did Peter and Jude attempt to prove the power of Christianity by performing miracles? No. They insisted that believers be on their guard, keep themselves in the love of God, and keep looking for Christ's return (Jude 21). The Roman Empire, consequently, marvelled. not at Christian miracles, but at Christian love.

During the Christmas holidays I met on the campus of one of our American colleges a friendly young Moslem student. When I began to witness to him, he asked, "Why should I become a Christian?" Should I have put on, if I could have, a demonstration of tongues? Heathen dervishes could have done that. Should I have professed to be a divine healer? Christian Science, Unity, New Thought, Mormonism and Father Divine's cult could have done that!

How did I answer him? First, I told him what Christ had done for me, and what He meant to me: that He had given me a new nature. freedom from the practice of sin, a measure of the "fruit of the Spirit," constant fellowship with God as my spiritual Father, and a powerful Gospel to preach. The young man didn't claim to have any of these blessings, and admitted that he didn't have my sense of security.

In subsequent correspondence with him, I called his attention to the fact that the Christian Scriptures, which he admitted were true, and his "Holy" Quran couldn't both be right. For this Turkish student denied the personality of the

Paraclete, as well as the deity of Christ. What he needed to see, therefore, wasn't low-grade miracles (which Satan could counterfeit), but the truth of the Gospel and the miracle of the new birth with the gracious fruit of the Spirit.

Sometimes we long for miraculous powers to help our neighbors, friends, and loved ones: alcoholics, mental cases, neurotics, cripples, the blind, young married couples who are having domestic troubles, and invalids. But the Gospel must come first. If God gives us a physical miracle now and then, we'll praise Him all the more. But Christ said that people who can't be helped by the Gospel wouldn't be helped by miracles: "If they hear not Moses and the prophets, neither will they be persuaded, though one rose from the dead." Consequently, our deepest need is a great revival of supernatural *love!* For we've left our "first love," that of the early believers. Satan can't counterfeit *love.*

15:45   *And so it is written, The first man Adam was made a living soul; the last Adam was made a quickening Spirit.*

We see the Holy Spirit here as the One through whom Christ becomes a life-giving Spirit. This must be so. In fact, the Nicene Creed statement was based on John 6:63 and this verse. If, then, the early church fathers took this as a reference to the Spirit, so can we. Again, incidentally, we perceive that Christ alone is not "the answer."

II. II CORINTHIANS—TWELVE REFERENCES

1:22   *Who hath also sealed us, and given the earnest of the Spirit in our hearts.*

This verse must be studied in the light of its context. A minority led by the Judaizers doubted Paul's sincerity. Accordingly, he sought to prove to them that he, Silas, and Timothy were sincere. To do this, he reminded them of three phases of the Paraclete's ministry in their lives: anointing, sealing, and assuring.

Anointing (v. 21) was based on God's Old Testament

promises concerning Christ (v. 20). The truth was that all God had ever promised either had been or should be fulfilled in Christ, and could be realized through Him by the Spirit. In faithfulness to these promises, God had given to Paul and his associates the graces and gifts of the Spirit; that is, the Spirit had made them partakers of the very life of God's *Anointed One* (Acts 10:38). In this way the Spirit had qualified them for special service. It was thus apparent to all that Paul was a man divinely fitted for the ministry he was so gloriously fulfilling. His fellowship with Christ, God's Anointed One— by means of the Paraclete—was so rich and full that he shared Christ's anointing.

When Paul declared, moreover, that God had "sealed" him and his co-laborers, he meant the Paraclete himself was God's seal of *ownership*. In other words, the indwelling presence of the Spirit had sealed to them the reality, truthfulness, purposes, and divine power of the Gospel; so their consciousness of salvation was the result of the Spirit's internal witness; and thus they were assured of being kept "unto the day of redemption" (Eph. 4:30). This assurance wrought by the Spirit's personal illumination was, in turn, an earnest of the glory which yet awaited them. (Concerning "earnest," see comment on II Cor. 5:5.) What Paul claimed for himself and his associates, he attributed likewise to his readers, and to all true followers of Christ (v. 21). Accordingly, the believers in Corinth could judge Paul's sincerity and also their own (13:5).

3:3 *Forasmuch as ye are manifestly declared to be the epistle of Christ ministered by us, written not with ink, but with the Spirit of the living God; not in tables of stone, but in fleshly tables of the heart.*

Paul declares here that the Corinthians themselves are his letter of commendation, composed and published by Christ, using him as His instrument and the Paraclete as His Agent. In other words, Paul's preaching of Christ was made effective and permanent by the power of the Spirit. Paul's letter wouldn't fade, therefore, as would one written with ink. Neither was his message written on tables of stone as were the Ten Commandments, but on living tables of sensitive human hearts. Charles R. Erdman was right, when he wrote: "The very best credentials of a Christian minister are to be found in the lives and characters of his people."

3:6 *Who also hath made us able ministers of the new testament; not of the letter, but of the Spirit: for the letter killeth, but the Spirit giveth life.*

Paul now has Judaizers in mind, false teachers who insist on an application of the Gospel apart from "the Spirit of grace." The result of their ministry, he says, is spiritual dormancy. The truth is, he implies: only "the Spirit of life in Christ Jesus" can mediate life to the human spirit.

3:8 *How shall not the ministration of the Spirit be rather glorious?*

Now Paul contrasts the glory of the new covenant with that of Moses' Law. Certainly the Spirit's control of human spirits is infinitely more glorious than the Law's control.[12]

3:17 *Now the Lord is that Spirit: and where the Spirit of the Lord is, there is liberty.*

In the context of this verse Paul uses the veil of Moses (Ex. 34:33–35) as an illustration of the difference between the Old Covenant and the New. Moses used a veil to keep the people from seeing the glory on his face gradually disappear. Similarly, the Old Covenant began to fade away as soon as it was given; but the New Covenant didn't—it "remaineth." The Old was glorious indeed, yet a ministration of death and condemnation. The New excells in glory because it reaches the "spirit" and gives "righteousness." Under the Old the people had no direct access to Jehovah, and were afraid to come nigh (Ex. 34:30); but under the New, we have free access—"there is liberty" and "great boldness of speech."

This verse 17 explains that the Lord, Jehovah of the Old

Covenant, is now working through the Spirit of Christ in the New Covenant, and is thus—as a Trinity—available for fellowship with men: "for where the Spirit of the Lord is, there is liberty." To paraphrase: "Now Jehovah deals with men by means of that wonderful New Testament ministry of the Spirit: and where the Spirit of Christ is working, there is freedom from fear, and full access to the grace and power of God." This was Paul's answer to the legalists, the ministers "of the letter" (3:6). Their mere outward application of the Law killed (Rom. 2:28, 29), but Paul's application of grace to the spirit gave life.

3:18 *But we all, with open face beholding as in a glass the glory of the Lord, are changed into the same image from glory to glory, even as by the Spirit of the Lord.*

Christians. saved by believing a Gospel of unfading glory, have not diminishing power. as did Moses who ministered a covenant of fading glory. So. with unveiled face we behold "the glory of God in the face of Jesus Christ." Thus, we're progressively and without interruption changed into the same image from one degree of glory to another. We. who "have this treasure in earthen vessels." are transfigured—Christ in us shines forth. This Christ-glorifying change springs from the work of "the Lord. the Spirit"; that is. from the hidden ministry of the third Person of the Godhead.

If we take the American Standard Version marginal rendering and read "reflecting as a mirror." the meaning is that our saved and sensitive hearts reflect as a mirror the glory of the Lord. This interpretation possibly suits the context better (see 3:2 and 4:6).

5:5 *Now he that hath wrought for us the selfsame thing is God, who hath given unto us the earnest of the Spirit.*

The work of the Paraclete in our hearts is the assurance, the pledge, and the token that God will finish the job and get us safely home to glory; that heaven will be a continuation and enlargement of the Spirit's blessings here. To wit. the

Paraclete in our hearts here on earth is an "earnest" of heaven hereafter.

6:6   *By pureness, by knowledge, by longuffering, by kindness, by the Holy Ghost, by love unfeigned.*

One of the many ways in which Paul and his associates commended themselves to others as God's ministers was "by the Holy Ghost." By the help of the Paraclete they were pure. understanding, long-suffering, and kind in their exercise of sincere love for others.

12:18   *Did Titus make a gain of you? walked we not in the same Spirit? walked we not in the same steps?*

(The American Standard Version margin capitalizes "spirit.") By the help of the same Holy Spirit who had empowered Paul, Titus admirably fulfilled his mission. Thus the Corinthians recognized the same single-mindedness and sincerity in him which they had seen in Paul.

13:14   *The grace of the Lord Jesus Christ, and the love of God, and the communion of the Holy Ghost, be with you all. Amen.*

By means of the person of the Paraclete in the Trinity, the Father and Son can and do fellowship with men. They did at Corinth. The hidden ministry of the Spirit flooded their hearts with the love of God in Christ. Exceedingly precious was this "commonwealth of the Spirit" (A. B. Come), despite radicalism.

Thus we've witnessed a church that seemed to be hopelessly divided and incurably carnal preserved and restored to purity. In the process, immature believers were shown the relative importance, proper place, and edifying value of gifts as well as "a *most* excellent way" to use them. In short, the power of God's glorious Gospel, made effective by His gracious Spirit, changed the whole church for the glory of God. Evidences of this success may be found in II Corinthians and Romans. II Corinthians, written only a few months after I Corinthians, doesn't mention tongues. Neither does Romans, written from

Corinth about twelve months after the writing of I Corinthians. We're especially grateful to God for this triumphant record, another thrilling episode of God's answer, even Christ and His Spirit.

A final word of appreciation should be given for the positive contribution of the extremists at Corinth: they emphasized the relation of the doctrine of the Paraclete to the doctrine of salvation and eternal life. Other groups since then have likewise laid special stress on the direct illumination of the Spirit while, on the contrary, Roman Catholic theology and post Reformation Protestantism have tended to restrict the Holy Spirit to the doctrine of the Trinity (*Twentieth Century Encyclopedia of Religious Knowledge*).

The Spirit in Paul's Epistles (Galatians Through Titus)—Divine Power Implied

PRIMARILY THESE EPISTLES, Galatians through Titus, give further light on the Paraclete's ministry to the individual believer. In them we learn conclusively that all human contact and fellowship with God depend at every point absolutely on the Spirit. Indeed, there's such a blending of the Spirit with the new nature that it is sometimes difficult to determine what is meant, the Holy Spirit or the regenerated human spirit. Expositors differ. Some suggest that Galatians 3:2, for example, should read like this: "Received ye the new nature by the works of the law, or by the hearing of faith?" Either way, however, Holy Spirit identifies with human spirit. God helps believers.

These epistles mention the Spirit as follows: Galatians, 16 times; Ephesians, 12; Philippians, 2; Colossians, 1; I Thessalonians, 4; II Thessalonians, 1; I Timothy, 2; II Timothy, 2; and Titus, 1. Philemon makes no mention. So, the Paraclete speaks of himself only forty-one times in these nine Christ-centered books. But Spirit-lit eyes see Him there more often, since the doctrine of the Spirit is *inferred*. For example, every time Paul gives a benediction, it's understood that the Spirit—who, notice, is never mentioned—transfers the "grace" and "peace" to the recipient: "Grace to you, and peace, from God our Father, and from the Lord Jesus Christ." The Paraclete remains hidden. As we've already said, anyway. His exceedingly precious ministry must be experienced to be known. Only thus does He make Christ "the answer."

I. GALATIANS—SIXTEEN REFERENCES

The issue in Galatians is legalism, the great religious sin. Is one saved and made spiritually mature by grace through faith alone, or is it by grace *and* law? Is the condition of salvation faith which works, or is it faith plus works? False teachers, called Judaizers, created this issue when they insisted on obedience to the Law in addition to faith. Paul responded by sternly denouncing them as accursed (1:8, 9). Incidentally, he never once prefixed "Holy" to "Spirit" in this epistle because that epithet was joyous; it was out of place in Galatians (J. F. B. Com.).

3:2 *This only would I learn of you, Received ye the Spirit by the works of the law, or by the hearing of faith?*

One question shows them their error: How did you become new creatures in Christ, receiving the Spirit and His gifts? Was it by doing good works, or by believing the Gospel? The only answer they could give was this: We became new creatures, not by works of merit, but by faith.

3:3 *Are ye so foolish? having begun in the Spirit, are ye now made perfect in the flesh?*

Here Paul reminds the Galatians that the Spirit also makes Christians mature by grace through faith alone. It wasn't good common sense to imagine that the grace principle which gave life could be superseded by the law principle, or that law could even help grace. The new nature certainly couldn't be "made perfect" by the old nature. That would be a foolish idea.

3:5 *He therefore that ministereth to you the Spirit, and work-eth miracles among you, doeth he it by the works of the law, or by the hearing of faith?*

Through His Gospel ministers God abundantly supplies the gifts and graces of the Spirit. (Evidently primitive Christians *consciously* received certain gifts at the time of conversion, sometimes extraordinary gifts, such as those listed in I Corinthians 12. So here again is the lesson of The Acts: early Christians knew Christ *in the power of His Spirit.*)

3:14 *That the blessing of Abraham might come on the Gentiles through Jesus Christ; that we might receive the promise of the Spirit through faith.*

Justification and friendship with God—all the spiritual promises God made to Abraham—are fulfilled to Gentiles, as well as to Jews, through faith. All received the Paraclete and His fulness (Luke 24:49; John 14:26; 15:26; and Acts 2:33-39) by believing on Christ Jesus (John 7:38; Rom. 8:2).

4:6 *And because ye are sons, God hath sent forth the Spirit of his Son into your hearts, crying, Abba, Father.*

Old Testament believers were minors; New Testament believers enjoy the position of adult sons. The Paraclete helps us to experience this spiritual maturity, giving us, at least to some degree, that filial love and confidence which exists between Christ and the Father. The Spirit is "the Spirit of God's Son," because He proceeds from the Son, as well as from the Father, forming the union of the believer with the Father in adult sonship.

4:29 *But as then he that was born after the flesh persecuted him that was born after the Spirit, even so it is now.*

The birth of Ishmael affords Paul a good illustration of legalism: Sarai and Abram tried to help God do the supernatural (Gen. 16:2ff.). They also attempted to deal with God on two principles at the same time, faith plus works. Years after Ishmael's birth by natural laws, however, Isaac was born according to supernatural laws. "Which things are an allegory" (Gal. 4:24). The results proved, Paul shows, that the two systems of law and grace cannot co-exist. Indeed, "Grace cannot act where there is either desert or ability. Grace neither helps the flesh nor accepts the help of the flesh. It is absolute. It does all" (Newell). Furthermore, legalism always spawns trouble. For, just as Ishmael persecuted Isaac (Gen. 21:9; Gal. 4:29), the Jews persecuted Paul. Legalism in Galatia, consequently, made it necessary for Paul to warn: ". . . if ye bite and devour one another, take heed that ye be not consumed one of another" (5:15).

5:5 *For we through the Spirit wait for the hope of righteousness by faith.*

Here are contrasted law and grace. Paul warns that one can't depend upon both circumcision and Christ; and that if he depends upon circumcision, "he is a debtor to do the whole law." In fact, those who substitute rites and ceremonies for fellowship with Christ (in the Spirit) and sole dependence on Him, "are fallen away from grace"; that is, they have forsaken the grace way. Instead, they hope to be found righteous at the judgment because of their works of merit. Paul declares however, that *we*, who've been declared righteous with the hope of being *made* righteous "through the Spirit by faith," patiently wait and firmly expect to be *found* righteous in Christ in that day (Rom. 8:23–25; Phil. 3:9).

To continue the contrast, the object of one's faith in grace is the glorified Man, Christ Jesus—a life-giving Spirit. In legalism, it is Christ on earth, an example. The principle of blessing in grace is living faith that liberates the Spirit in our lives; in legalism, it's works that grieve the Spirit. The method of action in grace is the Paraclete working through the redeemed human spirit; in legalism, it's the flesh working through ceremonies and mere human wisdom. The realm of activity in grace is the supernatural; in legalism, it's the natural. The motive in grace is love; in legalism, fear. What a difference! The results in grace are the effects of God's righteousness imputed by the Father and imparted by Christ in the Spirit: blessedness, freedom, fellowship, love-works, "fruit of the Spirit," heaven; in legalism: bondage, formality, law-works, "works of the flesh," God's curse, wretchedness, and, if not repented of, hell.

Grace means that Christ (in the Spirit) is not only necessary but enough. Legalism implies that Christ's provision at Calvary (applied by the Spirit) is not enough, but that religious works must be added; and it presumes there is some strength in us to do these works. Legalism, by ignoring the Spirit, truly makes void the grace of God; it is, alas, the great "religious" sin. Help us to avoid it, Lord!

Legalism is worse than murder, adultery, stealing, or lying. And only "religious" people can be guilty of it. Doubtless the practice of this sin is damning more people than any other is. And, to one's great surprise, the very people who most desire to do the will of God are often the ones most easily deceived by this accursed doctrine. It's the wretched mistake of earnest people; it's the temptation that bewitches folk who long to be filled with the Holy Spirit; it's the Satan-inspired error that destroys Christian joy, and stirs up the lusts of the flesh. Within the space of thirty words, notice, God twice announces His curse upon the legalist: "Let him be accursed . . . let him be accursed" (Gal. 1:8, 9).

Yet many people are guilty of this grievous sin because they don't know Christ in the Spirit; some are sincere and some are not. There was the Turkish Sultan, for example, who spent most of a certain night in revelry. The next morning he overslept the hour for early prayers. But, surprisingly, Satan soon woke him up. Why? So that he would keep up his vain form of religion, lest his conscience be awakened and he really repent!

In such a vein Paul wrote to the Galatians: "Ye observe days, and months, and times, and years. I am afraid of you, lest I have bestowed upon you labor in vain." Legalism, you see, makes one religious but not spiritual; it is indeed Satan's counterfeit for the Spirit's power. Really, there's as much difference between being religious and being spiritual as there is between heaven and hell. For mere observance of private devotions, or Sunday, or Christmas, or Easter, or Lent, or a holy year can never be a subtitute for warm friendship and ennobling partnership with the God-Man in the Spirit. Demons could be one hundred percent in Sunday school, "training union," and other humanly standardized religious practices. The Pharisees, who "by the hand of lawless men did crucify and slay" our Lord, were, remember, strict tithers; they "washed oft," and "made long prayers."

Devotions, tithing, church affiliation, Christian works—all are good and necessary *as a means* of fellowship with and obedience to Christ in the Spirit; but they are *accursed as a substitute*. Does a wife appreciate candy and flowers from her husband when she knows he loves another woman? So, many people are insincerely legalistic.

But there are sincere legalists, and these need our sympathy. I talked with a friendly young man in the Y.M.C.A. in Washington, D.C. Lamenting the fact that his team had just lost a ball game, he exclaimed, "I knew I should have gone to Mass last Sunday!" He sincerely believed, you see, that the game was lost because he didn't go to Mass. He didn't understand that God's favor comes to us solely because of what Christ did for us at Calvary. He evidently knew Christ was necessary but did not know that He (in the Spirit) was enough. He honestly imagined that blessings come through faith plus meritorious works. He did not know we can't add to the value and power of Christ's blood, and that whatever good works we do are really caused by the Spirit of grace who is in us (I Cor. 15:10). Unwittingly, he was, besides, presuming there was some good in himself, in his flesh, and that he could merit favors from God.

Truly, legality is Satan's most wicked doctrine, even his fatal "religion." It's no wonder Paul denounced Satan's teachers as "false apostles, deceitful workers, fashioning themselves into the apostles of Christ" (II Cor. 11:13, A.S.V.). Rightly he labeled them Satan's "ministers." For our welfare in time and eternity, we should give good heed to Paul: "Behold, I Paul say unto you, that if ye be circumcised, Christ shall profit you nothing. For I testify again to every man that is circumcised, that he is a debtor to do the whole law" (Gal. 5:2, 3). "If it be by grace, then it is no more of works: otherwise grace is no more grace" (Rom. 11:6). So, Gospel-intelligent Christians "wait for the hope of righteousness," not through the flesh by works, but "through the Spirit by faith."

5:16–18 *This I say then, Walk in the Spirit, and ye shall not fulfil the lust of the flesh. (17) For the flesh lusteth against the Spirit, and the Spirit against the flesh: and these are contrary the one to the other: so that ye cannot do the things that ye would. (18) But if ye be led of the Spirit, ye are not under the law.*

The only way to maintain freedom from the bondage of legalism is to order our conduct, step by step, choice by choice, according to the freedom of the Spirit. This makes necessary constant "reckoning" on (that is, counting as *true*) the facts of the Gospel. For, in every saved person there are two contrary principles, or powers, or natures. In deadly fear of the "flesh" and in utter despair of our old nature, we must depend wholly on Christ and His Spirit. Thus we keep indwelling sin dormant, and consequently delight in Christ's freedom. When the Spirit works in us on the principle of grace, we're not subject to the law-principle (cf. I Cor. 15:56).[1]

So the responsibility is ours; we must keep our wills on God's side; that is, we must activate our faith, in order that the Paraclete may work out for us the victory. When, consequently, our dependence on grace is constant and full, so is our freedom.

5:22, 23 *But the fruit of the Spirit is love, joy, peace, longsuffering, gentleness, goodness, faith, (23) meekness, temperance: against such there is no law.*

The result of walking after the Spirit is "the fruit of the Spirit." Fruit, in contrast with works, implies the supernatural in experience. Man can attach artificial fruit to a tree; only God can grow fruit there. The flesh can produce religious works, but only the Paraclete can produce spiritual fruit. Our responsibility is to submit to purging, to stay clean, and to abide in the Vine (cf. John 15:1–4). Legality, with all its religious activity and mere church work, cannot bear fruit any more than can a peach tree severed from its roots produce peaches. Christian fruit grows through reliance on Christ in the Spirit, and abiding in Him.

5:25 *If we live in the Spirit, let us also walk in the Spirit.*

Paul here exhorts the Galatians to continue as they had begun, walking, step by step, on the grace-Spirit principle.

6:8 *For he that soweth to his flesh shall of the flesh reap corruption; but he that soweth to the Spirit shall of the Spirit reap life everlasting.*

What a warning! It is true for the world as well as for the churches: he who cherishes and practices the things of the old nature shall reap the things of the old nature and eventually go to hell; whereas, he who cherishes and practices the things of the new nature shall reap the things of the new nature and eventually go to heaven.

We close our study in Galatians with a few undocumented quotations from men who knew the full answer. W. S. Hottel: "The Holy Spirit is the vital energy of the new life in Christ Jesus, and, He is the Spirit of sonship, who makes believers conscious of their place in the family and of their nearness to God." A. C. Gaebelein: "The Holy Spirit is sufficient and no law, no ordinances, no holy days or other ordinances, are needed to help the believer in a life before God." L. S. Chafer: "The Spirit becomes the indwelling presence in every individual who is saved and at the moment he is saved." Andrew Murray: "The idea of effort is the great hindrance of the Christian life.... There are two great divisions among religious people: Those who serve God legally and those who serve Him lovingly." This precious observation of Murray brings us to the core of the Spirit's significance in Galatians; that is, the condition of blessing isn't mere human effort; it's Christ-conscious obedience in the power of the Spirit.

II. EPHESIANS—TWELVE REFERENCES

In Ephesians we continue to study the work of the Paraclete in relation to individuals, but it's individuals as members of the Church. Because the Church has the Spirit, individuals have the Spirit (Eph. 2:22). Emphasis on individual life in the Spirit is now "supplemented by a new interest in the unity and catholicity of the Church" (Thomas). This is the place where it is definitely shown that the doctrine of the Holy Spirit is related to the Church, as well as to the Trinity and to salvation.

Ephesians also introduces us to God's sphere of gracious activity, "the heavenlies." This is the realm of the Holy Spirit and all human spirits connected with Christ. It also includes the region of wicked spirits (Eph. 6:10–18). For, remember, it was in Ephesus that God empowered Paul to make miraculous use of handkerchiefs and aprons to expose Satan-energized magicians. Indeed, Paul wrought there the "signs of an apostle" in great victory. So our study deepens, becomes richer.

References are as follows: 1:13, 17; 2:18, 22; 3:5, 16; 4:3, 4, 30; 5:18; and 6:17, 18. In these passages we find several new aspects of the Spirit's ministry; such as sealing, illuminating, serving as the dynamic of the Church, empowering, creating unity, grieving over the sins of saints and strengthening us through Christ to stand against demons.

1:13 *In whom ye also trusted, after that ye heard the word of truth, the gospel of your salvation: in whom also after that ye believed, ye were sealed with the Holy Spirit of promise.*

In Ephesians 1:3–14, perhaps the Bible's richest exposition of God's *grace*, all three persons of the Godhead are shown to be active in our redemption: the Father purposes, the Son provides, and the Spirit applies. Here the presence in our lives of the Holy Spirit of promise is God's seal of ownership. Whereas circumcision was the seal in the Old Testament (Rom. 4:11), the Spirit is the seal in the New Testament (Eph. 4:30): "... in whom, having also believed, ye were sealed with the Holy Spirit of promise" (A.S.V.). God does the sealing at the time of salvation by sending the Spirit to take up His abode in our hearts.

1:17   *That the God of our Lord Jesus Christ, the Father of glory, may give unto you the Spirit of wisdom and revelation in the knowledge of him.*[2]

The Ephesians already possessed the gift of the indwelling Paraclete. This passage, therefore, speaks of something additional: that is, the Spirit's ministry of illumination. We must cooperate with Him in this special phase of His work. When we do, we see things through Spirit-lit eyes. We are not ready, for instance, to study God's Word until we've recognized the Paraclete as our Teacher. For He alone can make real to us the hope and power of God's great salvation. He alone can fill our bosoms with the hope produced by God's calling; that is, the hope arising from the knowledge of what we inherit in Christ. Only He can show us the riches of the glory of Christ's inheritance in us, the joy He experiences in saving us. And only He can persuade us of God's ability to accomplish all things for us. The Paraclete wants to be, and will be, "the spirit of wisdom and revelation in the knowledge of [God]" to us, but we must acknowledge Him as such. We must not keep Him busy at something else, such as convicting us of sins and restraining us from carnality. We must be humble students of the Word, making private fellowship with Him the sweetest, most profitable, time of the day. Thus the Father speaks, the Son mediates, and the Spirit illuminates. He is the light, so to speak, in which we see God in Christ.

One glad day I sat in a library in Washington, D.C., studying Bishop Moule's exposition of this passage. As I meditated, the Paraclete spoke to me about receiving Him definitely as the One to help me in Bible study. I bowed my head and, by faith, did so. I shall always praise God for that invaluable experience.

2:18   *For through him we both have access by one Spirit unto the Father.*

Both Jews and Gentiles have access through Christ unto the Father in "the vital sphere or element" of the Spirit. God is in fellowship with redeemed men by the Paraclete who makes all one in Christ: "That he might create in himself of the two one new man, so making peace; and might reconcile them both in one body unto God through the cross."

2:22 *In whom ye also are builded together for an habitation of God through the Spirit.*

The Church is a holy temple identified with and united in Christ Jesus. Believers today, like the Ephesian believers in Paul's day, are being builded together to be God's dwelling place. "In the Spirit" (A.S.V.) signifies that it's in and by the influence of the Paraclete that we're built in Christ, that we form a habitation of God, and that God dwells in us.

3:5 *Which in other ages was not made known unto the sons of men, as it is now revealed unto his holy apostles and prophets by the Spirit.*

God's plan of making "no difference" between Jews and Gentiles in this age was not revealed in the Old Testament. But God revealed it to the New Testament apostles and prophets by His holy Agent, the Paraclete. Peter, taught by the Spirit, learned it through his vision of the "great sheet" and his experience with Cornelius. Paul received the full revelation and confirmed it among the other leaders (cf. Gal. 2). This was the Spirit's part in "the revelation of Jesus Christ" (Gal. 1:12).

3:16 *That he would grant you, according to the riches of his glory, to be strengthened with might by his Spirit in the inner man.*

This verse begins Paul's earnest prayer that we may be "empowered with strength in the inner self" (Berkeley V.), that we may receive power to know and to show divine love. Indeed, verses 16–19 outline "God's mode of development of Divine life in the saint" (Bishop Moule). The Corinthians who were overdoing speaking in tongues had not passed this way! All extremes in the name of the Holy Spirit can be avoided by taking heed to this significant passage.

To begin with. the Paraclete deals with us until we're able to realize. cherish. and commune with Christ dwelling in our hearts by faith; until by faith we perceive His presence. His excellence. and His glory. all the while receiving and returning, if feebly, expressions of mutual love. Thus He begins to empower us. We're in "to the ankles" (Ezek. 47:3). so to speak. This phase of the Spirit's empowering continues until we're firmly established in love for God and others. Faith grows. Prayer becomes spontaneous. Love deepens.

Thereafter. the Spirit continues developing. strengthening. and enlarging our minds, giving us fuller capacity to grasp mentally and to experience in some degree the surpassing magnitude of Christ's love for us. He explains. in addition. that Christ's love passes knowledge. not only because He himself is infinite. but because the humiliation and sufferings to which His love led. and the blessing which His love secured. are beyond our comprehension. The Paraclete enables us to perceive how wonderful. how free. how long-suffering, how manifold. and how constant our Saviour's love is; and how utterly measureless. We keep on believing. He keeps on filling.

Thus gradually we become "filled with all the fulness of God." with all His suitable graces and powers. Our hearts melt. our attitudes change. our wills grow strong; the Spirit eventually fully controls and uses us. filling us with God's revealed perfections: love. wisdom, power. grace. goodness. patience. and holiness.

4:3 *Endeavoring to keep the unity of the Spirit in the bond of peace.*

Verses 1 and 2 specify phases of diligence to be used in promoting unity among believers. the unity already created by the Spirit. This verse 3 exhorts us to cherish and to manifest Christian unity in the sphere and practice of peace. To this the Spiirt-filled believer is dedicated; in fact. this endeavor flows from his control by the Spirit. It should be said, moreover, that the only unifying power on earth—for homes, churches, communities, nations, and mankind—is the Spirit of God's Christ. He alone can illumine and enable us concerning, for example, the exceedingly important distinctions between constructive denominationalism and grievous sectarianism. He alone can make us show transdenominational unity and love—fellowship with each other above man-made divisions.

4:4 *There is one body, and one Spirit, even as ye are called in one hope of your calling.*

Verses 4 and 5 illustrate and emphasize the exhortation of verse 3. That is, all Christians constitute "one body," indwelt, moved, and empowered by "one Spirit"; and unified in the moral element of "one hope." They have, furthermore, one divine object toward whom their faith is directed, the Lord Jesus Christ (v. 5). There follows one common experience and confession of "faith" in Him, since all have been baptized into Him. "As there was one Lord and one faith in Him, so was there one and only one baptism into Him (Gal. 3:27), one and only one *inward* element, one and only one *outward* seal" (Ellicott). In this way all Christians have one sovereign God (v. 6) and spiritual Father eternally existing in three Persons: "above all, and through all, and in you all."

4:30 *And grieve not the holy Spirit of God, whereby ye are sealed unto the day of redemption.*

By the Paraclete's presence, influence and power, believers have been "sealed," certified, in view of the day of redemption. Meanwhile, God, in the Spirit, develops fellowship with us. And the Spirit's nature is such that He can be "grieved" by evil and worthless words and other sins. Wherefore, we're exhorted to go along with the Spirit as He uses the Word to cleanse and to insulate us. We are not to grieve Him: we must not hinder His work of removing the things of the flesh and supplying His things instead.

5:18 *And be not drunk with wine, wherein is excess; but be filled with the Spirit.*

This verse speaks of two kinds of control, one by wine and the other by the Paraclete. We should be continually "intoxicated" with the things of the Spirit that the "rivers" may flow (John 7:38).

This exhortation is given to all believers: wives, husbands, fathers, children, employers, and employees, as well as to the ministers of the Gospel. The "religious" claim, therefore, that the Holy Spirit's fulness is only for those "who have abandoned the ordinary vocations in favor of the various holy orders" is clearly unbiblical.

6:17 *And take the helmet of salvation, and the sword of the Spirit, which is the word of God.*

Christian warfare is carried on, in the last analysis, in the spiritual realm, "the heavenlies"; for it is primarily a clash with Satan and his demons. Wherefore, the Paraclete enables us to "put on the whole armor of God, that ye may be able to stand against the wiles of the devil." Thereafter, He supplies us with our only offensive weapon, the spoken word, the right text to use at the right time. Thus we overcome in times of temptation, we "bind the strong man" on behalf of others, and we "make known with boldness the mystery of the gospel." [3]

6:18 *Praying always with all prayer and supplication in the Spirit, and watching thereunto with all perseverance and supplication for all saints.*

"Prayer is the key to the use of the whole armor" (Edward Stelling). It is to be all kinds of prayer and at all seasons; there are times to "wrestle," for example, and there are times to rest. The Paraclete will show which kind at each particular season; He will supervise and help us to prevail (Rom. 8:26, 27). It's to be non-sectarian prayer, "for all the saints." God always leads such prayer warriors "in triumph in Christ, and maketh manifest through us the savor of his knowl-

edge in every place." Such are seated with Christ in the heavenlies. in the position of universal authority. "For the weapons of
our warfare are not of the flesh. but mighty before God to the
casting down of strongholds." This. of course. isn't legalistic
praying but that of happy warriors.

Now, in view of all this. what should be our outlook for
the Church as manifested in the churches today? Are there
not good reasons why we should see genuine revival and
mighty awakening in any assembly that will meet the conditions? Shall the gates of hell prevail against Christ's Church?
Couldn't Paul's prayers for the churches in his day be answered
for the churches in our day? Is it not still possible for Christ
to "bind the strong man"? Don't we have the power of attorney
in prayer? Isn't the "sword of the Spirit" just as effective as
ever? Is not Christianity supernatural? Is it not God's plan to
consumate all things in Christ?

III. PHILIPPIANS—TWO REFERENCES

Paul wrote this joy-filled epistle while he was in prison
at Rome. and the occasion was a gift from his friends at
Philippi. Paul's own life at that time strikingly illustrated true
Christian experience in the power of the Paraclete: "not something that is going on around the believer. but something which
is going on within him."

1:19 *For I know that this shall turn to my salvation through
your prayer. and the supply of the Spirit of Jesus Christ.*

Although Paul was kept under guard. the Gospel was being
preached by others in Rome. Some were actually preaching
Christ with impure motives of envy and contention. suppos-
ing they were making Paul's bondage more bitter and his
chains more galling. In such a situation Paul relied on the
prayers of his friends and the consequent supply of all his
needs by the Paraclete. who abundantly transferred to him
the things of Christ: wisdom, strength. liberty. authority, joy,
hope. Note that Paul here describes the Paraclete as "the
Spirit of Jesus Christ." That is, as we've seen, the Eternal

Spirit proceeds from Christ who "gives Himself spiritually in and with the Holy Ghost" (Ellicott).

2:1 *If there be therefore any consolation in Christ, if any comfort of love, if any fellowship of the Spirit, if any bowels of mercies. . . .*

In this spirit, Paul begins his exhortation to unity and meekness. He appeals to them on the basis of their mutual relationship in Christ, the constraints of love, the hidden Paraclete's commonwealth, and the tenderness of sympathy. It's another instance of God's fellowship with men by means of His Spirit. In this way, and in this way only. are men lifted from their inherent disunity, frustration, pride, and strife. This communion with the Father and the Son which the Spirit creates and sustains among believers makes it possible for Paul to write: "Rejoice in the Lord alway: and again I say, Rejoice."

IV. COLOSSIANS —ONE REFERENCE

The fact that Paul mentions the Paraclete only once in this Christ-centered epistle suggests that the Colossians are already well acquainted with Him; also that the doctrine of the Spirit is here implied. Consequently, it's here that we see more clearly than anywhere else the preeminence of Christ: Chief in the revelation of Deity (1:15a), Chief in creation (1:15–17), and Chief over His Church (1:18–23). For, to exalt and magnify Christ is the hidden Spirit's delight.

1:8 *Who also declared unto us your love in the Spirit.*

The Spirit confronted the heresy at Colosse with love in the hearts of the Christians. In the power of the Paraclete, they were "lovingly attached to the truth." Paul had heard of this love: ". . . love which ye have to all the saints," and he had also struggled in prayer for them "that their hearts might be comforted, being knit together in love" (2:2). Thus, they earnestly contended for "the faith which was once delivered unto the saints." This was Paul's way, Peter's way (II Pet. 3:17, 18), and Jude's way (22, 23) to combat heresy.

V. I AND II THESSALONIANS—FIVE REFERENCES

These early epistles imply a full knowledge of the Paraclete on the part of Paul's readers. First, the inherent power in the Gospel was made effective by the Spirit in the establishing of the church in Thessalonica:

1:5   *For our gospel came not unto you in word only, but also in power, and in the Holy Ghost, and in much assurance; as ye know what manner of men we were among you for your sake.*

Next, we see the Paraclete giving joy in affliction:

1:6   *And ye became followers of us, and of the Lord, having received the word in much affliction, with joy of the Holy Ghost.*

Again, and primarily, He is the Agent in sanctification:

4:8   *He therefore that despiseth, despiseth not man, but God, who hath also given unto us his Holy Spirit.*

For exposition, see on II Thessalonians 2:13.

5:19   *Quench not the Spirit.*

Here "the Eternal Spirit is represented as a fire which it was regarded possible to extinguish by a studied repression and disregard of its manifestation, arising from erroneous perceptions and a mistaken dread of enthusiasm" (Ellicott). In other words, dare we put out the fire of the Holy Spirit in our lives or the lives of others?

2:13. (II Thess.)   *But we are bound to give thanks always to God for you, brethren beloved of the Lord, because God hath from the beginning chosen you to salvation through sanctification of the Spirit and belief of the truth.*

Let us look at this verse in the light of I Thessalonians 4:1–8. I Thessalonians 4:1 exhorts us to attain more and more perfection in living Christ; for indeed, it's always possible for consecrated believers to become more consecrated. Verse 3 tells of God's will that we abstain from all sexual vice, dedicating ourselves to the most thorough purity. If we disregard this instruction, Paul says, we disregard not man but God (v. 8), whose Spirit is holy, chaste, pure.

These verses, therefore, emphasize *our part* alongside the Spirit's part. To wit, diligent cooperation of the human will with the divine is necessary (II Pet. 1:5). The sanctifying work of the Spirit depends primarily, however, upon our "belief of the truth," our conscious reliance on Christ (II Thess. 2:13). Yet ultimately all depends on "the God of peace himself," who alone can sanctify us wholly (I Thess. 5:23).

VI. I AND II TIMOTHY—FIVE REFERENCES

These Scriptures were addressed to ministers and they emphasize: the pattern of faith, I Timothy 3:16; the warning against apostasy, I Timothy 4:1; the gift of power, II Timothy 1:7; the guarding of doctrine, II Timothy 1:14; and the experience of renewal, Titus 3:5. Therefore, it is especially important for ministers to honor the Paraclete.

3:16 *And without controversy great is the mystery of godliness: God was manifest in the flesh, justified in the Spirit, seen of angels, preached unto the Gentiles, believed on in the world, received up into glory.*

Early Christians believed that God was manifested in human form in the person of Jesus Christ, and was vindicated as such in the realm of the Paraclete's ministry. Then, after crucifixion, "according to the Spirit of Holiness [He] was openly designated as the Son of God with power when He was raised from the dead" (Rom. 1:3, 4, Berkeley V.). Angels witnessed His resurrection (Matt. 28:2–7) and ascension (Acts 1:10, 11). Again, on the day of Pentecost the Paraclete vindicated Christ by inaugurating the worldwide preaching of the Gospel. This constitutes the pattern of faith.

4:1 *Now the Spirit speaketh expressly, that in the latter times some shall depart from the faith, giving heed to seducing spirits, and doctrines of devils.*

The Spirit of inspiration definitely expressed himself to Paul and the other apostles to the effect that the future of Christianity would be marred by a Satan-inspired falling away of professed believers. Thus He warned against apostasy.

1:7 (II Tim.) *For God has not given us the spirit of fear; but of power, and of love, and of a sound mind.*

The presence of the Spirit is here definitely *implied*. Paul alludes to the same truth in Romans 8:15, where adult sonship is created by the Paraclete. Here the Paraclete develops power, love, and a wholesome outlook.

1:14 *That good thing which was committed unto thee keep by the Holy Ghost which dwelleth in us.*

Ony the Paraclete is wise and strong enough to enable Christians in general and ministers in particular to "guard that precious entrusted deposit." the "faith once for all delivered." Paul here exhorts Timothy regarding the Word spoken through Christ and His apostles. It was first the spoken Word, then the Church created by the spoken Word received through faith, and finally the written Word of the New Testament.

3:5 (Titus) *Not by works of righteousness which we have done, but according to his mercy he saved us, by the washing of regeneration, and renewing of the Holy Ghost.*

The experience of renewal comes after regeneration; it's the development and extension of regeneration. These two aspects of the Paraclete's work are implied in the terms "washing" and "renewing."

Those who presume to find in this verse the interpretation that "baptism is the instrument or means of regeneration" fall into the fatal error of ancient Pharisaism, which regarded circumcision as insuring salvation. irrespective of personal character. For outward baptism is only a figure of the inward cleansing of the Spirit (John 3:5; I Pet. 3:21). No mere figure can regenerate: only the Paraclete can do that, and the Gospel is His instrument (I Pet. 1:23).

How fitting to conclude Paul's 108 references with these five from the Pastoral Epistles. They climax Paul's rich and comprehensive doctrine of the Spirit. And since the Pastorals are addressed to ministers and concern churches. it may be pertinent to ask. incidentally. if they teach organizational unity of all churches. Or. do the "offices" referred to exercise authority beyond the local assembly? The answer in the case of Timothy is No; that of Titus. a qualified Yes. That is. the influence Titus wielded over the church on Crete was spiritual. not ecclesiastical. Indeed. ecclesiasticism never arose until the second century. but it has been a pressing danger ever since. Not church union. but "the unity of the Spirit" was the emphasis in Paul's day—and also in John's (Rev. 2 and 3).

Thus we have clearly seen in Paul's epistles the wide *meaning* of full redemption: Christ indwelling believers in the person of the Holy Spirit and forming them into local churches "zealous of good works," especially fishing for men (Tit. 2:14). We're now prepared to study our very present God's part in the *exhortation* of redemption, as set forth in the General Epistles: helping us to give "all diligence" (II Pet. 1:5) to blazing (Heb. 6:1), even when our faith is "tried with fire" (I Pet. 1:7).

10

The Spirit in the General Epistles and The Revelation—Divine Power Essential

WE SHOULDN'T BE SURPRISED in our study of the Spirit through the Bible to find Him exhorting us at the last, over and over, to lay hold of Christ, to use fully our riches in Him. In Hebrews we're urged and warned and instructed repeatedly to "draw nigh" and worship "in Spirit and in truth," entering into "the holiest of all"; in James we sense the jealous yearning of the Paraclete for the entire devotion of our hearts; in I Peter we behold Spirit-wrought glory resting upon those who suffer with Christ; in II Peter we review the Spirit's inspiration of Scripture; in I John we experience the witness of the Spirit in fellowship; in Jude we learn how to "contend for the truth"; and in The Revelation, we hear (seven times) "what the Spirit saith unto the churches."

There are twenty-two references to the Spirit in the General Epistles, the theme of which is the exhortation of redemption—living faith in Christ or else: seven in Hebrews, one in James, five in I Peter, one in II Peter, six in I John, none in II and III John, and two in Jude. The Revelation, which concerns the consummation of redemption, contains seventeen.

I. HEBREWS—SEVEN REFERENCES

Since Hebrews sets forth Christ as our great High Priest, the Paraclete's indwelling ministry to the individual believer has no place there; so the references are principally historical.

2:4 *God also bearing witness, both by signs and wonders, and with divers miracles, and gifts of the Holy Ghost, according to his own will?*

This verse completes a long question which began with verse 2: If wilful sinners didn't escape judgment under law, how shall we under grace escape. "if we neglect so great salvation"? For this salvation was first spoken by Christ himself, and confirmed by them that heard Him; and God bore witness to it *"according to his own will."* That is. it was God's will to bear witness to the Gospel in the early days of Christianity "with signs and wonders, and with divers miracles, and gifts of the Holy Ghost." The word "first" in verse 3, notice, doesn't imply that it was God's will so to witness at first but not now; it simply means the Gospel "first began to be spoken by the Lord." So this passage does not teach, as some have imagined, that Christianity is less supernatural now than then. No. indeed. God will still bear witness to His Gospel. *"according to his own will."* "To each is granted the evidence of the Spirit for the common welfare" (I Cor. 12:7, Berkeley V.).

3:7 *Wherefore (as the Holy Ghost saith, To day if ye will hear his voice....*

Here is an instance of the Spirit's use of the Word to warn us believers. all professing believers: against hardening our hearts. against trying the Lord. against erring in our hearts, against an evil heart of unbelief. and against the deceitfulness of sin.

This is to say. it is essential to make much use of the Word in our times of "drawing near" so the Spirit will have a chance to apply it; otherwise. sin will harden our hearts. Sin hardens us in various ways: "because of delayed judgment. by making sin appear harmless. by promising good or enjoyment, by taking advantage of our ignorance of the Word, and by encouraging us to violate our conscience, and, thus, slowly stupify it" (Newell). We err in our hearts by remaining ignorant of God's Word. and by dissipating our hunger for personal fellowship with God through the Word. The Spirit would also use the Word to warn us against an evil heart of unbelief. For not all who *profess* to be Christians are really born again; many are like Judas and those illustrated by the Parable of the Sower. We see, then, why it is tragic to ignore the Word: if we do so, the Paraclete can't warn us of these perils. And observe that we live in the dispensation, the *today*, of the Paraclete's speaking.

6:4–6 *For it is impossible for those who were once enlightened, and have tasted of the heavenly gift, and were made partakers of the Holy Ghost,* ... (6) *If they shall fall away to renew them again unto repentance.*

This verse, you know, was addressed to Hebrews who had confessed faith in our Lord Jesus Christ. Whereas they all *professed* to be Christians, there's evidence that the writer feared some weren't really born again. He warns, therefore, against apostasy, the wilful casting away of known revealed truth. In so doing, he implies a person can go a long way in spiritual things without being saved: he can taste without really drinking; he can be made a partaker of the Paraclete's ministry to a certain degree, as, for example, Saul in the Old Testament and Judas in the New; he can have a Spirit-wrought view of Christ, and knowledge of His earthly Messiahship, death and resurrection. But if, under persecution and discouragement or for any other reason, he wilfully turns away from Christ and becomes utterly indifferent to his fruitless state toward God, he becomes a hater of the light, an apostate, to whom God will not permit renewal unto repentance (6:3). For apart from the power of the Gospel, his heart bears "thorns and briars" (v. 8). Thus the Spirit's use of the Word preserves mere professors from apostasy until they become born again; until they become "partakers of Christ" and hold "the beginning of [their] confidence steadfast unto the end" (3:14). Then it can be said, "But, beloved, we are persuaded better things of you, and things that accompany salvation, though we thus speak" (6:9). To "fall away" from the power of the Paraclete's use of the Gospel, however, means eternal doom.

9:8   *The Holy Ghost this signifying, that the way into the holiest of all was not yet made manifest, while as the first tabernacle was yet standing.*

Old Testament tabernacle worship, provided by the Holy Spirit, signified in type the Old Testament believer's distance from God: he didn't have the high privilege of intimate fellowship, of coming "boldly unto the throne of grace" (4:16), of "drawing near" (10:22).

9:14   *How much more shall the blood of Christ, who through the eternal Spirit offered himself without spot to God, purge your conscience from dead works to serve the living God?*

Here we see, incidentally, among many other precious things, all three Persons of the Godhead active in our redemption, the deity of the Spirit being implied: "eternal Spirit." Mainly, however, Christ accomplished our eternal redemption "through the eternal Spirit"; that is, through the eternal Spirit, Christ as a *human Being*, was able to offer himself without spot to God. And He did this in order to cleanse our conscience from legal obedience to serve our living God according to grace. The Eternal Spirit, take note, also makes the finished work of the Man Christ Jesus eternal in the experience of true believers.

10:15   *Whereof the Holy Ghost also is a witness to us. . . .*

Scripture, inspired by the Holy Spirit, testifies to the fact that Christ's once-for-all sacrifice sanctifies believers (positionally) once for all (10:10, 14). This verse also implies the deity of the Holy Spirit, for He is here identified with the Lord of Jeremiah 31. Furthermore, reference to the Holy Spirit in connection with the two covenants mentioned by Jeremiah implies the divine inspiration of Jeremiah's prophecy and Hebrews, and, therefore, Scripture in general.

10:29 *Of how much sorer punishment, suppose ye, shall he*
be thought worthy, who hath trodden under foot the Son
of God, and hath counted the blood of the covenant, where-
with he was sanctified, an unholy thing, and hath done
despite unto the Spirit of grace?

This reference should be studied in the light of the whole
paragraph, verses 26–31. It is another warning against apostasy
(see 6:3–8). The words "sin wilfully" don't refer to sins
committed inconsiderately and from ignorance or weakness;
instead, the context shows they refer to voluntary, wilful
turning away from Christ and back to Judaism. This is to say,
people who *profess* to be Christians for a time and then wilfully repudiate Christ, thereby outrage the Spirit of grace,
and also deliberately and permanently spurn the privileges
of the manifest presence and power of the Paraclete in a day
of grace. Furthermore, they show contempt of the grace of
God, and of that which He has done in the Person of Jesus,
in order to deliver them from the consequences of disobedience
(Darby). Since God has no other sacrifice for sins, all that
remains for those who thus finally reject Christ is "a certain
fearful expectation of judgment, and a fierceness of fire which
shall devour the adversaries."

II. JAMES—ONE REFERENCE

4:5 *Do you think that the scripture saith in vain, The Spirit*
that dwelleth in us lusteth to envy?

"That Spirit which he made to dwell in us yearneth for
us even unto jealous envy" (A.S.V., margin). "Or do you
suppose the Scripture speaks to no purpose? The Spirit, which
took up His abode in us, yearns jealously over us" (Berkeley V.).
A footnote adds: "No quotation, but a summary of Old Testament teaching: God wants all of a person, our undivided
loyalty."

Thus again we see the ministry of the Spirit implied. For
certainly James, the half-brother of our Lord, knew the Spirit
in power. Observe how his teaching fits into Paul's: the Holy

Spirit who inspired all Scripture and who indwells all true believers does all that is consistent with our freedom of will to conform us to the image of God's Son.... This great passage (James 4:1–10) will bring genuine revival to all who will really apply it.

III. I AND II PETER—SIX REFERENCES

1:2 *Elect according to the foreknowledge of God the Father, through sanctification of the Spirit, unto obedience and sprinkling of the blood of Jesus Christ: Grace unto you, and peace, be multiplied.*

Peter, of course, also knew the Spirit in power. Study this meaty salutation until you see Paul's Gospel shining through. "Foreknowledge of God the Father" is the gracious basis of election, "sanctification of the Spirit" is the efficient means of election, and "obedience" is the glorious purpose of election. Whereas election under Law was national and by Jehovah, election under Grace is individual and by the Father. Another contrast: consecration under the Law was through ordinances; under Grace it's through the Spirit, resulting in whole-hearted faith-obedience.

1:11 *Searching what, or what manner of time the Spirit of Christ which was in them did signify, when it testified beforehand the sufferings of Christ, and the glory that should follow.*

Several versions translate "when *it* testified," leaving room for some interpreters to question the personality of the Paraclete. But some, including Rotherham, Moffatt, and Weymouth, do otherwise; for example, Weymouth says, "They investigated the time which the Spirit of Christ within them kept indicating, or its characteristics, when He solemnly made known beforehand the sufferings that were destined for Christ and the glories which would follow."

1:12 *Unto whom it was revealed, that not unto themselves, but unto us they did minister the things, which are now*

*reported unto you by them that have preached the gospel
unto you with the Holy Ghost sent down from heaven;
which things the angels desire to look into.*

Here Peter encourages his readers concerning the great
salvation of this day of grace. Note several things about God's
Spirit: He is "the Spirit of Christ"; He worked in the Old
Testament prophets; He testified to them "the sufferings of
Christ, and the glory that should follow"; He disclosed to
the prophets that this great day of grace was not for them
but for us; He empowered the early preachers of the Gospel;
and He was "sent down from heaven." So here again the
whole New Testament doctrine of the Spirit is implied; that
is, He "came" on the day of Pentecost in the sense that He
took over on earth for the once-crucified Christ now in glory.[1]

3:18 *For Christ also hath once suffered for sins, the just
for the unjust, that he might bring us to God, being put
to death in the flesh, but quickened by the Spirit.*

In general, there are two interpretations of this much-
disputed passage (I Pet. 3:18–22). The older one claims that
Christ, by the Spirit, preached through Noah. The view held
by the majority of modern exegetes is: Christ, in His human
spirit quickened by the Holy Spirit, visited the prison of evil
spirits to proclaim victory over them. This He did while His
incorruptible crucified body lay in Joseph's tomb. Some translations which favor this latter position are: American Standard
Version, Amplified, Berkeley, Phillips, New English Bible and
Weymouth.[2]

4:14 *If ye be reproached for the name of Christ, happy are
ye; for the Spirit of glory and of God resteth upon you.*

We capitalize "spirit" here with the American Standard
and many other versions. The Berkeley Version says, "the Spirit
of glory, yes, the Spirit of God, is resting on you." In other
words, we're encouraged to maintain a testimony worthy of
persecution, because that is a sign of spiritual prosperity and
power.

1:21 (II Pet.) *For the prophecy came not in old time by the will of man: but holy men of God spake as they were moved by the Holy Ghost.*

This verse declares that prophecy didn't come from man, that no part of it came from human wisdom or effort; but that it did come—all of it—from God. "Men spake from God" (A.S.V.); that is, men, human instruments with human literary talents and human vocabularies, were so miraculously used by the Paraclete that our Christian Scriptures, in their original languages, came to us without error, infallible.

IV. I JOHN—SIX REFERENCES

According to the American Standard and other versions, the Paraclete is mentioned in I John six times in five verses. . . . And herein our attention is directed to the Spirit's work of producing faith in Christ and of inspiring belief in the supernatural character of Christianity. Thus we see more of the Paraclete as "the Spirit of truth," as mentioned in John's Gospel.

3:24 *And he that keepeth his commandments dwelleth in him, and he in him. And hereby we know that he abideth in us, by the Spirit which he hath given us.*

By the Spirit's help Christians lovingly obey God's grace-commandments (3:23) and hence enjoy a sense of His presence and fellowship. In this manner the Triune God "comes unto" us and makes His abode with us (John 14:21-23).

4:2 *Hereby we know the Spirit of God: Every Spirit that confesseth that Jesus Christ is come in the flesh is of God.*

Since Christian love should abound "in all judgment" (Phil. 1:9), John teaches us how to discern the "many false prophets [which] have gone out into the world" (4:1). We recognize God's true ministers by their confession to the full deity and perfect humanity of Jesus Christ. Ministers controlled by the Spirit do this because the Spirit glorifies Christ. It is His nature and habit to do so. "Hereby we know the spirit of truth and the spirit of error." So we judge the false in the light of the true. John, the apostle of love, would have us beware, not of what preachers say about Christ, but what they leave unsaid; for, "Every spirit that confesseth not that Jesus Christ is come in the flesh is not of God." Notice that Spirit-wrought love insists on loyalty to the Christ of God.

4:13   *Hereby know we that we dwell in him, and he in us, because he hath given us of his Spirit.*

God gives himself unto us (in applied redemption and realized fellowship) in the person of His Spirit (see I John 3:24).

5:7, 8   *And it is the Spirit that beareth witness, because the Spirit is the truth. (8) For there are three who bear witness, the Spirit, and the water, and the blood: and the three agree in one* (A.S.V.).

The Paraclete begets and develops our confidence in the facts of Christ's earthly life and ministry, and also in the value and power of His shed blood, as appropriated in Christian experience. Wherefore there are really three witnesses to the supernatural character of Christianity: the Spirit, Christ's earthly ministry ("the water"), and Christian experience ("the blood"). And these three agree in one united testimony, that "God gave unto us eternal life, and this life is in his Son." The Paraclete, therefore, is "the Spirit of truth" in the sense that He persuades us of the veracity of Gospel facts. And in doing this, He so distinguishes Christianity from all mere religions that John concludes: "My little children, guard your-selves from idols."

V. JUDE—TWO REFERENCES

The first mention of the Paraclete by Jude is connected with a warning against apostate religious leaders (v. 19) and the second with instruction about how to "contend for the faith" (v. 20).

v. 19   *These be they who separate themselves, having not the*
        Spirit.

Jude cries, "Remember" that there will always be apostate
leaders in the churches! These leaders, he says, separate themselves from the main current of Christianity, and lead others
after them; because they have never been born of the Spirit.
and, consequently, aren't led by Him.

v. 20   *But ye, beloved, building up yourselves on your most*
        holy faith, praying in the Holy Ghost.

The Paraclete's help is central in obedience to Jude's
chief exhortation ". . .that ye should earnestly contend for
the faith which was once delivered unto the saints." The context (vv. 17–23) shows that He enables us to contend in the
right spirit: (1) Remember that our Lord's apostles warned
that apostate leaders would come—those who "bend their
tongues . . . for lies" (Jer. 9:3), (2) "Keep yourselves in the
love of God," and (3) "have compassion" on the lost. And
the text (v. 20) reveals the crux of the whole exhortation,
". . .praying in the Holy Ghost" (see Rom. 8:26, 27).

VI. THE REVELATION—SEVENTEEN REFERENCES

The fitting function of the Spirit in The Revelation is
that of consummation. He is. therefore, seen as the Agent
in God's culminating government, both of the world and the
churches in the world. The great issue is: "Who shall reign,
Satan through man. or God through Christ?" And The Revelation answers this age-old question by unveiling the glorified
God-Man and His divine program of last things. In this program the Spirit plays an active role throughout. not as
indweller of believers. but as Christ's Agent in world government. This character of the Spirit is symbolized by the unique
designation. "the seven Spirits" (1:4; 3:1; 4:5; 5:6).

1:4   *John to the seven churches which are in Asia: Grace be*
      unto you, and peace, from him which is, and which was,

and which is to come; and from the seven Spirits which are before his throne.

This portrait of the Paraclete is that of the sevenfold Spirit resting upon "the prince of the kings of the earth" (1:5). Zechariah witnesses to this governmental operation in these words: "Not by might, nor by power, but by my Spirit, saith the LORD of hosts" (4:6). (See comment on Isaiah 11:2.)

1:10 *I was in the Spirit on the Lord's day, and heard behind me a great voice, as a trumpet.*

In the power of the Paraclete to inspire. John on Patmos became ecstatic; he entered into a trance, "becoming thereby receptive of the vision or revelation to follow" (Alford). This happens three other times in The Revelation: 4:2; 17:3; and 21:10 (see A.S.V.). (Compare Ezek. 8:3; 11:24; 37:1; 43:5; and II Cor. 12:2.)

2:7 *He that hath an ear, let him hear what the Spirit saith unto the churches.*

Notice that our glorified Lord does not say, "He that hath an ear, let him hear what the Spirit saith unto *this church*." No, the point is that the Paraclete enables born-again. attentive Christians to know His voice in all Scripture. Objective truth or revelation mediated by Christ and produced by the Spirit is heard with spiritual ears opened by the self-same Spirit of Christ. Each and every local church, therefore, is directly responsible to Christ the Head of the Church. Consequently, Christ here exhorts the man with the spiritually attentive ear, the "messenger" (angel) of each church, to discern when the Spirit is speaking to his church. It's a solemn responsibility; neglect to heed could mean loss of the church's testimony for Christ.

2:11 *He that hath an ear, let him hear what the Spirit saith unto the churches.*

This call to heed the Paraclete's voice in the Scriptures is identical to each of the seven churches, the two cited, and those referred to in 2:17; 2:29; 3:6; 3:13; and 3:22. There is, however, a significant change in the placing of the call. In His messages to Ephesus, Smyrna, and Pergamum, Christ gives the exhortation to the whole church before He gives the promise to overcomers; but thereafter the call appears to be to overcomers only.

3:1 *And unto the angel of the church in Sardis write; These things saith he that hath the seven Spirits of God, and the seven stars.*

The God-Man in glory possesses the perfections of the Spirit of God; in this character He exercises lordship over "the seven stars," "the angels [messengers] of the seven churches" (1:20). He is well-qualified, therefore, to enable the Sardis-type church to perfect her works before God.

In Revelation 1:4, 5 the three Persons of the Trinity are presented as equal; here the Paraclete is pictured as subordinate, but only in the plan of redemption. "The Spirit is subordinate to the Son, as the Son to the Father, in the Divine creative and redemptive arrangements, although all are equal in fact of Deity" (Newell).

4:2 *And immediately I was in the Spirit: and, behold, a throne was set in heaven, and one sat on the throne.*

See comment on Revelation 1:10.

4:5 *And out of the throne proceeded lightnings and thunderings and voices: and there were seven lamps of fire burning before the throne, which are the seven Spirits of God.*

Here is symbolized the Paraclete's ministry of illumination in heaven; the judgments of God's throne are made in the light of His infinite wisdom.

5:6 *And I beheld, and, lo, in the midst of the throne and of the four beasts, and in the midst of the elders, stood a lamb as it had been slain, having seven horns and seven eyes, which are the seven Spirits of God sent forth into all the earth.*

Our Lord on earth, the Lamb of God, was rejected and crucified by His own world; consequently, He is now a King in exile from His own earthly kingdom. This verse, therefore, pictures the time, yet future, when, God's throne of grace having been changed into a throne of adjudication, Christ shall begin to establish righteousness and peace on earth. In doing so, He shall manifest perfect power, "seven horns," and utter discernment in earth's affairs, "seven eyes."

14:13 *And I heard a voice from heaven saying unto me, Write, Blessed are the dead which die in the Lord from henceforth: Yea, saith the Spirit, that they may rest from their labors; and their works do follow them.*

The Spirit of inspiration reveals that after God's throne has become a throne of adjudication (during the Great Tribulation), death for those "in the Lord" will be better than life.

17:3 *So he carried me away in the Spirit into the wilderness.*

See comment on Revelation 1:10.

21:10 *And he carried me away in the Spirit to a great and high mountain, and showed me that great city, the holy Jerusalem, descending out of heaven from God.*

See comment on Revelation 1:10.

22:17 *And the Spirit and the bride say, Come. And let him that heareth say, Come. And let him that is athirst come. And whosoever will, let him take the water of life freely.*

Note first that Revelation 22, the last chapter in the Bible, is full of the promise of Christ's second coming: "Behold, I come quickly" (v. 7); "And, behold, I come quickly" (v. 12); "I am the root and the offspring of David, and the bright and morning star" (v. 16); and "Surely I come quickly" (v. 20).

Observe next that the Paraclete is foremost in inviting Christ back, being joined by the Church. "There is also the exhortation to every uninstructed *hearer*, who may read or hear read this great book of The Revelation with its mighty consummation in Christ's second coming—he is exhorted to join the Spirit and the Bride in inviting Him back: 'Let him that heareth, say. *Come*' " (Newell).

This is indeed a fitting view of the Spirit's distinctive New Testament ministry. On the day of Pentecost He became present in the world in a special way to call out and to prepare the Church for her absent Lord. How appropriate for Him here to desire the coming of the Bridegroom for the Bride!

As in Genesis we saw "God stepping out of eternity into time," so, here we see Him "stepping back out of time into eternity" (Wm. Evans). and taking the redeemed with Him for fellowship. Our transcendent, immanent, provident, Triune God has brought man to his "chief and highest end," even to "glorify God, and fully to enjoy Him forever." "Behold, the tabernacle of God is *with* men, and he will dwell *with* them, and they shall be his people, and God himself shall be *with* them, and be their God."

Now what shall we conclude from this inductive study of the Spirit? We say this chiefly: It's a hidden Spirit who glorifies Christ in us and thus makes Him the answer for all our needs. For the Spirit mentions himself in only 322 of more than 31,000 verses. This is, indeed, significant, and we dare not dispute the fact; for we do so at our own peril. Rather, we must respect the different functions of Christ and His Spirit, as Bernard Ramm implies:

> The great mystery of the Christian religion is God manifest in the flesh. in the flesh of Jesus of Nazareth. The Son of God is the manifesting One and the manifest One. But the mystery of the Holy Spirit comes from the fact that he is the power of God present and active, the executive of the Divine will, the Lord of all life, and the immediate bearer and communicator of salvation. but yet remains hidden. Here the Son and the Spirit remain at antipodes.[3]

Wherefore let's glance at this strategic implication in history (chapter eleven) and doctrine (chapter twelve) and then peruse the Spirit's method in making Christ God's answer (conclusion).

Synopsis of the Spirit in Christian History

THE NEW TESTAMENT CLEARLY PORTRAYS Christ in the power of the Spirit as God's answer in the first century. There's no doubt about this.

I. The Spirit in the Second and Third Centuries—His Presence Enjoyed. Early Christian writers, those who immediately succeeded the apostles, didn't give much attention to the doctrine of the Spirit. The doctrine of Christ claimed their attention. rather; no heresies had arisen to force upon the churches a doctrinal statement concerning the Spirit. These early Christians, as we today often do, enjoyed the presence and power of the Spirit without giving Him due recognition doctrinally. We shall not be surprised, consequently. to find false and extravagant notions about His person and work.

A. Clement of Rome. Clement lived in the first century about 30–100. but he is commonly classed with the so-called Apostolic Fathers. who belong as a body to the second and third centuries. Brief samples of these men will suffice. Clement wrote thus to the Corinthians:

> Content with the provision which God had made for you, and carefully attending to His words. ye were inwardly filled with His doctrine, and His sufferings were before your eyes. Thus a profound and abundant

180

peace was given to you all, and ye had an insatiable desire for doing good, while a full outpouring of the Holy
Spirit was upon you all.[1]

B. Ignatius of Antioch. We don't know the date of Ignatius' birth. He died approximately 107.

The joy of the Spirit's presence and some of the secrets of
that joy appear in *The Epistle of Ignatius to the Ephesians*:

> But ye, being full of the Holy Spirit, do nothing ac-
> cording to the flesh, but all things according to the
> Spirit. Ye are complete in Christ Jesus. . . . But the
> Holy Spirit does not speak of His own things, but those
> of Christ, and that not from himself, but from the Lord;
> even as the Lord also announced to us the things He
> received from the Father.[2]

C. The Shepherd of Hermas. Hermas, a pastor in Rome,
composed this remarkable work—a sort of "Pilgrim's Progress"
of the early churches—about 140–160. The joy of the Holy
Spirit is everywhere exhibited. The most helpful gleanings,
perhaps, may be classified as "Marks of the Spiritual Man":

> Both these are grievous to the Holy Spirit—doubt
> and anger. Wherefore remove grief from you, and crush
> not the Holy Spirit which dwells in you, lest he en-
> treat God against you, and he withdraw from you. For
> the Spirit of God which has been granted to us to dwell
> in this body does not endure grief nor straitness. Where-
> fore put on cheerfulness, which always is agreeable and
> acceptable to God, and rejoice in it. For every cheerful
> man does what is good, and despises grief; but the
> sorrowful man always acts wickedly. . . . Try the man
> who has the Divine Spirit by his life. First, he who has
> the Divine Spirit proceeding from above is meek, and
> peaceable, and humble, and refrains from all iniquity
> and the vain desire of this world, and contents himself
> with fewer wants than those of other men.[3]

D. The Apologists. Thorough study of the person of Christ necessitated at least casual consideration of the Spirit's relation to Christ. Thus Justin Martyr of Palestine (100?–165?) reasoned with Trypho, a Jew, as follows:

> The Scripture says that these enumerated powers of the Spirit have come on Him, not because He stood in need of them, but because they would rest in Him, i.e., would find their accomplishment in Him, so that there would be no more prophets in your nation after the ancient custom: and this fact you plainly perceive. . . . Accordingly the Spirit rested when Christ came, after whom, in the times of this dispensation wrought out by Him amongst men, it was requisite that such gifts should cease from you; and having received their rest in Him, should again, as had been predicted, become gifts which, from the grace of His Spirit's power, He imparts to those who believe in Him, according as He deems each man worthy thereof.[4]

Irenaeus of Greece (130?–202?) had quite a bit to say about the Spirit in dealing with the heresy that "Christ was one and Jesus another." "The Apostles teach that it was neither Christ nor the Saviour," he asserted, "but the Holy Spirit, who descended upon Jesus." The descent of the Spirit as a dove at our Lord's baptism, he reasoned, was a blessed necessity:

> For as a compacted lump of dough cannot be formed of dry wheat without fluid matter, nor can a loaf possess unity, so, in like manner, neither could we, being many, be made one in Christ Jesus without the water from heaven. . . . The Lord, receiving this as a gift from His Father, does Himself also confer it upon those who are partakers of Himself, sending the Holy Spirit upon all the earth.[5]

Irenaeus, however, didn't hold to the scriptural doctrine of the personality of the Spirit; yet he sensed the presense of the Spirit. Christian leaders at this time were still giving their chief thought to the personality of Christ. Newman states: "The Holy Spirit, according to Irenaeus, is identical with the Wisdom of the Old Testament, and is God manifest in Providence. revelation, and the human conscience. The Trinity of Irenaeus would therefore be: God in the world, God in Christ, and God in himself." [6]

E. Gnosticism. Influence of Gnosticism on Christian thought and life was widespread during most of the second century and part of the third. This manifold enemy of the Gospel, with its emphasis on human wisdom, naturally radiated no spiritual joy. Simon Magus (Acts 8:9–24) illustrates the nature of this misunderstanding of the Spirit. which eventually made necessary a doctrinal statement.

According to Newman:

> This Simon of Samaria is said to have associated with himself a disreputable woman named Helena. and the two are said to have been worshipped by many of the Samaritans as the male and female principles of deity. He is said to have claimed to be the Word, the Paraclete, and the Omnipotent One, and to have declared Helena to have been the first conception of his mind. Through her the angels and powers of the. lower world had been produced. and through these angels the world had been framed. He himself and not Jesus. whom he regarded as a mere man who had received a divine impartation at his baptism. was the true Redeemer of mankind.[7]

Another sect of this period, and a branch of Gnosticism. was started by Mani, a Mesopotamian. Mani "regarded himself . . . as the promised Paraclete." [8]

F. Montanism. Montanists divorced the Word from the Spirit, and, consequently, developed an unwholesome emotionalism. Priscilla and Maximilla, women who claimed special enlightenment by the Paraclete. presumed that God had fulfilled to them personally Christ's promise in John 16:12, 13: "I have yet many things to say unto you, but ye cannot bear them now. Howbeit when he, the Spirit of truth, is come, he will guide you into all truth."

With this imagined authority, the Montanists insisted upon certain extremes, such as legalistic separation, and frequent and long-continued fasts; also the speedy end of the present dispensation. Their one-sided enthusiasm and fanaticism eventually led to monasticism, in which experience of the Spirit's presence, to say the least, was not robust.

G. *Monarchianism.* This heresy also shows the growing need for a scriptural doctrine of the Spirit. Theodotus and Paul of Samosata regarded Jesus as a mere man energized and exalted by the divine Spirit. Praxeas, Noetus, and Sabellius saw in the incarnation only a mode of divine activity and manifestation, and, consequently, overlooked trinitarian truth with its fulness of joy.

H. *Tertullian of Carthage, about 145–216.* Newman classifies Tertullian as a polemical writer who decried alarming conditions within the churches. Tertullian believed the greatest danger to Christianity was, not persecution from without, but laxity of discipline from within. This conviction finally led him into Montanism with its over-emphasis on the Spirit's gift of prophecy.

Tertullian believed the Spirit of God and the waters of creation had an essential unity, and that "the primeval hovering of the Spirit over the waters was typical of baptism." He contended, in accordance, that water baptism prepared one to receive the Holy Spirit. No other Apostolic Father went to this extreme.

Tertullian is refreshing, however, in his repeated references to the "Vicar of the Lord":

> The reason why the Lord sent the Paraclete was, that, since human mediocrity was unable to take all things at once, discipline should, little by little, be directed, and ordained, and carried on to perfection, by

that Vicar of the Lord, the Holy Spirit.... What then is the Paraclete's office but this: the direction of discipline, the revelation of the Scriptures, the re-formation of the intellect, the advancement toward the 'better things'? [9]

I. Clement of Alexandria, about 153–217. Clement was another who enjoyed the Spirit without giving Him due recognition. It has been pointed out that well over four hundred large double-column pages given to Clement in *The Ante-Nicene Fathers* have no statement that enables us to see, for instance, whether he distinguished the work of the Holy Spirit from that of the "Logos." Here's a typical saying of Clement: "There is one Father of the universe; there is also one Word of the universe; and one Holy Spirit, who is everywhere."

J. Origen of Alexandria, about 185–254. Origen was one of the first to attempt a "systematic exposition of Christianity as a whole." Consequently, we find more about the Holy Spirit in Origen than in any other writer of this era. Newman gives this summary:

> The Holy Spirit Origen regarded as the first and most exalted of all beings produced by the Father through the Son. His activity differs from that of the Logos, in that the latter extends to all creatures, whereas the former appears only in connection with the dispensation of God's grace.[10]

Origen's idea of the way man appropriates God's grace smacks of Romans 8: "The power to will and to do good comes from God; choice of good rests with man; after choice for good, all needful assistance in the perfecting of Christian character is furnished by the Holy Spirit." [11]

In writing of "what the Spirit is," Origen speaks of "authority and dignity" and the Spirit's place in the Trinity:

> The person of the Holy Spirit was of such authority and dignity, that saving baptism was not complete except by the authority of the most excellent Trinity of them

all, i.e., by the naming of the Father, Son, and Holy
Spirit, and by joining to the unbegotten God the Father,
and to His only-begotten Son, the name also of the Holy
Spirit. Who, then, is not amazed at the exceeding
majesty of the Holy Spirit, when he hears that he who
speaks a word against the Son of man may hope for
forgiveness; but that he who is guilty of blasphemy
against the Holy Spirit has not forgiveness, either in
the present world or in that which is to come.... All
knowledge of the Father is obtained by revelation of
the Son through the Holy Spirit.... We must understand, therefore, that as the Son, who alone knows the
Father, reveals Him to whom He will, so the Holy Spirit,
who alone searches the deep things of God, reveals God
to whom He will: 'For the Spirit bloweth where he listeth.' We are not, however, to suppose that the Spirit
derives His knowledge through the revelation from the
Son. For if the Holy Spirit knows the Father through the
Son's revelation, He passes from a state of ignorance
to one of knowledge; but it is alike impious and foolish
to confess the Holy Spirit, and yet to ascribe to Him
ignorance. For even although something else existed
before the Holy Spirit, it was not by progressive advancement that He came to be the Holy Spirit; as if one
should venture to say, that at the time when He was
not yet the Holy Spirit He was ignorant of the Father,
but that after He had received knowledge He was made
the Holy Spirit. For if this were the case, the Holy Spirit
would never be reckoned in the unity of the Trinity, i.e.,
along with the unchangeable Father and His Son, unless
He had always been the Holy Spirit.[12]

K. Novatian, 210–280. The writings of Novatian, like
those of other Apostolic Fathers, contain much that is unprofitable for us today. Although he wrote little about the Spirit, we
do find in his "Treatise Concerning the Trinity" this high-
level statement:

This is He who, after the manner of a dove, when our Lord was baptized, came and abode upon Him, dwelling in Christ full and entire, and not maimed in any measure or portion; but with His whole overflow copiously distributed and sent forth, so that from Him others might receive some enjoyment of His graces: the source of the entire Holy Spirit remaining in Christ, so that from Him might be drawn streams of gifts and works. while the Holy Spirit dwelt affluently in Christ.[13]

These Apostolic Fathers, therefore, enjoyed the presence of the Spirit but had no clear-cut doctrine of His person and work; consequently, as Swete says, "The spiritual giants of the Apostolic age [Matthew, Mark, Luke, John, Peter, James, Paul] were succeeded by men of lower stature and poorer capacity."

The Spirit's place in remaining Christian centuries we merely outline, for this sketch of the second and third centuries suffices to show the need and possibility for a mature doctrine of the Spirit.

II. The Spirit in the Fourth and Fifth Centuries—His Deity Affirmed. The Spirit receives fuller discussion. Heresies force attention to the Spirit. Unbelief in His deity develops. Leading writers of fourth century: Eusebius, Bishop of Caesarea; Cyril of Jerusalem; Athanasius; the Cappadocians—Basil of Caesarea, Gregory of Nazianzus, Gregory of Nyasa.... Deity of the Spirit affirmed at Council of Constantinople, 381.... Leading writers of fifth century: Theodore of Mopsuestia, 392–428; Theodoret. 432–458; Ambrose of Milan; Augustine of Hippo.... Deity of Spirit permanently decided upon at Council of Chalcedon. 451.

III. The Spirit in the Next Ten Centuries—His Relation to the Father and to the Son Discussed. Eternal procession from the Son as well as from the Father. This doctrine gets into the Creed—perhaps at Council of Toledo in Spain, 589. The doctrine lies dormant; streams of thought run sluggishly. Mediaeval mysticism and preparation for the Reformation.

IV. The Spirit in the Reformation—His Work Emphasized: by vindication of authority of Scriptures; by setting forth doctrine of justification; by affirming God's sovereignty; by admitting man's weakness; by exalting Christ above Church; by Luther, Calvin, and other leaders; by various Reformed Documents.

V. The Spirit in Seventeenth and Eighteenth Centuries— Excesses, Reactions, Revivals. Relation of the Spirit to the will of man. Re-emphasis on man's need of the Spirit. Connection of the Spirit with Scripture. Rise of Rationalism. Deism and Infidelity join Rationalism. Spiritual blight falls on England. Movements of revival: Pietists in Germany, Methodists and Evangelicals in Great Britain, men used of God in America, the missionary movement.

VI. The Spirit in Nineteenth and Twentieth Centuries— Progress Toward New Testament View of Spirit. Apostolic succession offers no help. Emphasis on feeling not to be trusted. Visions and revelations must be tested by Scripture. Plymouth Brethrenism rediscovers much truth. Nineteenth-century revivals represent clear progress. Rise of Bible schools, conferences and radio programs. Rally of evangelicals; mid-century evangelism.

VII. Lessons from History: human wisdom tends to supplant the Spirit, human energy hinders the Spirit, overuse of human authority grieves the Spirit, religious formality quenches the Spirit, sectarianism insults the Spirit, emotionalism ignores the Spirit's relation to Scriptures, fanaticism ignores Spirit's relation to Christ, work of the Spirit should become more constant in experience, and secret of spiritual blessing is found in gracious cooperation with the Spirit.

The Spirit stands ready to make Christ God's answer now— just as in the first century. Why not?

12

Synopsis of the Spirit in Christian Doctrine

NOTICE HOW IMPORTANT is the fact that the Spirit is a divine person. This fact is the key that unlocks the rivers of living water, making Christ God's answer. For, since Pentecost, it is faith in Christ glorified in heaven that causes this divine person on earth to act on our behalf.

I. The Personality of the Spirit. Is the Holy Spirit a power for us to use, or is He an almighty Person who longs to use us? Is our problem in spiritual efficiency one of getting more of Him, or of His getting more of us?

A. The Meaning of Personality. We don't mean, of course, the Spirit has a body like people on earth. Corporeality is not essential to personality—a corpse isn't a person. We don't mean He has limitations as do people on earth; for He is unlimited in intelligence, judgment, will-power, and so on. We don't mean He is another God, that Christianity has three Gods (Deut. 6:4, 5; Mark 12:29, 30; John 14:18). We don't mean He is another individual; individuality and personality in the Godhead are two different things (Acts 5:3, 4; Matt. 28:19).

When we say the Holy Spirit is a person, we mean He possesses personal distinctions in the Godhead, that He has qualities distinct from those of the Father and the Son. These qualities, however, are only relatively independent within the Godhead; that is, the Spirit can pierce the wall of self-

189

consciousness in the Father or the Son; whereas you and I can't pierce that wall in each other (II Cor. 13:14; Matt. 28:19; John 14:16). Also we mean the Spirit is a center of self-conscious life in the Godhead, that "there are three centers of self-consciousness in the one self-consciousness of God." [1] (See Matt. 3:16, 17.)

In other words, our Christian God is a personal Being, infinitely rich and full, who can be received, enjoyed, and fellowshipped (Acts 2:38; 19:2; Rom. 5:5; I Cor. 6:19; Gal. 3:2). "The transcendence of the Deity is expressed by the Father; the expression of the Deity is represented by the Son; while the truth of the immanence of the Deity for man's moral and spiritual life is that for which the Holy Spirit stands. And thus the Holy Spirit is at once the personal, energetic life of God and the 'Executive of the Godhead' in relation to man." [2] Compare John 16:7 with 14:18 (A.S.V.).

B. The Marks of Personality. Scripture reveals the personality of the Spirit by use of masculine gender and pronouns (John 14:16, 17, 26); by ascribing to Him intelligence (I Cor. 2:10, 11; Isa. 11:2; Neh. 9:20; Mark 13:11; John 14:26; 15:26); by attributing to Him judgment (John 16:13; Acts 13:2; 15:28; 20:28); by assigning to Him will-power (Gen. 6:3; John 16:7–11; Acts 7:51; I Cor. 12:11; Gal. 5:17); by speaking of His personal activities (John 16:13–15; Acts 8:29; 10:19; 16:6); and by referring to His personal feelings (Isa. 63:10; Matt. 12:31; Acts 5:3; Eph. 4:30; Heb. 10:29).

II. The Deity of the Spirit. "The Scriptures do not stop to prove either the personality or the deity of the Holy Spirit. Everywhere, such truth is clearly expressed and constantly implied that men must be blind to miss or deny it. Quite confidently, Bible writers speak of the Spirit as God, know Him as God, and give Him the position of equality with the Father and the Son." [3]

A. Scripture Implies the Deity of the Spirit by:

　　1. Giving Him divine titles: "The Spirit of God" (Matt.

3:16); "The Spirit of Christ" (Rom. 8:9); "The Lord the Spirit" (II Cor. 3:18. A.S.V.).

2. Presenting Him as equal with Jehovah: compare Isa. 6:8–10 with Acts 28:25–27; see II Cor. 3:18.

3. The idiomatic expression in John 14:18.

4. Associating Him with the Godhead: in baptism of Christ (Matt. 3:16. 17); in Christian baptism (Matt. 28:19); in Christian comfort (John 14:16); in witnessing (John 15:26); at Pentecost (Acts 2:32. 33); in church discipline (Acts 5:3. 4); in Christian unity (I Cor. 3:16); in spiritual gifts (I Cor. 12:4–6).

5. Assigning to Him attributes of Deity: as eternal (Heb. 9:14); omnipresent (Rom. 8:26. 27); omnipotent (John 3:5; Rom. 8:11; Matt. 12:28); omniscient (I Cor. 2:10. 11).

B. *Doctrine Affirms Deity of the Spirit, as in:*

1. Nicene Creed. A.D. 325, and at Constantinople. A.D. 381: "I believe in the Holy Ghost. the Lord and Life-Giver. Who proceedeth from the Father and the Son, Who with the Father and the Son together is worshiped and glorified. Who spake by the prophets."

2. Doctrine of Trinity: There is but one God. the Father and the Son and the Spirit is each God, and the Father and the Son and the Spirit is each a distinct person.[4] This doctrine of the Trinity is found in solution. so to speak: unity of God (Rom. 3:30; I Cor. 8:4; Gal. 3:20); Godhead of Christ (John 1:1; Rom. 9:5; John 5:18; Titus 2:13; John 10:30; Phil. 2:6; Col. 1:15); three persons in One individual (I Thess. 1:2–5; Titus 3:4–6); the plural form of divine name *Elohim* used with singular verb (Gen. 1:1); plural pronouns used to designate single individual (Gen. 1:26; 3:22); plural verbs used with plural *Elohim* to show majestic. eternal. supernatural powers of God (Gen. 20:13; 35:7); repetitions of name of God (Gen. 19:24; Ps. 45:6. 7); threefold formulas (Num. 6:24–26; Isa. 6:3).

There are no real analogies for the Trinity. Augustine favored threefold nature of man—spirit. soul and body—as psychological analogy; but man is not three persons in one individual. Roger Bacon suggested three equal angles of the equilateral triangle; but there's no life, light, love, majesty, or power in a triangle. Memory, understanding, and will imply oneness and also threefoldness; but none of these powers, separately taken, constitutes a man. An actor who plays three parts in a drama won't do: he's only one and the same person. Aspects of sun, such as heat, light, vitamins, remain aspects only: the three Persons of the Deity are not mere aspects.

Perhaps the clearest idea of the Trinity and the Spirit's place in Godhead may be had from Matthew 28:19: "Go ye therefore, and teach all nations, baptizing them in the name of the Father, and of the Son, and of the Holy Ghost." This, observe, does not say "in the names," or "in the name of the Father, Son, and Holy Ghost." For God is one God, existing in three Persons with a single name. the distinctness of each Person being emphasized by the repeated article: "In the name of *the* Father, and of *the* Son, and of *the* Holy Ghost."

3. The doctrine of eternal procession of the Spirit (John 15:26; Ps. 104:30; I Cor. 2:11, 12; Gal. 4:6; Rom. 8:9; John 16:7—note use of present tense).

C. *Christians Enjoy Deity of the Spirit by:*

1. Experiencing the new birth (John 3:5).

2. Inward revelation of God (Eph. 1:17). (Christ has revealed Him outwardly—John 1:18.)

3. His advocacy in soul (Rom. 8:26, 27). (Christ is our Advocate in heaven—Rom. 8:34.)

4. Active cooperation with Spirit (Rom. 8:4). (We are passive in finished work of Christ—Rom. 7:25.)

5. Progressive sanctification by the Spirit (Eph. 4:25–32). (Our positional sanctification in Christ is once-for-all—Heb. 10:10.)

6. Graces produced by the Spirit (Gal. 5:17–26). (The Spirit makes positional crucifixion with Christ real in experience—Gal. 2:20.)

7. Spiritual worship of God (II Cor. 13:14).

> Praise God, from whom all blessings flow;
> Praise Him. all creatures here below;
> Praise Him above. ye heav'nly host;
> Praise Father, Son, and Holy Ghost.

III. The Work of the Spirit: it's a continuation of Christ's ministry to obedient believers; for He promised, "I will not leave you desolate: I come unto you" (John 14:18. A.S.V.).

A. *Work of the Spirit in Creation Included*:

1. Infinite works of generation (Ps. 104:30).
2. "Confusion and emptiness" brought to order (Gen. 1:2).
3. Beautification of nature (Job 26:13).

B. *In Inspiration*:

1. Scriptural testimony (I Cor. 2:13).
2. Meaning of inspiration (II Tim. 3:16a).
3. Result of inspiration (II Tim. 3:16b, 17).

C. *With Individuals in General Before Pentecost*:

1. Striving with men (Gen. 6:3).
2. Temporary indwelling of men (Ezek. 2:2).
3. Temporary filling of men (Ex. 28:3).

D. *With Our Lord Jesus Christ*:

1. In preparing for His birth (Matt. 1:18–20).
2. In His public ministry (Luke 4:18).
3. In His redeeming work (Heb. 9:14).
4. Since Pentecost (John 14:18).

E. *With Believers* (since Pentecost):

1. See Chapter Five: blessed and manifold ministry of Paraclete—promised.
2. See Chapter Six: "arrival" of another Person of Godhead—Pentecost.
3. See Chapter Seven: eighteen aspects of applied redemption—Romans.

4. See Chapter Eight: nine new phases—Corinthians.

5. See Chapter Nine: other precious ministries of other Comforter—Galatians through Titus.

6. See Chapter Ten: consummation miracles of the Holy Spirit of God—General Epistles and The Revelation.

7. See Conclusion: Scripture's greatest text on how to be filled—how the Spirit makes Christ God's answer (John 7:37. 38).

When we see and heed the Spirit's relationship to Christ after Pentecost, the "rivers" begin to flow—we give evidence of baptism in the Spirit (Mt. 3:11).

Conclusion—How the Spirit Makes Christ God's Answer

BIBLE BELIEVERS MAY DIFFER on minor doctrines. But there's one great fundamental on which we all agree, namely, "Christ is the answer."

Yet, perhaps to our surprise, we have discovered that Christ *alone* is not the answer. For Scripture, Christian history and theology testify that Christ alone is merely the potential answer, whereas Christ *in the Spirit* is the actual answer. This is true. No thoughtful person would dare say otherwise. Wherefore, the different functions of the persons in the Godhead must be respected. For we're Trinitarians, and, as Griffith Thomas says, "The Holy Spirit is the unique element of Christianity as a living power today." [1] Could our oversight here be the missing note in our testimony? And is there clear, unmistakable Scripture pointing in this direction? In other words, should we expect the Spirit to make Christ God's answer, and the only answer, to the needs of the world? Yes, there is Scripture, and thus basis for such an expectation.

For this "radical and sustaining" nature of the Spirit's ministry is set forth by our Lord himself in a word picture a child can understand—a picture of many beauties and values. It rightly relates the Spirit to Christ, it avoids extremes, it gives balance, it magnifies Christ, it's not abstracted from our total concern for the Christian faith, and it happily emphasizes the Spirit's hiddenness. Also this remarkable text might help to conciliate Pentecostals and non-Pentecostals. There's even a possibility that, pondered and believed, it might mark the dawning of a new day for biblical Christianity.[2]

This simple yet profound picture, which Scofield rightly describes as "the great prophecy concerning the Holy Spirit for power," is found in John 7:37–39:

> (37) *In the last day, that great day of the feast, Jesus stood and cried, saying, If any man thirst, let him come unto me, and drink.* (38) *He that believeth on me, as the scripture hath said, out of his belly shall flow rivers of living water.* (39) *(But this spake he of the Spirit, which they that believe on him should receive: for the Holy Ghost was not yet given; because that Jesus was not yet glorified.)*

Watch this passage unfold. First, that Christ alone isn't the full answer is signified by verse 39. In fact, we get the thrust of verses 37 and 38 only in the import of verse 39. Who makes us thirsty for power? Verse 39 answers. "The Spirit." Who brings us to the source of power? Who enables us to receive power? Who keeps us believing for power? Who sends forth the rivers of living water? In each case, verse 39 answers, "The Spirit." Without question, this verse points to Pentecost. For the gist of it is: "But this spake he of the Spirit's filling." This function of the Spirit, doubtless, is what our risen Lord had in mind when He charged the apostles. saying, "And, behold, I send the promise of my Father upon you: but tarry ye in the city of Jerusalem, until ye be endued with power from on high." In other words, Christ *in the Spirit* is truly God's answer, both potentially and actually.

How Christ in the Spirit is the answer, moreover, is implied is verses 37 and 38, so we need not guess. We can be as certain about the filling of the Spirit as we are about the birth of the Spirit. For, let me repeat, our Lord himself here teaches us the way, the sane, simple, sure way to power. And we travel this way. as parenthetical verse 39 indicates, under the guidance of the Spirit. Here are the steps the Spirit takes in supplying our need through Christ Jesus:

1. *"Thirst"*—He brings us under conviction for power.

2. *"Come unto me"*—He brings us to Christ glorified as the source of power.

3. *"Drink"*—He enables us to appropriate Christ for power.

4. *"He that believeth on me"*—He keeps us believing for power.

5. *"Rivers of living water"*—He produces the evidences of power.

I. Reasons Why We Need Power. A Christian must become convinced of this need to be filled with the Spirit just as he became convinced of his need to be born of the Spirit. Consider, therefore, five of the many reasons why we need to be empowered:

A. To Control Self. The Spirit slew me with Romans 7:14–25. For both personal experience and modern psychology helped me to understand what Paul was talking about in this passage. I believe he implies here what psychologists now recognize, namely, that a person hasn't one ego but many, and that, in the normal person, one ego, the innermost self, is usually dominant. I believe, besides, that Paul is here teaching that the regenerated ego can't dominate us except the Holy Spirit enthrone Christ in our hearts.

Furthermore, psychology's probing of the subconscious makes me tremble until I reckon the indwelling Spirit can handle those dimensions of my personality also. How I need His power! I can't, for instance, think one right thought without the Spirit's power. J. Stafford Wright illustrates the importance of the subconscious and how essential it is, therefore, to have the Spirit's aid in this area:

> All these groups [of psychiatrists] are firmly convinced of the importance of the Unconscious. If one compares the mind of man to an island, the conscious part represents the comparatively small piece of land above water. The Unconscious is the far greater part that goes down to the bed of the ocean.... The Uncon-

scious is the seat of the impulses, drives, and neuroses.
It is, in fact. the powerhouse of the life.[3]

Yes, we must have the Spirit's power; for only He can
restrain the wrong energies and create the right drives in what
Freud called our subconscious "id"; only He can produce
the "fruit" we call Christian character.

B. To Grow Up. There can be no maturing apart from
power, and apart from maturity there can be no proper showing
of our unity in Christ. We see this emphasized in Ephesians
3:14–19, where the Greek aorist tense of the verbs implies
definite progress in spiritual development. The Ephesians,
note, were those who could appreciate "the heavenlies," and
"comprehend with all saints" some degree of the love of
Christ. On the other hand, the Corinthians were carnal and
immature, neglecting the graces of the Spirit and misusing
His gifts. Paul consequently could not speak wisdom among
them. So we must have this power, I repeat. both to grow
up and to "be one" with other Christians.

C. To Overcome Satan. There can be no victory apart from
power. Ephesians 6:10–18 constantly warns us that we have
not the slightest chance of surviving in this great spiritual
warfare unless we're "strong in the Lord, and in the power
of his might." Satan is intelligent. deceitful, fearsome, mighty,
our adversary. We're sinful, foolish, weak. We must keep
filled with the Spirit to cope with Satan and his demons.

D. To Speak with Authority. Only the Spirit can enable
us to "speak as the oracles of God"; only He can demonstrate
Christ as the spiritual power needed by the world today.[4]
You'll agree with me that relatively few men and churches
today speak to the multitudes with Christian authority—so
hearers are conscious of Christ speaking to their hearts. Many
preach the *words* of Scripture, but not many preach the *Word*
of Scripture. Many magnify a "Baptist" Christ or a "Methodist"
Christ or a "Presbyterian" Christ or a "Roman" Christ, ad in-
finitum. But how many magnify the Christ of God, to whom

"all power is given ... in heaven and in earth"? And why do we miss the mark? Why are we failing? We're failing because: "Authority in the Church, together with vitality and solidarity, is the work of the Holy Spirit." [5]

E. To Avoid Chastening. Ephesians 5:18 should keep us constantly alert lest we grieve and quench the Spirit of the living God. We need supernatural help every moment to obey our Father, who scourgeth every son whom He receiveth. We know it's God's will for us to be Spirit-filled, and we should be steadfastly aware of James 4:17: "Therefore to him that knoweth to do good, and doeth it not, to him it is sin."

Also, since "judgment must begin at the house of God" (I Pet. 4:17), churches as well as individual Christians should fear God's discipline. George A. Miles, president of Washington Bible College, charges: "The local church is defeating its own purpose of evangelizing the world by substituting organization for the *sovereignty* of the Spirit, ritualism and talented men for the *power* of the Spirit, and human wisdom for the *sword* of the Spirit." He declares: "We neglect the *program* of the Spirit. Instead of *going*, we stay at home; instead of *giving*, we spend it on ourselves; instead of *sending missionaries*, we construct ornate buildings." Such makes it necessary for God to chasten.

"You can lead a horse to water, but you can't make him drink," is an old maxim. True, but you can salt him. May God be pleased to "salt" the Christians of this generation and make us thirst for His power in our lives and ministries.

II. Way to Recognize Christ Glorified as Source of Power. Something went wrong at a manufactoring plant. Hundreds of employees stood idle: no company machinst could locate the trouble. So a master mechanic from across town was called in, and, after fifteen minutes, he yelled, "Start 'er up."

Motors hummed. Everybody went back to work; the company quit losing money.

When the superintendent asked the master mechanic what

he owed him, he replied, "A hundred dollars and fifty cents."

Curious, the superintendent inquired, "Why a hundred dollars and fifty cents? Why not a hundred five or a hundred ten dollars, even?"

"Fifty cents for the work I did," answered the expert, "and a hundred dollars for knowing how to do it."

So it is very important to know God's way to power.

A. Wrong ways to Recognize Christ Glorified as Source: tarrying, as though Pentecost hadn't already come; fasting in the spirit of pharisaism; seeking "tongues" or some other ecstasy instead of doing business with God by faith; "praying through" in the manner of Baal's prophets (I Kings 18:26–28); legalistic restitution and reconciliation; "getting empty," as though you weren't a new creation in Christ; presuming that being filled with the Word (Col. 3:16) means being filled with the Spirit (Eph. 5:18ff.); that is, failing to see the Word as the instrument and the Spirit as the Agent.

B. Right Way to Power Is Simple, Wholehearted Faith.

    1. *"Come"* with right motive:
        * humbling yourself "under the mighty hand of God," I Peter 5:6; aim to make a good private in God's army; He doesn't need many generals.
        * seeking to obey lovingly, John 14:21.
        * counting the cost: *"And others had trial of cruel mockings and scourgings, yea, moreover of bonds and imprisonment. . . ."* Not all Spirit-filled people fare alike.

    2. *"Come"* on the principle of grace, receiving:
        * *G*od's *R*iches *A*t *C*hrist's *E*xpense, Rom. 3:24;
        * power without meriting it, Rom. 11:6;
        * the message of grace, Gal. 3:2–5;
        * what Abraham was promised, Gal. 3:14;
        * conscious nearness to God, Heb. 7:18, 19.

    3. *"Come"* to a glorious Person, who is:
        * Commander-in-Chief, Matt. 28:18–20;

* the exalted God-Man, Phil. 2:9–11;
* Head of creation and the Church, Col. 1:15–19;
* living Judge of the churches, Rev. 1:12–16;
* KING OF KINGS AND LORD OF LORDS, Rev. 19.

III. How to Believe on Christ for Power. Believe on Him according to the facts of the Gospel. Take Romans, for instance, and consider the possibilities implied by the climax of the epistle in 15:13—"Now the God of hope fill you with all joy and peace in believing, that ye may abound in hope, through the power of the Holy Ghost." Here are some of the facts about yourself in Christ: I am the righteousness of God in Christ (1:17); I am Abraham's heir in Christ (4:16); I enjoy peace with God in Christ (5:1); I have access to grace in Christ (5:2); I rejoice in troubles in Christ (5:3–5); I have received the Holy Spirit in Christ (5:5); I shall be saved from wrath through Christ (5:9–11); I have "much more" victory in Christ than I had defeat in Adam (5:17); I reign in life through Christ (5:17, 21); I died to sin with Christ (6:2); I was buried with Christ (6:3); I was raised with Christ (6:4); I share His risen life (6:8); I'm alive unto God in Christ (6:11); I've been made free from practice of sin in Christ (6:18); the Spirit enables me to realize this freedom (8:1–11); the Spirit helps me live "in the heavenlies" in Christ (8:12–25); the Spirit intercedes for me in Christ (8:26, 27); all things work together for good to me in Christ (8:28); God is for me in Christ (8:29–32); Christ himself intercedes for me (8:33, 34); I'm eternally secure in Christ (8:35–39). Do this: you can't help but be filled. But if you need further instruction:

A. Meditate Prayerfully on Christ's Promise to Empower, as did the 120 before Pentecost: "Verily, verily, I say unto you, he that believeth on me, the works that I do shall he do also; and greater works than these shall he do; because I go unto my Father . . . I will not leave you orphans: I will come to you . . . because I live, ye shall live also . . . ye shall know that I am in my Father, and ye in me, and I in you . . .

I will manifest myself to him . . . my Father will love him, and we will come to him, and make our abode with him . . . peace I leave with you, my peace I give unto you . . . I am the vine, ye are the branches: he that abideth in me, and I in him, the same bringeth forth much fruit: for without me ye can do nothing."

B. *Agree to Make Wrong Things Right*—as He directs. "If I regard iniquity in my heart, the Lord will not hear me." Also take good heed to Matthew 5:23, 24; 18:15–17; and Luke 19:8.

C. *Believe on Christ Glorified for Power*—just as you believed on Him crucified for salvation. This simple distinction, be assured, makes the salient difference between "life" and "life more abundantly." You've seen Him in His humiliation and sacrifice; now behold Him in His glory and power.

A glimpse of God the Son in the physical realm helps me to cherish Him more in the spiritual. So consider Him as "both the first principle and the upholding principle of the whole scheme of creation"; for "in him all things hold together." Light from the sun, traveling 186,000 miles per second, reaches us in eight minutes; but it takes light from Proxima Centauri, earth's nearest star, four years to reach us. This is true because Proxima Centauri is 270,000 times more remote than the sun.

Yet earth's nearest star is only one in 100 billion others in our galaxy, the Milky Way. And there are tens of billions of other galaxies, or star families, within reach of Palomar's two-hundred-inch telescope. No one, of course, can even calculate how many more galaxies there are beyond. Fantastic, we say. But so the astronomers keep telling us; and more: that the stars differ in weight, size, speed, color and glory. Sirius, some claim, is the brightest, and that it sweeps through the heavens at 1,000 miles a minute. Others estimate that Arcturus is eighty times as large and 8,000 times as brilliant as the sun, and that it shoots through space at the unbelievable speed of more than 300 miles a second. Scientists also describe for us the spectral colors: bright yellow, light yellow, pale yellow, and yellowish white and purple; pale grey, light grey, red and white.

Hold dear fellowship with this Lord of Glory who placed all those stars out there in space and who keeps them in orbit, whose brilliance and splendor surpass the brightness and variegated beauties of them all; associate, I say, commune, participate with Him believingly—this makes the Spirit take possession of you. Believe until you become conscious of the Lordship of Christ. Keep on "drinking" until you believe you're filled. Then you *are* filled. Then the Spirit has made Christ the secret and the center of your entire personality. You're now ready to suffer with Him joyfully, and, if necessary, to die for Him gloriously. Thus the gracious principle operates: living faith in Jesus glorified as a Man in heaven releases streams of spiritual blessings *on earth*—blessings from the Christ of God who "maketh Arcturus, Orion, and Pleiades" (Job 9:9).

D. Often Prayer, and Sometimes Prayer with Fasting, is necessary to build up this faith for enduement: ". . . how much more shall your heavenly Father give the Holy Spirit to them that ask him?" . . . "And when they had prayed, the place was shaken where they were assembled together; and they were all filled with the Holy Ghost, and they spake the word with boldness." . . . "Who, when they were come down, prayed for them, that they might receive the Holy Ghost" . . . "According to your faith be it done unto you."

E. Whereas Scripture Exhorts Us to Confess Christ Boldly, It Is Silent About Our Testifying to God's Power in Our Lives. Rather, just as a chief mark of the Spirit is hiddenness, so are we reticent about this "ability to bring things to pass by way of heaven." (See V. on "Evidences of Power.")

IV. How to Stay Empowered. To distinguish between initial filling and continuous filling, compare once-for-all thirst and drinking (Gr. aorist verb) in John 4:14 with uninterrupted thirsting and drinking (Gr. present imperative) in John 7:37. Also notice that the Greek participle translated "believeth" in

John 7:38 denotes continuous action or fixed attitude. This implies that we're to continue to believe by "reckoning," "yielding" and "walking after the Spirit" (Rom. 6–8). Let's be assured, therefore, that the first filling is not a terminal experience; it's the mere beginning of a lifelong process of believing on:

* Christ our Righteousness, as in Romans
* Christ our Wisdom, as in I Corinthians
* Christ our Strength, as in II Corinthians
* Christ our Freedom, as in Galatians
* Christ our Position, as in Ephesians
* Christ our Goal, as in Philippians
* Christ our Head, as in Colossians
* Christ our Hope, as in Thessalonians
* Christ our Great High Priest, as in Hebrews
* Christ our Coming King, as in The Revelation

V. Evidences of Power. Just as there are various marks of the birth of the Spirit, there are, likewise, unmistakable signs of the filling. Let's look at these evidences from five points of view: as to tongues, soul winning, normalcy, blessedness, and "rivers."

A. Is Speaking in Tongues the Evidence? First, the Bible doesn't so teach. For in The Acts the three instances of tongues (2:4; 10:46; and 19:6) seem to have dispensational significance only. Note that believers generally had no special manifestation: 2:41, 42, 47; 4:4; 6:3; 8:15–17; and so on. In the next place, in I Corinthians, which discusses tongues, the record shows that all didn't receive the gift: ". . .do all speak with tongues? do all interpret?" Again, certain contemporary Pentecostal leaders have acknowledged that tongues aren't essential evidence (see p. 137). Still again, be it observed, that not all empowered men have spoken in tongues; for instance, Luther, Calvin, Knox; missionaries like Carey, Hudson Taylor and Judson; evangelists like Wesley, Whitefield, Finney, Moody, Spurgeon, Torrey, Sunday, and others.

B. Others Claim Soul-winning Is the Evidence. Again we don't agree; because, in the first place, some men full of the Spirit don't win many souls. Judson labored seven years in Burma before he baptized his first convert. In the second place, some men who do win souls aren't spiritual men; sometimes they're like those ministers Christ spoke of in Matthew 7:21–23. (It's true, however, that all Spirit-filled people do witness.)

C. But There Are Evidences on Which All Can Agree. Examine, for instance, the record in The Acts. When we look behind the spectacular dispensational "scaffolding," here's what we find: witnesses faithful unto death, use of the tongue for the glory of God, Holy Ghost conviction, steadfastness, heavenly accomplishments with no earthly explanation, gladness, determination to know and to do the will of God despite all opposition, great courage, great liberality, and the like. This is to say, we discover normal Christian experience—spiritual qualities which can't be forged by Satan.

After all, by the way, Spirit-filled Christians are only normal Christians. So it was in New Testament times. So it is now. To test ourselves we may ask the following questions: Am I winning constant victory through Christ in the Spirit? Do I know how to rejoice in troubles? Do I love to witness for Christ? Am I able, by God's grace, to transform handicaps and weaknesses into spiritual assets? Is worship of God my chief delight? Is my testimony unmarred by such things as questionable habits, unconfessed sins, and need to make some things right with others? Do I think of myself as a Christian rather than as a Baptist, or "member" of some other denomination? Am I faithful to God in apparent failure before men? Do I suffer persecution? (II Tim. 3:12). If you can answer "yes" to these questions, you *are* empowered, you're a normal believer.

But if you suffer from periods of wretched despondency and frantic desperation, you're not dominated by God's Spirit. If you can't make financial ends meet, if you're considering divorce, if you're contemplating suicide, if poor health or anything else is defeating you in the work to which God has called you, or if your ministry is cold and unfruitful, you need power.

D. *Do the Beatitudes Suggest Fulness?* Yes, for who but the Spirit can make us "poor in spirit," giving us such a sense of our own spiritual poverty as to make us beggars at the throne of grace? Who but the Spirit melts our hearts over our relative failure amid the world's exploding masses? He is the only One who can make us truly "mourn" with Christ's compassion. Indeed, when He controls we become really "meek," we "hunger and thirst" to know the righteous One better, we show mercy toward sinners and backsliders, and we maintain Christ-honoring and neighbor-loving motives.

E. *Finally, No One Will Deny That Christ Draws Us a Picture of Power in John 7:38.* And in this picture He himself indicates plainly what the evidences are—they are rivers of living water, as promised in the Old Testament:

... in the wilderness shall waters break out, and streams in the desert (Isa. 35:6).

When the poor and needy seek water, and there is none, and their tongue faileth for thirst, I the LORD will hear them, I the God of Israel will not forsake them. I will open rivers in high places, and fountains in the midst of the valleys: I will make the wilderness a pool of water, and the dry land springs of water (Isa. 41:17, 18).

For I will pour water upon him that is thirsty, and floods upon the dry ground: I will pour my Spirit upon thy seed, and my blessings upon thine offspring (Isa. 44:3).

And the LORD shall guide thee continually, and satisfy thy soul in drought, and make fat thy bones: and thou shalt be like a watered garden, and like a spring of water, whose waters fail not (Isa. 58:11).

"As the scripture hath said," these rivers flow from within those who continue to believe on Christ Jesus: from their consciences, unvarying fidelity; from their judgments, pure and holy decisions; from their affections, love for that which He loves and hatred for that which He hates; from their desires, a passion for His will to be done; from their memories. gratitude for His benefits; from their thoughts, meditation upon His excellencies; and from their hopes, a longing for His return. (All this without effort. mind you. for rivers flow without effort.)

I've discovered seven such rivers: (1) The all-important river of grace-caused dedication. Romans 12:1, 2. (2) The joyful river of real humility, Romans 12:3–8. "Oh. the joy of having nothing and being nothing. seeing nothing but a *Living Christ in glory*, and being careful for nothing but His interests down here" (J. N. D.). (3) The fruitful river of Spirit-wrought love. Romans 12:9—15:33. (4) The peaceful river of Christian unity, Ephesians 4:1–16. (5) The clean river of Christ-honoring separation. Ephesians 4:17—5:17. (6) The beautiful river of sincere worship. gratitude and mutual submission. Ephesians 5:18—6:9. (7) The mighty river of power through prayer. Ephesians 6:10–18.

The beds of these rivers may be broadened by taking heed to the exhortations of God's Word, and the volume may be increased by digging deeper into the doctrines of grace. Accordingly. we're to keep on thirsting, keep on coming. keep on drinking; in short. keep on believing for power.

Thus we obey the Great Commission. For these rivers flow deeper and deeper into the "deserts" of sin all around us. Spirit-controlled believers look with compassion on the unsaved masses:

* Increasing at the alarming rate of well over fifty million a year—estimates reach 192.000 a day
* One-third dominated by atheistic Communism
* 700,000,000 in Red China. and 1.000 scattered tribes without one missionary. and
* Nearly 2.000 dialects without any Scripture

Spiritual men also make the Gospel relevant to the rising tidal wave of crime and immorality, which:

* Adds 1,200 new alcoholics daily to America's 5,000,000, costing more than one billion dollars a year
* Increases four times faster than the population, costing taxpayers twenty billion dollars a year
* Spawns an unprecedented emergency of juvenile delinquency
* Includes 20,000 suicides annually, with another 100,000 Americans suspected as "hidden suicides"
* Boosted illegitimacy twenty-four percent since 1960, with 286,000 infants born out of wedlock in 1964

All these things, plus the plague of broken homes; the victimized children of divorced couples; the overflowing insane asylums; the crowded jails; the class hatreds; the greedy warfare between capital and labor; the restless masses; the cheapness of human life; and the threat of total war with thermonuclear bombs, chemicals and bacteria—all these challenge normal Christians to apply the Gospel.

"Overcomers," furthermore, strongly resist the current all-out attack upon and crisis within biblical Christianity:

* Philosophy, scientism and communism
* Counterfeit religious reformation
* Do-it-yourself religion
* One-religion-for-one-world-ism
* Legalism, sectarianism and pharisaism
* Widespread failure of our churches
* Complacency and general unbelief

For, men with God's answer know God's Christ in the power of God's Spirit; they discern two kinds of power in the Gospel—divine facts and a divine Agent to use those facts. Such men don't regard this Agent as the "spare tire"; they honor Him as the "ignition system."

Emphasis on Pentecost Fire

(I) WHY WE NEED TO BLAZE

Look at this section from three points of view: (1) What it means to blaze, (2) blazing as evidence of baptism in the Spirit and (3) reasons why we should blaze.

Our sad plight: lack of dedicated human ability *plus* God's action (Ex. 6:1-8; Jer. 51:20-24; II Cor. 2:14-17). Since our wonderful Lord promised that Spirit-filled believers would do "greater works" than He did—because our works would be in the spiritual realm and not by one Person but by many (Jn. 14:12)—we have not only the right but also the responsibility to expect joyful *action* in our churches, action which the civic clubs can't match: radiant influence, enthusiasm, passion, and power which can't be explained except by way of heaven.

So, every preacher needs to set his pulpit on fire with Christ's love and keep it blazing until the people in the pews glow with heavenly sunshine.

There is no other way to evoke and clearly display our unsearchable riches in God's glorious Christ (Eph. 3:8; Col. 2:3). This alone produces the proof and demonstrates the evidence of our baptism in the Spirit—Pentecostal fire stirred into a blaze:

(1) Miraculous cleansing of selfishness, dross, fear of men's faces, drugs, alcoholism, illicit sex, profanity, irritability, hate, racism (Mt. 3:11; Job 23:10; Jer. 1:8; Jn. 17:17; Acts 9:9-20; II Tim. 1:7). Only God's Gospel saturated with Pentecostal power can do this (Rom. 8:13).

(2) Holy boldness (Acts 3:12-26; 4:13, 29, 31; 5:29-33; II Tim. 4:2). Human courage is necessary but not enough: "little

is much if God is in it." Such courage flouts fear! . . . Evidence of Spirit-baptism (Rom. 8:15).

(3) *Spiritual power*: Gospel facts (Col. 3:16) infused by God's Spirit (Eph. 5:18) make hearts burn with God's love (Lk. 24:32; I Cor. 2:4, 5; 12:7; Eph. ·1:19; 3:16; Phil. 3:10; I Thes. 1:5; II Tim. 1:7). Men are melted and moved to believe for God-glorifying miracles (Jn. 14:12-14). . . . All is grist for their mill. . . . They use the gifts of the God who came at Pentecost (I Cor. 12:7). . . . "The Word by the Spirit and the Spirit in the Word are *always* effective" (Clark H. Pinnock, emphasis mine). . . . Certain evidence of the baptism (Rom. 8:16, 17). . . . See Foreword by John Gilmore. (Ill.) by Wm. Arthur, *The Tongue of Fire*, p. 309.) Do many "fundamental" Bible conferences and churches merely store up kegs of unused powder—never strike fire to the Gospel?

(4) *Non-sectarian love* (Jn 13:35; Rom. 12:20; Gal. 5:22-6:1; Eph. 3:17-19; II Tim. 1:7; I Jn. 2:10; 3:23; 4:7-12). Love for God's will made known in His Word, love for God's children assembled in His church, and love for God's purpose to evangelize His world—this is irrefutable evidence. The greatest thing in the world is our love soaked in God's love: it's the hallmark of true Christianity.

(5) *God-given insight* into Scripture—received by a "sound mind," (II Tim. 1:7; Acts 2:16; 3:13, 18-24; 4:11, 12; 7:37; 9:20; 15:13-18; Gal. 1:12). Even trenchant and astute minds are obtuse here; we must have heavenly wisdom to discern the significant nuances of God's Word. . . . Evidence often ignored.

(6) *Spirit-inspired hope* for the Church in general (Mt. 16:18; Rom. 15:13; Heb. 9:11; Mk. 9:49; Lk. 12:49; Rev. 22:16, 17). Christ's prayers (Jn. 17:21-23) and Paul's prayers for the Church (Eph. 1:17-19; 3:16-21) will yet be answered (I Jn. 5:14, 15). . . . Chirst's Church is made up of people who are "more than conquerors" (Rom. 8:37) and "overcomers" (Rev. 2 and 3). . . . The Reformers led the Church out of "Egypt." Who will lead it into "Canaan"? This rules out the pessimism of some premillennialists. No matter what our theory of the millennium, there is yet a future "fulness" for us Gentiles (Rom. 11:25)

and thereafter a "fulness" for Israel (Rom. 11:12). We must remember that Paul wrote before the millennial theories were born. (Ill. *I will Build My Church*, Alfred F. Kuen, Moody Press, 1970)

(7) Spirit-inspired hope for our own local church: "salt of the earth," "light of the world," "pillar and ground of the truth," Christ's church (Rom. 16:16), God's church (I Cor. 1:2; II Thes. 1:1). . . . Pulpits blazing. . . . Kindness. . . . Radiance. . . . Labors of love. . . . "Rich in good works" (I Tim. 6:18). . . . "First love. . . first works" (Rev. 2:3, 4). . . . "Fishers of men." Things happen, heavenly things, things that couldn't happen in a religious *club*! Attention, friends of God's Christ! Let's determine to claim and use our full share of "the riches of the Gentiles" (Rom. 11:12).

(8) Virile ability to fish for men (Mt. 4:19—the first and most important thing our dear Lord asks us to do). If we're not soul winners, we're not filled with the Spirit (Eph 5:18); if we're not filled with the Spirit, we're quenching the Spirit (I Thes. 5:19); if we're quenching the Spirit, we're sinning (Jas. 4:17). We ought to be getting people saved (Jn. 14:15); there's something bad wrong if we're not reproducing (Jn. 12:24, 25; II Cor. 5:11-15). If you're not a fisher of men and are not willing to become a fisher of men, you may be headed toward the lake of fire (Mt. 7:21-23; Rev. 21:7, 8). Take heed! And certainly you will be put on the shelf (Rev. 2:5). All normal Christians bear fruit (Jn. 15:2). . . . Primary evidence of the baptism.

(9) Loving obedience to the Great Commission—despite Communism and other hindrances. The God who·is here longs to help us finish the job assigned by our triumphant Lord Jesus: see *New Scofield Reference Bible* note on Luke 24:51 (Jn. 14:12; Acts 1:8; II Tim. 3:9). . . . "World evangelism is war—God's war!" (Pray earnestly for the great armies marching today toward this battlefield.)

(10) Visible progress beyond human ability (I Tim. 4:15; Josh. 1:8d; Phil. 3:10-17). Ministry vibrant—not humdrum. "Moralizing and lecturing are two main weaknesses in today's preaching.". . . There's oak-tree type of growth, discipline; no shortcut to radiant power. (Lord Spirit, please show us how to incite this evidence of the baptism.)

(11) Use of spiritual gifts (Acts 2:4; 10:46; 19:6; I Cor. 12:7-10; 28-30; I Pet. 4:9-11). . . . Undisputed evidence.

(12) Joyful endurance of suffering which has characterized the spread of Christ's fire (Mt. 5:10-12; 20:22; Mk. 9:49; Lk. 12:49, 50; 14:26-33; Rom. 5:3-5; II Cor. 1:5; 4:10; Phil. 1:29; 3:10; Col. 1:24; II Tim. 2:10; Jas. 1:2-4; I Pet. 4:13, 14). . . . Fifty million martyrs in early Christianity; more in our century. . . . Raymond Lull, Christ's apostle to the Moslems (1235-1315), joyfully chose the martyr's crown. Would he have done this without the baptism?

Such are the staples of New Testament Christianity, the full evidence of baptism in the Spirit (Mt. 3:11; Lk. 3:16). This heavenly testimony, moreover, is not divisive, terminal, or questionable; but tends to "help others grow in the Lord, encouraging and comforting them" (TLB, I Cor. 14:3). This is what Paul understood the baptism to mean, and this is what it means to honor God's fiery Agent—He's not "the spare tire."

Witness Samuel Chadwick: "The commonest bush ablaze with the presence of God becomes a miracle of glory" (Ex. 3:2). *Witness Helmut Thielicke:* Spurgeon "kindled . . . an inexaustible blaze that glowed and burned on solid hearths. . . . Here was the miracle of a bush that burned with fire and yet was not consumed." *Witness Charles H. Stevens:* "If one should be asked to name the weakness that characterizes historical New Testament Christianity as it prevails today, it would have to be the lack of radiance and heavenly fire that was so evident in the early church."

How about this heavenly radiance in your life, dear reader? In your church? In your prayer meeting? Wake up! Only thirteen percent of college students in Africa, for instance, believe that we Christians really try to live up to what our triumphant Lord teaches for His triumphant Church (survey for SIM *Africa Now*).

Yet God's Gospel proclaims abundant provision in Christ for all those who are *determined* to blaze with Pentecostal fire (I Jn. 5:12; Gal. 2:20; Phil. 1:21; 4:13). We don't have to *get* the fulness; we have already got it *in Christ* (Col. 2:9, 10)—we only need to reckon on it (Rom. 6:11) and demonstrate it (Jn. 16:14; Gal. 3 and 4; Eph. 5:18).

Remember: Truth without power is "the letter that killeth" (I Cor. 2:4, 5; II Cor. 3:4-6. See pp. 141-143). Even Apollas (Acts 18:24-26) will not do; we *must* have Paul's Gospel combined with Pentecostal power—or we'll continue to have deceived "church members" (Jas. 1:22-25) and dead churches (Rev. 3:1).

(II) HOW TO BLAZE

Let me repeat: We possess Pentecostal fire *in Christ* (Jn. 1:14; Col. 1:19; 2:9, 10). For instance, our problem is not the same as Elijah's was, to pray down God's fire. God's fire fell for us at Pentecost, and is now incorporated in Christ, the second Adam (Rom. 5:12-21; I Cor. 15:45); and we are members of His Body (I Cor. 12:27; Eph. 5:30). (See p. 135)

Paul explains all this in his epistles. Pentecostal fire blazed in "The Acts of the Apostles," climaxed by the ministry of Paul. He understood Pentecost. He refers to the Spirit after Pentecost more times (108) than all other New Testament writers put together (93). Indeed, Paul, writing many years after Pentecost, standardized Christian experience. Consequently, we must shift emphasis from the first half of Acts to the last half, the historical context of Paul's epistles. Truly, "the only hope of Christianity is in the rehabilitating of the Pauline theology" (Francis L. Patton, late president of Princeton University).So, let's interpret Matthew 3:11 from Paul's point of view (Rom. 3-23; I Cor. 12:13; II Tim. 1:6, 7; Tit. 2:11-15).

Simple, yet whole-souled, *faith*, step by step, was the sole condition by which Paul blazed with Pentecostal fire (II Cor. 5:7; Rom. 8:4). His faith was the kind that Abraham exercised— which included repentance (Josh. 24:2; Mt. 21:32; Lk. 13:3, 5; Acts 20:21; I Thes 1:9); was apart from works, ordinances and law (Rom. 4:1-15); was inspired by grace to expect miracles (Rom. 4:16, 17); and which waxed stronger and stronger crisis after crisis (Rom. 4:18-21). His fiath was the kind the Apostle John wrote about in his Gospel (using the word 100 times)—a committing of ourselves unreservedly to God's Christ (Rom. 1:17; 6:13; 12:1, 2). Paul's faith transformed him, a persecuter

unto death of Christians, into a love-slave of Christ and a debtor
to all men. It issued in grace-obedience (Rom 1:5; 6:15-23; 8:4,
13; 16:26). Paul knew by faith when to rest (Mt. 11:28-30) and
when to wrestle (Eph 6:10-18). By faith he walked "in newness
of life" (Rom. 6:4), triumphing day after day (II Cor. 2:14). This
kind of faith, of course, is better experienced than analyzed.
Really, we can't describe a sunset or rainbow to a blind person.

Walking "not according to the standard of the flesh" (Rom.
7), but "according to the standard of the Spirit" (Rom. 6 and
8), Paul blazed with Pentecostal fire in Philippi, Corinth, Ephesus—everywhere "turning the world upside down" (Acts 17:6.
See pp. 90- 92). Dreadful, bitter, prolonged Roman persecution
couldn't stamp out Paul's Gospel ignited by Pentecost's fire: by
A. D. 312 (debatable) even Emperor Constantine confessed faith
in Christ and offered every soldier in his army 20 pieces of gold
and a baptismal robe if he would do likewise.

We, too, must enter into the blessings of Acts 2:4 through the
Pauline gateway of Romans 8:4. By full-orbed, living faith our
determined, steadfast attitude must be:

• I am *in Christ*, just as my arm is in my body. I have the
same relationship to the Father that Christ has (Rom. 3:24 and
8:1). Moreover, I enjoy the privileges and responsibilities of an
adult son (Gal. 4:4-7).

• I died to sin with Christ, I was buried with Him, I was raised
with Him to "walk in newness of life," and I share His resurrection life and power (Rom. 6:1-10).

• Christ lives in me, just as the vine lives in the branch through
sap; just as my body lives in my arm through blood (Rom. 8:10;
Gal. 2:20). Christ exercises His wisdom and power in and through
me by His Spirit (Rom. 8:2; I Cor. 15:45)—Who "efficaciously
unites us to Himself" (Calvin. See p. 111).

• Christ has baptized me in Pentecostal fire, and constantly
helps me to keep it blazing (Phil. 4:13; II Tim. 1:6, 7.

Just to be sure, let's change the figure from blazing to boxing:
you're a member of Christ's Body, just as your arm is a member
of your body. If your arm is normal, it represents normal Christian experience: it simply needs to be developed, disciplined,

trained to win the boxing match. But if it is shriveled, diseased, injured, or has a tourniquet on it; it must have appropriate treatment. You must arrange to let the vigor of your body flow into your arm. Likewise "let" yourself be filled with Christ by the Spirit (Eph. 4:28-5:18; Gal. 4:19).

William R. Newell *let* the Spirit fill him by mailing a confession to a man whom he had cheated. Len G. Broughton and W. W. Hamilton began their remarkable ministries by *responding* to A. C. Dixon's two-hour message on Pentecostal power. Charles G. Finney let the Spirit give him evidence of the baptism by *believing* God could use him more profitably as a revivalist than as a lawyer. C. I. Scofield taught that God's Word does not "exhort believers to seek . . . the baptism of the Spirit," but to "be filled with the Spirit": grieve not the Spirit, quench not the Spirit, yield, believe, pray (*Plain Papers on the Doctrine of the Holy Spirit*, pp. 53-69). Using the term "baptism" in the sense of "filled," R. A. Torrey preached God's Christ around the world by *adding* the message of Pentecost to that of Calvary. (Ernest M. Wadsworth, who knew Torrey personally, wrote a long article in the *Sunday School Times* affirming this. Wadsworth was director of the Great Commission Prayer League in Chicago.) The Ephesians let the Spirit keep them filled by *heeding* Paul's epistle to them. All these members of the Body of Christ cooperated with the Spirit by letting, yielding, responding, believing, walking, adding, heeding. They developed strong arms, as it were, like a boxing champion.

If we, too, "walk after the Spirit," He will (1) fulfil the requirement of the Law in us, (2) create the right purpose in life, (3) enthrone Christ in our hearts, (4) make Christ our life, (5) help us realize our adult sonship, (6) give us courage, (7) witness to our security, and (8) fill our hearts with hope (Rom. 15:13. See pp. 111-120 and 122). (What better evidence of baptism in the Spirit could we want?)

But if you're still not "endued with power from on high" (Lk. 24:49), and if you really mean business with the God who empowers, check your "ignition system," as it were, by mulling over these 40 questions: (1) Are you unquestionably saved? (Parable of the Sower and Heb. 12:6-8, 29 imply that most professing Christians are not actually saved—churches are most strategic mission field.) (2) Do you ignore the Person, presence and office of the God who is here—treat Him like He is an old "spare tire" (see pp. 69, 70)? (3) Are you grieving Him by failing to *be* what you are in Christ (Eph. 4:30)—free from the power of indwelling sin (Rom. 6:18, 22), honest on income tax returns? (4) Are you quenching Him by refusing to *do* what you should for love of Christ (Mt. 4:19; I Thes. 5:19)? (5) Are you fishing for men? If not, you are both grieving and quenching the Spirit; so stop studying right here and begin practicing Matthew 4:19.

(6) Are you receiving God's grace in vain (II Cor. 5:11, 14; 6:1-10)? Grace made a love-slave and debtor out of Paul. Is there any good reason why it shouldn't do the same for us? (7) Are you under Satan's spell (II Tim. 2:24-26)? (Meditate on Mt. 12:29)... Is your church under Satan's power? (Plead Mt. 16:18) (8) Do you loathe yourself apart from Christ (Job 42:6; Isa. 57:15; 66:2)? The more mature Paul got the more sinful he felt (I Cor. 15:9; Eph. 3:8; I Tim. 1:15). (Obey I Pet. 5:6) (9) Are you ignoring the necessity of *two* kinds of heavenly power: Gospel facts—which believers knew before Pentecost (Lk. 24:49)—steeped in the Spirit's ability (I Cor. 2:4, 5; I Thes. 1:5)? Some Christians need more Gospel content; others need more fire; all need both. (10) Do you know the difference between "happy flesh" (Ex. 32:6, 19) and holy fire (I Cor. 12:2, 3)?

(11) Are you despising the Spirit's offer of gifts for empowered service (I Thes. 5:20); for instance, are you trying to preach without the gift of prophecy (I Cor. 14:1)? (12) Are you obeying Romans 6:11 and 12:1, 2? (13) Do you maintain the attitude of love outlined in Romans 12:9-21? (14) Do you magnify Christ in citizenship, and in love toward your neighbors (Rom. 13)? (15) Are you right regarding debatable things (Rom. 14)? (You Catholic charismatics are hurting your testimony with cigarettes and cocktails.)

(16) Are you believing the deeper meaning of the Gospel (Rom. 6-8) that your state by nature may be superseded by your standing in Christ (Rom. 12:21; 13:14; Eph. 4:21—6:17)?

That is, do you know and reckon on your oneness with Christ in glory? Have you yielded once for all to God for holiness (Rom. 6:13)? (17) Are you giving radiance and heavenly fire in your testimony priority over denominational differences, separation, methodology, and personalities (Gal. 5:15)? (Heed Lk. 24:49) This, of course, is not to compromise on essentials about God's Christ (II Jn. 9, 10). God forbid. We certainly can't blaze apart from Him. It's His fire of love. (18) Do you really desire to enjoy "the unsearchable riches of Christ" (Eph. 3:8; Col. 2:3)? If, perchance, you are a Catholic friend and neighbor, are you willing to break with tradition and face up to Scripture only concerning: Salvation by sovereign grace through living faith plus nothing? Mary born a sinner just like the rest of us? The pope, too, liable to error in faith and morals? No physical presence of Christ in the bread and wine? No true sacrifice in the Mass? Mary is not the Queen of Heaven? Worship of images is idolatry? Why not "Launch out into the deep" (Lk. 5:4)? (19) Are you afraid or chary of the Spirit and His gifts (I Cor. 14:39)? (Rely on I Jn. 4:18) (20) Are you snared in unscriptural marriage, an unequal yoke, or work requiring evil practices (II Cor. 6:14-7:1)? (II Tim. 2:21 will help)

(21) Have you repented of personal responsibility for the deplorable conditions in Christian circles today (Jer. 4:8; Dan. 9:3-10; Lam. 5; II Tim. 3:1-9)? (22) Do you maintain a loving attitude toward Christians with whom you do not agree (Mk. 9:38-41; Mt. 18:15-17; Tit. 3:10)?

> He drew a circle that shut me out,
>   Heretic, rebel and thing to flout.
> But Love and I had the wit to win:
>   We drew a circle that took him in.
>
> —Anon.

(23) Are your teaching and preaching an end in themselves (II Tim. 4:2)? Are they legalistic (Gal. 1:6-9)? Socialistic (cp. Tit. 2:11-15)? Is your ministry in a rut (God loves variety)? Is it arid? Banal? Baneful? Bigoted? Chauvinistic? Craven? Deceitful? Empty? Factious? Garish? Harsh? Impractical? Inept? Jaded? Lukewarm? Maudlin? Mundane? Prolix?

Prosaic? Provincial? Repetitive? Sectarian? Snide? Stilt-
ed? Trite? Turbid? Venal? Thank God, Pentecostal fire
burns out all such dross and we diligently apply Paul's Gospel
in the fervent love of God. Let's ask the God of Pentecost
to help us evoke and stir up this wonderful fire—which we
have in God's Christ—into glorious, ambient flames. This God
who is here makes us piquant witnesses. Read Acts and see.
(24) Do you appreciate the local church (I Cor. 3:9-17)? (25)
Do you contend that *all* God's work should be sponsored
by local churches (Mt. 13:11; Acts 8:38)?

(26) Do you know how to apply God's Gospel in love so
the Spirit can strike fire to it (Acts 2:37; 5:33; 7:54; Rom.
8:4)? (27) Do you have a perennial sense of need (Rom.
7:18; Phil. 3:10-17)? (28) Do you confess public sins publicly
(II Sam. 12:13; Ps. 51:3; I Jn. 1:9)? (29) Do you believe
denominations can please God (I Cor. 3:21-23)? (30) Are you
mature enough to fellowship with people on the other side of denominational fences (Eph. 4:11-16)?

(31) Are you praising God that Christ's fire will ultimately
rout out Satan's fire, even in this "World Aflame" (Billy Graham) and despite "Worldwide Turmoil in the Churches" (*U.S.
News and World Report*)? Descry Matthew 3:11; 16:18; Luke
12:49; Romans 5:20; 8:37; II Timothy 3:9; Revelation 19:16.
(32) Are you willing to pay any price God asks for victory
(Jer. 12:5; Ezek. 4:9-15; II Cor. 2:14-16)? (33) Are you willing
to be despised for Christ's sake (I Cor. 4:9-13)? (34) Are
you willing to get into "the refiner's pot" and stay there
until the Comforter says "Enough" (Job 23:10; Prov. 17:3)?
(35) Do you honestly crave a testimony that men like Lenin
and Neitzsche would respect (Tit. 2:5)? Lenin: "If ever I met
a Christian, I'd become one." Neitzsche: "Show me first that
you are redeemed; then I'll listen to talk about your redeemer."

(36) Do you live an effective life of prayer (see pp. 120,
121)? (37) Is baptism in the Spirit once for all—100 %, and
filling progressive (Mt. 3:11; Eph. 5:18)? (38) Is your home
life growing sweeter (I Pet. 3:1-7)? (39) Are you balancing
your responsibility as a Christian with God's sovereignty (Ex.
6:1; Jer. 24:7)? (40) Do you cherish the "blessed hope":

that we shall be caught up (I Thes. 4:13-18) and that an actual Man shall come in the clouds to receive a worldwide kingdom (Rev. 19:1-6)? Profit from David H. Adeney's view of this soon coming event: "The Communist revolution is not radical enough. The Christian's hope of Christ's return must be persuasively proclaimed to those who find it hard to accept the idea of divine intervention in human history." If our answer to any of these questions is wrong, we're quenching and grieving the Spirit of the living God—and contradicting the evidence of our Spirit-baptism.

Again, meditation on Pentecostal facts will help release the power of this "ignition system." • *God's love has been poured out in my heart* (Rom. 5:5). Yes, the God who is here busted (Smoky Mountain English) a barrel of celestial (much better than sourwood) honey in my heart. "Oh, taste and see that the LORD is good." (See pp. 102, 103) "He is altogether lovely."

• *I died to sin with Christ; I was buried with Him; I was raised with Him to walk in newness of life: I share His resurrection power—I'm one with Him in Glory* (Rom. 6:1-11). (See pp. 103-108) *I'm free from the power of sin that dwells within me* (Rom. 6:18, 22).

• *My spirit is enshrined in the warm, tender care, discipline and sublimating power of the completing Agent of the Godhead* (Rom. 8:9; see pp. 10-12). (I like this pregnant word *sublimate*; in this context it magnifies Christ in our bodies according to Rom. 12:1, 2; II Cor. 3:18 and Phil. 1:20.)

• *The eyes of my heart are more and more illumined by this fiery Completing Agent* (Eph. 1:18). • *My inner man enjoys the ever-developing power of Pentecost* (Eph. 3:16). • *Christ loved me to the death—and still loves me infinitely* (II Cor. 5:14; Rev. 1:5). • *The God who is here enables me to prevail in prayer* (see pp. 120-121). *The God who empowers coaches me when fasting is necessary* (Mt. 6:16-18; I Cor. 7:5). • *I have not only the right but also the responsibility to believe for miracles every day—the miracles God wants to perform for me* (Jn. 14:12-14).

Beware lest television steal your precious time to meditate. Listen to Norman E. Allison; he knows the value of solitude:

"Do you think you could ask God to make your life into one that *must* give time to Him? Turn the thought over in your mind. It has to be a prayerful, firm, binding determination—yes, a transaction made with God at the very seat of all human action, your will. . . . Are you ready for this? When you are, God will respond." (Ill. Back-of-head picture of Carl Sandburg, Pulitzer poet, 1951)

Finally, be wary of wildfire. Satan would be a poor devil if he didn't try to counterfeit and counteract Pentecostal fire. . . . Paul portrayed wildfire as "a zeal for God, but not according to knowledge" (Rom. 10:2)—a human fervor constantly fanned by demons (II Cor. 11:13-15; Phil. 3:6; II Pet. 2:1; I Jn. 4:1). Our Lord warned against wildfire (Mt. 7:15; 24:24). . . . Christ started His "pure celestial fire" at Pentecost. Since then fervid human ability filled with the Holy Spirit has time and again stirred up an "inextenguishable blaze."

Illustrations of Wildfire: Will worship of Nadab and Abihu (Lev. 10:1-5). Frenzy of Baal's prophets (I Ki. 18:26-28). Pagan religionists, Hindu holy men, Mormons, psychedelics—speaking in tongues. "Zeal to make converts, enumerate baptisms, count noses, and publish results that sound more like man than God" (Charles H. Stevens). Jumpers and Barkers of 1760. Buddhist burnings. Pakistan cruelty. Hare Krishna, Zen, Yoga, witchcraft, Satanism, astrology.

Characteristics: Vagrant allusions to God but no allegiance to God's Christ. False doctrine of many ways to God (Acts 16:16-18). Prate about ritual, observances, pet doctrines (Gal. 1:6, 7). Preachers and singers avoid vital truth and indulge in toxic trivia (cp. I Cor. 2:4, 5). Addled prayer (Dan. 10:13, 14). Indecent and disorderly "worship" (I Cor. 14:32-40). Complacency, atheism, man's religion (I Tim. 5:6; II Tim. 3:1-8).

When holy fire comes on the scene to do something about a bad situation, wildfire shows up to counteract: Wildfire often lurks in women teachers; holy fire exudes from men teachers. Wildfire ignores the place and importance of the local church; holy fire honors the local church. (The N. T. knows nothing of the Robinson Crusoe type of Christian—the unaffiliated religious prig.) Wildfire discloses Satan's many demons; holy fire reveals God's *one* Spirit. Wildfire incenses apart from God's Word; holy fire spreads only through God's Word. (Hear this: It certainly isn't God's will for us to try to ride fiery stallions without bridles.) Wildfire feeds on legalism; holy fire illuminates the finished work of Christ. Wildfire garbles our feelings; holy fire guides our conscience and will. Wildfire directs attention to our group apart form Christ; holy fire to the unity of all believers. Wildfire makes us mulish and proud; holy fire makes us pliable and humble—there's no "super-spirituality" in true spirituality (Francis Schaeffer). Wildfire puffs up self in us; holy fire magnifies Christ in us. Wildfire struggles at things which only God can do; holy fire rests in assurance of Christ's eventual triumph.

Detect wildfire—just as you recognize counterfeit money—by having a thorough knowledge of heaven's fire: it is Christ's fire, zeal imbued with His person and work (Jn. 16:14). Only God's Spirit witnesses to His Christ and His Spirit witnesses to His Christ only (I Jn. 4:2).

> *There is only one thing in which God is interested and that is the exaltation and glorification of His Son. He is not interested in glorifying any individual, group, movement, body of people, or ecclesiastical system, apart from Christ. He is interested in these only to the extent they exalt and glorify His Christ.*
>
> *—Anon.*

The God who empowers makes Christ our Lord indeed (I Cor. 12:3). The God who illumines gives discernment (I Jn. 4:1-6). The God who came at Pentecost promotes unity in the Body of Christ (I Cor. 12:12, 13, 27; 13:1-13; Eph. 4:1-6; Jn. 17:20-23; Mt. 5:23, 24; 18:15-20; II Thes. 3:6; II Tim. 2:24-26; Rev. 2:2).(Is not God's Christ the only issue important enough to divide us? See Preface to this edition. We may not see fit to work with some Christians (Acts 15:39) or be able to eat the Lord's Supper with some "brethren" (I Cor. 5:11), but shouldn't we pray for them (Mt. 18:17) and warn them (Tit. 3:10)? It is certainly our responsibility "to preserve the unity of the Spirit in the bond of peace.")

To sum up: Believe now for Pentecostal fire to begin blazing in your life and ministry: by faith begin to "walk after the Spirit." Double check your faith. Increase your faith. Be on guard against noxious extremes (Ill. by late president of Asbury, Henry Clay Morrison). Ask the God who is here to teach you how to blaze step by step, decision by decision. That's what He's here for—Blessed Teacher!

* Be a burning bush
* Strike fire to the Gospel
* Be an activist for Christ
* Prove your baptism in Pentecostal fire
* Act your faith in the whole Gospel: "walk after the Spirit"

(III) HE WHO BLAZES SHOWS PLAINLY THAT HE'S BEEN BAPTIZED IN FIRE

Whether or not you agree, please weigh with an open mind and heart the following exposition, humbly suggested with irenic amity toward and fervent love for those who may disagree.

First, we receive the baptism subconsciously (cp. Unger, *The Baptizing Work of the Holy Spirit*, p. 16) the moment we become members of the Body of Christ (Rom. 12:5; I Cor. 6:17; 12:13; Eph. 4:4; 5:30; Col. 1:24; 3:15). For example, take believers at Pentecost. They were conscious of the filling (2:4), but we would never know that they were baptized then too if it were not for Acts 11:16 (see pp. 72-74 and 82). Again, Romans 6:3 implies that we must be taught this baptism. So, we must distinguish between the fact and the evidence. Furthermore, evidence of this baptism may be consciously experiencd at the time of conversion or later (Acts 8:14-17; 10:44-47; 19:4-6). Let Paul be our example here. Was he not justified, forgiven, taken out of Adam and placed in Christ Jesus, baptized in fire, born again, sealed and anointed there in the dust on the road to Damascus (Acts 9:6)? Did not the God who is here begin to indwell him at that sublime moment? If not then, when? Who burnt out of his sincere (but terribly wrong) soul the wildfire and self-righteousness and legalism and pride and prejudice and sectarianism and blasphemy and cruelty and murder (Acts 9:9)? Who prepared him to be filled with the Spirit three days later (Acts 9:17)? When was God's love poured out abundantly (perfect tense) in Saul's heart (Rom. 5:5-10)? When did he become fully conscious of this love? Three days later, when Ananias addressed him as "Brother Saul," and he realized that he was accepted by Christians—whom he had hated—then he began to delight in God's Calvary love. Thus he was filled consciously three days after he was baptized subconsciously. And thus his state by nature was blessedly brought up to his standing in Christ: that which was latent became patent; nascent life and love blazed (Col. 2:10; 3:5-4:6; Eph. 4:20-6:18).

Christian history testifies to this fact: some believers have indeed had "a distinct experience separate from salvation." To name a few: Len G. Broughton, Wilbur Chapman, A. B. Earle, Jonathan Edwards, Christmas Evans, Finney, Moody, A. T. Pierson, John R. Rice, Scarborough, A. B. Simpson, Spurgeon, Billy Sunday, Truett, W. W. Hamilton, A. C. Dixon, R. A. Torrey.

Others blazed, however, without this "distinct experience subsequent to salvation": A. J. Gordon, Billy Graham, F. B. Meyer, Andrew Murray, C. I. Scofield, Oswald J. Smith, Wesley, Whitefield, Gypsy Smith, Charles Fuller, Luther, Calvin, Knox, Hudson Taylor, Judson, Carey, Goforth. (Yes, all these glowed with heavenly fire, and without speaking in tongues.)

Finally, perhaps the most convincing reason for believing we are baptized in celestial fire at the moment of salvation is the plain fact that those who never receive this baptism (Mt. 3:11) must suffer the "unquenchable fire" (Mt. 3:12; Lk. 3:17; Mk. 9:43, 48; Rom. 6:23; Rev. 21:7, 8). "The Pentecostal distinction between a prior baptism *of* the Spirit—in which the Spirit is the agent—and a subsequent baptism *in* the Spirit—in which Christ is the agent—has no support in New Testament grammar or texts" (Brunner).

In the second place, there's overwhelming conviction on the part of Bible students that "fire" in Matthew 3:11 and Luke 3:16 symbolizes the Pentecostal ministry of the God who is here:

This baptism is church truth which exploded in the hearts of believers at Pentecost. Witness Walvoord: "We search the prophetic Scriptures in vain for any reference to the baptism of the Spirit, except in regard to the church, the body of Christ" (*The Holy Spirit*, p. 231). • The context contrasts two kinds of people— good and bad fruit, wheat and chaff; two kinds of fire; two kinds of baptism; two baptizers; two activities on Christ's part: He "baptizes" in holy fire in connection with His first advent (v. 11) and He "burns up" with hell-fire in connection with His second advent (v. 12). • "Fire" in Matthew 3:11 cannot mean the same as "fire" in Matthew 3:12 because baptism in the fire of the Spirit implies a transient act, whereas burn up in unquenchable fire describes an eternal condition. Is the lake of fire ever referred to as a baptism? Or, is it reasonable to imagine a baptism lasting throughout the Tribulation period?

• This mode of speech was common in Bible days: "He will baptize you in the Holy Spirit and fire." "Dead Sea literature makes it perfectly clear that this is a hendiadys" (*The Anchor Bible*). Examples: We drink from *cups and gold*, for *golden cups; deceit and words*, for *deceitful words; Holy Spirit and fire*, for *fire of Holy Spirit*. Phillips: "He will baptize you with the fire of the Holy Spirit." TLB: "He will baptize you with fire—with the Holy Spirit" (Lk. 3:16).

•The best English versions—Davidson, Harper, Jerusalem Bible, Moffatt, Nave's, New American Bible, New American Standard, Newberry, Noyes, Rheims, Rotherham, Worrell's, Wyclif—have no second preposition, as "with" (in italics) in the King James Version. "So it is in all Greek, Latin, Syriac, Arabic, Persian, Egyptian, and Ethiopic versions" (Lapide). John didn't say, "He will baptize you in the Holy Spirit or in fire." Neither did he say, "He will baptize some of you in the Holy Spirit and some of you in fire."

• Augustine: "The Spirit is Himself the love of God; and when He is given to a man, He kindles in him the fire of love to God and his neighbor." • *Biblical Illustrator*: "Baptism with the Holy Ghost is not one thing and baptism with fire another, but the former is the reality of which the latter is the symbol."

•Calvin: Christ "baptizes us in the Holy Spirit and fire, . . . and he consecrates us, purged of worldly uncleanness." •*A Catholic Commentary on Holy Scripture* (1954): "The baptism of the coming Messias will be a steeping in the Holy Spirit, a profoundly purifying fire." *James Elder Cumming: "Suffering in view of purification." *Samuel Chadwick: "The baptism of the Spirit is the baptism of fire. Spirit-filled souls are ablaze for God. They love with a love that glows. They believe with a faith that kindles. They serve with a devotion that consumes. They hate sin with a fierceness that burns."

*C. J. Ellicott: "The baptism 'with fire' would convey, in its turn the thought of power at once destroying evil and purifying good." William Evans: "This cleansing is done by the blast of the Spirit's burning. Here is the searching, illuminating, refining, dross-consuming character of the Spirit." *Wilfred J. Harrington (R. Catholic): "Spirit and fire stand in apposition ('the fire of the Spirit') and refer to the outpouring of the Holy Spirit of Ac. 2:3." *Maynard James: "The emblem of the Holy Ghost . . . was the roaring of the divine fire that gave a 'sound' as of rushing wind."

*Jamieson, Faussett and Brown Commentary:". . . the fiery character of the Spirit's operations upon the soul—searching, consuming, refining, sublimating; as nearly all good interpreters understand the words." (Of 400 interpreters researched, 317 took this view; 83 that "fire" in verses 11 and 12 meant the same thing, judgment.) R. C. H. Lenski: ". . . judgment is never conceived as a baptism with fire or any other element; baptism and baptizing always imply cleansing and not destruction." *New Bible Commentary: "The Holy Ghost and fire are identical. He is the fire of God that burns up the dross in the believer's life and sets him ablaze for God."

*William L. Pettingill (*Bible Questions and Answers,* 1965 ed.): "The reference is to the baptism of the Holy Spirit as our Energizer and Purifier. 'Quench not the Spirit' (I Thes. 5:19) means 'Don't put out the fire.' " (He changed his conviction after writing *Simple Studies in Matthew.*) *Ivor Powell (1965): "Of all the synonyms used, none is so expressive as that of fire, which destroys, softens, purifies, cheers, heals, defends, illumines, and supplies power." *Philip Schaff (Lange's translator): Differs with Lange, saying in a footnote, "It is harsh to separate 'the Holy Spirit' and 'fire,' as referring to opposite classes of people, when they are clearly united in *humas* [Gr. for *you*], and by the copulative *kai* [Gr. for *and*] (not the disjunctive *e* [Gr. for *or*])."

•John Wesley: "He shall fill you with the Holy Ghost, inflaming your hearts with that fire of love which many waters cannot quench." •*New Scofield Reference Bible*: The cross reference connects "fire" in Matthew 3:11 with Acts 2:3. •This conforms to C. I. Scofield's position: "To quench the Spirit, therefore, is to resist His fiery energy, His consuming and purifying work. We are baptized with the Holy Ghost and with fire" (*Plain Papers on the Doctrine of the Holy Spirit*, Revel, 1899, p. 57. An excellent little book, especially on how to be filled. Hope you have it). •John R. W. Stott, rector of All Souls Church, London, Honorary Chaplain to the Queen of England and author of *Basic Christianity* and many other books, understands "fire" in Matthew 3:11 correctly. Hear him on Revelation 3:16: "The Greek words are striking, and we are left in no doubt about their meaning. 'Cold' means icy cold and 'hot' means boiling hot. Jesus Christ would prefer us to boil or to freeze, rather than we should simmer down into a tasteless tepidity. . . . Our inner spiritual fire is in constant danger of dying down. It needs to be poked and fed and fanned into flame. . . . True, the Christian Church has often been scared stiff of 'enthusiasm'. John Wesley and his friends had reason to know this. So have many others both before him and since. But enthusiasm is an essential part of Christianity. Christ warmly approves of it even if the Church disapproves. His message to us in our sleepyheaded lethargy and chilliness is His message to Laodicea years ago: *be zealous and repent* (v. 19). Zeal, heat, fire, passion—these are the qualities we lack today and desperately need" (*What Christ Thinks of the Church*, Eerdmans, 1972, pp. 116, 117).

Questions: Is not this first reference, Matthew 3:11, the key to the doctrine of the baptism in the Spirit? Does it not give a basis for Paul's attitude of triumph for Christ's Church (Mt. 16:18), apostasy to the contrary? Did not power become available at Pentecost which had never before been within the reach of believers?

I am fully convinced so. Furthermore, I suspect that Satan has adroitly cast a spell of prejudice on many Christians concerning Pentecostal fire, for I have never known a great text like Matthew 3:11 to be so misinterpreted by so many otherwise good expositors. (Most books on the Holy Spirit, however, just skip this great Gospel prophecy.)

Thirdly, let's take a fresh, closer, unbiased look at I Corinthians 12-14, in the light of what Herman Bavinck, B. B. Warfield and others have written about the gifts of the Spirit discussed therein. It just may be that the Pentecostals are partly right and partly wrong and that we non-Pentecostals are partly right and partly wrong about tongues. If we could agree that blazing with Pentecostal fire, including genuine tongues, is the all-inclusive evidence of baptism in the Spirit, faster progress could be made toward carrying out the Great Commission.

And let's understand that we're considering the "spirituals" of I Corinthians 12-14 only. We're not thinking about the evidences of our Lord's deity (Jn. 20:30), or the "special miracles" of the apostles (Acts 5:12; 19:11)—"dispensational scaffolding" (Charles H. Stevens), as it were. No, we're examining Christ's gifts to His Body, the Church. When He ascended He gave gifts to men (Eph. 4:8); He granted to each believer "the evidence of the Spirit for the common welfare" (I Cor. 12:7). And our use of these gifts displays God's power through us.

Now was Herman Bavinck, a Dutch theologian, including these gifts, these *charismata*, in his famous statement at the beginning of this century? In answer to this question, we quote at length from Klaas Runia, formerly a theologian in Australia and now in the Netherlands ("The Third Work of the Spirit," *Eternity*, Jan. '72):

> Special revelation has been given in the form of an historical process, which reaches its end-point in the person and work of Christ. Added to this were the outpouring of the Holy Spirit and '*the extraordinary* working of the powers and gifts through and under the guidance of the Apostolate.' But when the Scriptures were completed, there was no longer need for such *special* signs and gifts (emphasis supplied).

Thus Ruina quotes Bavinck. Our question: Did Bavinck include these gifts of I Corinthians 12-14? If he did, and if he is correct, then you and I today, living hundreds of years after the apostles died, would have to read I Corinthians 12:7 differently, like this: "But the manifestation of the Spirit *was* given to every man to profit withal." The gifts were for them but not for us. The infant Church didn't get to keep and develop and use the *charismata*. (See Paul's solution of the whole problem of "spirituals," pp. 148, 149.)

B. B. Warfield, a theologian at Princeton Seminary shortly after the turn of the century, went so far as to say, "The *charismata* belonged, in a true sense, to the apostles. . . . they were distinctively the authentication of the Apostles" (Ruina). But Clark H. Pinnock, recently a professor of theology at New Orleans Baptist Theological Seminary and now at Trinity Evangelical Divinity School, Deerfield, Illinois, rejects "as empirically and exegetically unsound the Warfield view" (*Christianity Today*, 12-8-72, p. 50).

Ruina also quotes *The New Bible Dictionary* (British Inter-Varsity Fellowship, 1965): "It is only in the presence of the apostles that these gifts are showered down." But he concludes, "In our opinion the Pentecostals are right when they say that the gifts are still present" (the editor of *Eternity* agreed).

We especially like the practical conclusion of Runia's article:

> To ignore the gifts means to slight the Giver. . . . A congregation that is aware of and using the gifts of the Spirit cannot help but be alive. . . . We can summarize it all in the words of Peter: "As *each* has received a gift, *employ* it for another, as good stewards of *God's varied grace*: whoever speaks, as one who utters oracles of God: whoever renders service, as one who renders it by the strength which God supplies; in order that in everything *God may be glorified* through Jesus Christ. To Him belong glory and dominion for ever and ever. Amen" (I Pet. 4:10, 11).

I Corinthians 12:12-27 shows that these gifts "are in Christ what the foot, the hand, the ear, the eyes are in the human body" (James M. Gray). "All gifts promote the health and strength of the whole body, therefore none can be safely dispensed with"

(A. T. Pierson). "We quench the Spirit when we . . . give no liberty for the ministry of the various gifts of the Spirit, thus imposing silence or inactivity on others" (C. I. Scofield).

In Chapter 13, Paul writes about seven gifts, three of which he had not mentioned in Chapter 12: understanding of mysteries, liberality, and martyrdom. There he contrasts gifts as being temporal with graces as being eternal, and points out that gifts without love are worthless. The meaning of the phrase "that which is perfect" in verse 10 is crucial. (See pp. 137, 138) We're certain that the "perfect" has not yet come because we still "see through a glass darkly," not "face to face"; we still "know in part," not "even as also we are known" (v. 12).

In Chapter 14 Paul mentions other gifts: "revelation" and "doctrine" (v. 6), "singing" (v. 15), and "giving thanks" (v. 16). Now if God withdrew all these gifts from the body of Christ after the death of the apostles, we today are not supposed to "desire spiritual gifts," especially "that we may prophesy." That Paul is not talking about prophesying (14:1) in the sense, for example, that Isaiah prophesied is clear from 14:3: "He that prophesieth speaketh unto men to edification, and exhortation, and comfort." Likewise, when he speaks of "revelation" in verse 6, he's not implying that we today can write books on a par with the Bible—Romanism's traditions, Mormonism's *Doctrine and Covenants, Pearl of Great Price,* and *Book of Mormon* notwithstanding. No, "Inspiration is gone with the apostles, but illumination still flows freely" (Leo Kidd). (Ill. Kidd and Comstock)

Finally, if we take Bavinck and Warfield to mean that all gifts, or some gifts, especially tongues, have been withdrawn, and if we agree with them; then we can't take Paul's attitude toward the problem: "covet to prophesy, and forbid not to speak in tongues" (14:39). And that's serious. If we can't take Paul's point of view, whose can we? Paul is the very one who explains Pentecost for this age (Rom. 2:16; 15:15-19; 16:25; Acts 13:38, 39; 15:15-18; Gal. 1:11, 12; 2:9; Eph. 3:3; Phil. 3:17; 4:9; II Thes. 2:13, 14; 3:9; II Tim. 2:8; II Pet. 3:15, 16). He shows that the Gospel is not a development from Judaism but a separate, new revelation (Eph. 3; cp. William R. Newell). Consider carefully

Paul's "no difference" doctrine of sin, Romans 3:22, and his "more than conquerors" doctrine of Pentecost, Romans 6, 7, and 8. Wherefore, let's adjust both Pentecostal and non-Pentecostal theology to Paul.

When Paul faced demon counterfeit tongues outside the church at Corinth (I Cor. 12:2, 3), he didn't denounce all tongues as Satanic; rather he laid down suitable safeguards: *The gift of tongues is not a mark of spiritual maturity (except at Pentecost). *May be fleshly and Satanic. "One kind of ecstasy is superficially very much like another" (F. F. Bruce). *Should not be magnified above prophecy. *No exhortation to seek tongues—as, for instance, prophecy. *Not for all believers (I Cor. 12:30). (There's no evidence that Christ ever spoke in tongues.) *Primarily for private worship (14:18, 19, 28)—except at Pentecost. *Wrong use can mar our testimony. Would Campus Crusade, for instance, enlist graduates of Oral Roberts University if they maintained Paul's attitude toward tongues? *The right use is always interpreted in public to edify our church—except no interpreters were needed at Pentecost. *Can be childish (14:20), but wasn't at Pentecost. *Not used to get people saved (14:24, 25)—as at Pentecost. *Not by women in public (14:34, 35). (How about "the women, and Mary, the mother of Jesus" on that remarkable day of Pentecost?) *By course (14:27). Was it by course on that day when 3,000 were saved and baptized? *The gift of tongues at Corinth was overemphasized, divisive, and had to be rebuked (14:36-38). How about the scores of tongues groups in our world today who are at each other's throats? *The same blessedness which is experienced in tongues unintelligently can be enjoyed intelligently apart from tongues, and is 2,000 times better (14:15-19). For example, Paul could straighten out the bad situation at Corinth, but the tongues speakers couldn't.

Some questions: If tongues at Corinth were earthly languages like they were at Pentecost, why would Paul delight in speaking them in private worship? How would that edify him? If we non-Pentecostals have had this baptism, where is the evidence in most of our lives? Where does Scripture teach us to "seek the baptism with tongues as the evidence"? Who "tutored the disciples on the day of Pentecost" to speak in tongues (Russell T. Hitt)?

When the ignition parts are working right and we're not out of gasoline, our car runs well; likewise, when Christians are normal, we blaze with holy fire. If we're not blazing, we're pouring cold water on Christ's fire (I Thes. 5:19), a grievous sin (Jas. 4:17). Yes, may the God who is here deal with us: for Christians to be cold, or even lukewarm, is SIN (Rev. 3:16). Grace, when rightly understood and appreciated, produces eager interest in "the things of the Spirit" (Rom. 8:5), energetic and unflagging witnessing for Christ (Mt. 4:19), and Spirit-empowered *action* (Eph. 5:18). Pride, prejudice, stubbornness, rebellion, complacency—God hates them! They put out the fire of Pentecost. But Pentecostal radiance and love get the job done—and they can't be counterfeited.

Additional sources of research: J. A. Alexander; Norman E. Allison; Sir Robert Anderson; James G. Andrews, Jr.; John E. Ashbrook; Glenn W. Barker; Don Basham; Raymond W. Beecher, Editor of *Voice* magazine; Loraine Boettner; Robert D. Brinsmead, Editor of *Present Truth* magazine; Percy S. Brewster.

Frederick Dale Bruner's *A Theology of the Holy Spirit* (Eerdmans, 1970, 390 pp. $8.95) was reviewed by Michael Harper, Editor of *Renewal Magazine*, London, and by Geoffrey W. Bromiley, Fuller Theological Seminary. Harper: "Here is a crucial book. It is the most detailed and thorough criticism of Pentecostal theology that has ever been published. . . . I fear this book does not help bridge the gap—it only widens the breach still further" (Oct. /Nov. issue, 1971). Bromiley: "It demands of Pentecostals more strenuous biblical and dogmatic study. . . . It demands of their critics an authentic acceptance of the biblical rule, a more profound thinking through of the issues involved, and a readiness to see the need that Pentecostalism is trying to meet . . . ." (*Eternity*, Oct. 1971).

Catholic Pentecostals, Charisma '72; David L. Cummins; R. L. Dabney; J. N. Darby; E. S. English; Felicitas D. Goodman; Paul R. Van Gorder; Greater Pittsburgh Charismatic Conference, 1972; Robert G. Gromacki; Franklin Hall; Wm. B. Hallman; James Hastings; R. C. Hazen; Carl F. H. Henry; James W. L. Hill; Charles and A. A. Hodge; Wade H. Horton; Ramon Hunston; Marcelus Kik; Kurt Koch; Harold Lindsell, Etitor of *Christianity Today*; Herbert Lockyer; C. S. Lovett; Bud Lyles.

David Mains; Henrietta C. Mears; C. John Miller; Watson Mills; G. Campbell Morgan; Nichol; Chris W. Parnell; Earl P. Paulk; Edward Plowman; Plummer; Pneuma '72; Allen Redpath; H. N Ridderbos; J. C. Ryle; William J. Samarin; Francis A. Schaeffer; Scroggie; the Society for Pentecostal Studies; Miles J. Stanford; Lehman Strauss; J. F. Strombeck; Vinson Synan; H. C. Thiessen; J. H. Thornwell; Merrill F. Unger; Wilbur B. Wallis; Wayne A. Webb; Wescott.

Acknowledgements

EXPOSITIONS IN CHAPTERS I through III are based chiefly on *The Pulpit Commentary* and Fausset's *Critical and Experimental Commentary*, and those in Chapter IV on A. T. Robertson's *Word Pictures in the New Testament*. Treatment of the pivotal Epistle to the Romans reflects the personal and written ministry of William R. Newell, and deals with the Spirit's work on the basis of the believer's identification with Christ Jesus.

Southern Bible Testimony is grateful to the writers and publishers listed in the "Notes" section of this book for brief quotations.

Notes

CHAPTER TWO

1. *Man in the Process of Time* (Grand Rapids: Eerdmans Publishing Company, 1956), p. 70.

CHAPTER THREE

1. *The Holy Spirit of God* (Chicago: The Bible Institute Colportage Association, 1913), p. 10.
2. *Studies in Isaiah* (New York: Loizeaux Brothers, n.d.), p. 388.
3. Ibid., p. 726.
4. *Scofield Reference Bible* (New York: Oxford University Press, 1909), p. 88.
5. E. Y. Mullins in *International Standard Bible Enc.* (Chicago: Howard-Severance Co., 1915), III, 1409.

CHAPTER FOUR

1. *Word Pictures in the New Testament* (New York: Richard R. Smith, Inc., 1930), I, 282.
2. Source unknown.
3. *Lectures on the Book of Acts* (New York: Loizeaux Brothers, 1945), p. 437.

CHAPTER FIVE

1. Denney, quoted by Thomas, *The Holy Spirit of God* (Chicago: The Bible Institute Colportage Ass'n, 1913), p. 61.
2. Stevens, quoted by Thomas, ibid., p. 66.
3. *The Spirit of Christ* (London: Nesbit and Co., 1888), pp. 52, 55.
4. Procession from both the Father and the Son is held by most theologians in the Western world; but the doctrine isn't accepted by many in the East, especially the Eastern Orthodox Church.

5. Certain modern interpreters—Bultmann, for example—have attempted to use such passages as John 14:18 against the traditional doctrine of the second coming. Bible-believing scholars, however, have exposed their error. For a "Critique of Rudolf Bultmann's Present Eschatology," see D. E. Holwerda's *The Holy Spirit and Eschatology in the Gospel of John* (Grand Rapids: Wm. B. Eerdmans Publishing Company, n.d.), pp. 113–126.

6. In his chapter on "The Holy Spirit and the World," Thomas convinces me on this point with statements like these: "The first thing to notice is that in the New Testament there is an entire absence of all cosmical relations of the Holy Spirit such as we find in the Old Testament. . . . No one has ever been led to Christ in the centre of Africa, or China, or elsewhere by the Holy Spirit apart from some testimony to Christ by life or word; the latter either spoken or written." [*The Holy Spirit of God* (Chicago: The Bible Institute Colportage Ass'n, 1913), pp. 185–189.]

7. W. T. Conner, *The Work of the Holy Spirit* (Nashville: Broadman Press, 1949), p. 84.

8. Islam claims "Comforter" is a corruption of one of the names of Mohammed. (*Quran*, ed. by A. Yusuf Ali, note on John 14:18.)

9. When John B. Marchbanks, my associate, was editor of "The Question Box" in *Our Hope* magazine, he gave, in my opinion, a careful and correct statement on this verse (July, 1956):

> When our Lord, on the evening of His resurrection, appeared to His disciples, "He breathed on them, and saith unto them, Receive ye the Holy Ghost" (John 20:22). This action was symbolic, we believe, showing that the risen Lord was the Giver of the Holy Spirit (cf. Acts 2:32, 33). It was also an anticipative action, looking forward to the coming of the Holy Spirit on the Day of Pentecost.
>
> Just prior to His ascension our Lord promised the disciples: "But ye shall receive power, after that the

236 / FIRE, RADIANCE, AND LOVE

Holy Ghost is come upon you: and ye shall be witnesses unto me" (Acts 1:8). This witnessing power was evidently the thing the Lord had in mind when "He breathed on them, and saith unto them, Receive ye the Holy Ghost," for He continued: "Whose soever sins ye remit, they are remitted unto them; and whose soever sins ye retain, they are retained" (John 20:22, 23). That is, the disciples were told that by the power of the Gospel message which was committed to them, sins would be forgiven or retained: forgiven, if the message was believed; retained, if the message was rejected.

W. T. Conner also connects John 20:22 with Christ's promise of Pentecost, saying, "After the resurrection he breathed on the disciples and said, 'Receive ye the Holy Spirit' (20:22). Pentecost was his gift to the infant church." [*The Work of the Holy Spirit* (Nashville: Broadman Press. 1949. p. 91).]

CHAPTER SIX

1. *The Book of Acts* in *New London Commentary of the New Testament* (London, Edinburgh: Marshall, Morgan and Scott, 1954), note on p. 177.

2. Philadelphia: American Baptist Publication Society, 1887, Volume on *Corinthians–Thessalonians*, p. 107.

3. Why do the first sixteen chapters of The Acts contain forty-eight references to the Spirit, whereas the last twelve speak of Him only twelve times? Did Paul's ministry begin to wane? I doubt it. For after this he wrote all his epistles with the possible exception of Galatians. Why then does the Spirit seem to fade out? I suggest again the doctrine of the Spirit is *implied*.

4. Ponder Professor Erdman's comment on this point:

There are men like Apollos in Christian pulpits but there are many more like these twelve 'disciples' in the pews of Christian churches. They are sincere men, they hate their sins, they believe in the teachings of Jesus, they admire the Sermon on the Mount, they yearn for the highest and best things, but they lack spiritual power. Why? Because they are 'disciples of John,' they have not fixed their hearts and their hopes upon a Divine, raised, glorified Christ; they do not know 'the grace of God.' When, however, they learn the full gospel and yield themselves to Christ, they are not merely baptized with water. but also by the Holy Spirit. [*The Acts* (Philadelphia: The Westminster Press, 1936), pp. 132, 133.]

5. F. F. Bruce sums up the matter very satisfactorily:

We should not conclude that this determination to go was disobedience to the guidance of the Spirit of God; this determination of his was the fruit of an inward spiritual constraint which would not be gainsaid. It was natural that his friends who by the prophetic spirit were able to foretell his tribulation and imprisonment should try to dissuade him from going on, but with a complete lack of concern for his own safety, so long as he could fulfil his sacred service, Paul, like his Master, 'steadfastly set his face to go to Jerusalem.' [*The Book of Acts* in *The New London Commentary on the New Testament* (London and Edinburgh: Marshall, Morgan and Scott, 1954), p. 421.]

6. J. B. Phillips makes a confession to which we all should say Amen:

We in the modern Church have unquestionably *lost* something. Whether it is due to the atrophy of the quality which the New Testament calls 'faith,' whether it is due to a stifling churchiness, whether it is due to our sinful complacency . . . , or whatever the cause may be, very little of the modern Church could bear comparison with the spiritual drive, the genuine fellowship, and the gay unconquerable courage of the Young Church. [*The Young Church in Action* (New York: The Macmillian Company, 1952), p. XVI.]

7. There is, for instance, the testimony of Bob Finley, staff member of the Inter-Varsity Christian Fellowship in the Far East:

> The [Korean] revival was accompanied by apostolic miracles. At a daybreak prayer meeting of Presbyterians and Methodists, a paralytic boy leaped to his feet and walked for the first time in his life.... Before he was healed I noticed that the Korean's right foot and arm were wrinkled and shriveled and hopelessly twisted. He had been carried thirty miles to the meeting on the back of another. Heads were bowed while prayer was made for the sick. When I opened my eyes and saw him standing, I could hardly believe it. I had thought that such miracles were only for the early church. Just to make sure I went up to him and examined his right hand and foot. I felt the new, solid flesh with my fingers. It was warm and whole as my own.... Then I believed ("The Korean Revival." *Christian Life* magazine. Aug. 1950).

8. Her own testimony written and published one year later follows:

> My doctor had given me up, and had told me that I could not be cured. I was far gone with diabetes, and also suffered much from arthritis. My doctor did all he could for me, but for months I was helpless, in much pain. and always had to have insulin for diabetes.
>
> One day when my faithful pastor came to see me. as he often did. to feed me on the Living Bread. I told him what my doctor had said—that I could never be cured. He answered me [and I must confess that my answer was more professional than sincere]. "Well, there is a Physician in Heaven who can cure you."
>
> When he left, I immediately took my Bible and began searching for the One who could heal me, and, praise God, I found Him. Many Scriptures told me of how Jesus had compassion on the people and healed them. I asked Him if He would heal me, too, and give me faith

to believe He would. I believed that He was "the same yesterday, and today, and forever," taking for my promise James 5:14, 15: "Is any sick among you? let him call for the elders of the church; and let them pray over him, anointing him with oil in the name of the Lord: and the prayer of faith shall save the sick, and the Lord shall raise him up; and if he have committed sins, they shall be forgiven him."

On Sunday, May 24, 1942, I was taken to the church where the deacons and pastor anointed me and prayed for me. God's presence and power were gloriously felt, and when I woke up on Monday morning I was completely healed. Praise Him forever!

Two days after my healing, my doctor came to see me. I told him what God had done for me, but he would not believe me. So he took my blood pressure, which had been far above normal for weeks, and he found it normal.

Though convinced that my blood pressure was normal, and that I no longer suffered from arthritis, my doctor believed that I still had diabetes and told me that I must continue with the insulin shots. This grieved me, for I believed that God had also healed me of diabetes.

Again I talked with my pastor about it and he advised me to continue with the insulin, believing that soon, in some way, God's complete healing would be manifest to the doctor. And it was. After some days of taking insulin, I became very ill from it. Then the doctor told me to stop using it.

How I thank God for His wonderful healing power to me. I am feeling well and stronger all the time. May God bless this testimony to His glory. Praise Him forever!

9. *Romans Verse by Verse* (Chicago: Grace Publications, Inc., 1938), pp. 462, 463.

CHAPTER SEVEN

1. Davison, quoted by Thomas, *The Holy Spirit of God* (Chicago: The Bible Institute Colportage Ass'n, 1913), p. 24.

2. We do not count *Spirit* in 8:1 because apparently it was added by some copyist.

3. Chicago: Moody Press, 1962, p. 1184.

4. Moule, quoted by Thomas, *The Holy Spirit of God* (Chicago: The Bible Institute Colportage Ass'n. 1913). p. 24.

5. Mrs. T. C. Rounds, founder and for twenty-five years superintendent of the Chicago Hebrew Mission, related an experience which illustrates the way of victory over indwelling sin when manifested as irritability:

> While attending the Female Seminary at Steuben-ville, Ohio, at the age of sixteen, I was suddenly told of the death of my dearly beloved father. The shock was so great that I fell to the floor, prostrated by the blow, striking my head on my trunk. This resulted in nervous prostration, and many years of suffering. . . . With naturally a sensitive disposition. Satan made good use of the circumstances, and the natural heart, to fasten upon me a very ungovernable temper. A match never took fire quicker than this phosphorescent "bundle of nerves."
>
> Time would fail to tell of the soul efforts, the soul agonies, the cries, the tears, the prayers, that went up for deliverance. but all to no purpose. Many were the times the writer would come down stairs [*sic*] from her knees. crying to God to be kept for the day, only to fall to pieces over a burnt bisquit or potato, or any other trifling thing. Do what I would there was always "a law in my members, warring against the law of my mind, bringing me into captivity to the law of sin" (Rom. 7:23).
>
> Upon an occasion that caused unusual disturbance, in a state of helpless hopelessness. crying to the Lord

for deliverance, *four points* were clearly given to me by the Spirit as a guide to the coveted blessing.

At this juncture Mrs. Rounds told how Romans 6:11 and 13 and related Scriptures were outlined in her mind to give her the Gospel attitude: *dead, alive, yield, let God work.* Then she continued her testimony, telling of a test which worked the deeper meaning from her head to her heart:

A few days after, I was awakened by a heavy crash in the hall. Half asleep I groped my way to the head of the stairs. Looking down I saw that my dear husband, attempting to take the lamp from its place in the hall, had let it slip from his hand, and to my horror I saw kerosene oil streaming down the stairs and over the hall carpet, with broken glass everywhere, and my husband frantically trying to repair the damage, all unmindful of my presence. In an instant I was thoroughly aroused, inside and outside, and notwithstanding all my "reckonings," etc., I was "mad." The old-time habit of giving a piece of mind on such occasions promptly presented itself for utterance.

I felt I must say, "Now, George, how *could* you be so careless!" (With proper emphasis on "could.")

But a voice whispered, "Yes, but that would not be Christ-like."

"I know," I responded, "but I think I ought to say something that would make him more careful in the future."

"Yes, but that would not be Christ-like," repeated my faithful monitor. . . . "Have you forgotten the four keys I gave you?" I went back into my room. In a moment, like Christian, I remembered, and I began to "reckon myself dead" to these thoughts that came rolling like sea billows over my soul . . . and I "reckoned myself alive" to the love that would say the kind thing. . . . Then I said, "I yield myself unto Thee, O Heavenly Father. Thou must work the wrong thoughts *out*, and the right thoughts in, for I *cannot*." Instantly, like a flash of lightning, it was done. . . . I went to the top of the stairs and called down in the sweetest of tones, for they came out of His heart: "Hello, George, what is the matter down there?"

With a look of agony and expectant reproof, he said: "I was trying to take the lamp down and it slipped out of my hand. Oh, it's too bad!"

"Yes, it is quite a muss," I said, "but never mind, we'll fix it up after breakfast."

A more relieved man never breathed. He looked up to see whether it could possibly be his wife. and the look spoke volumes of gratitude. (*The Broken Lamp*, Chicago Hebrew Mission)

6. Read Wm. R. Newell, *Romans Verse by Verse* (Chicago: Grace Publications, Inc., 1938), pp. 101–106, 191, 391–393.

This is not to say that certain Reformers themselves didn't go on from justification by faith to "the fulness of the blessing of the Gospel of Christ." Luther did. And other individuals have done so down through the years. Walter Marshall, toward the end of the seventeenth century, wrote of the "life more abundant" in *The Gospel Mystery of Sanctification*. Later W. E. Broadman, Robert Pearsall Smith and Hannah Whitall Smith sowed the seed of the Keswick movement which has reached the spiritually elite around the world through the messages of men like Evan H. Hopkins, A. T. Pierson, F. B. Meyer, H. W. Webb-Peploe, J. Stuart Holden, W. Graham Scroggie, A. C. Dixon, R. A. Torrey and J. Elder Cumming. [Consult Herbert F. Stevenson, *Keswick's Authentic Voice* (Grand Rapids: Zondervan Publishing House, 1959), pp. 5–14.]

7. The real issue in Romans 7:14–25 is not whether the passage describes Paul's pre-Christian experience or an experience he had after he became a Christian. There are good expositors on both sides of this question. But we believe the point God wants us to see is that no man *in himself*, whether Christian or not, can do the will of God. Christ and His Spirit

are man's *only* hope. For a scholarly discussion of the two interpretations. see articles by C. Leslie Mitton on "Romans XII. Rediscovered" in *The Expository Times* (Edinburgh: T. and T. Clark), vol. LXV, nos. 3, 4, 5, Dec., 1953 and Jan. and Feb., 1954.

8. For an exhaustive discussion of this subject, consult Richard N. Longenecker, *Paul, Apostle of Liberty* (New York, Evanston and London: Harper and Row, 1964), pp. 160–170.

9. For an excellent explanation of "adoption," a major New Testament term, see Skevington Wood, *Life By the Spirit* (Grand Rapids: Zondervan Publishing Company, 1963), pp. 80–82, 89.

10. Chicago: Moody Press, 1962, p. 1220.

11. *Romans Verse by Verse* (Chicago: Grace Publications, Inc., 1938), pp. 536, 537.

CHAPTER EIGHT

1. Albert Barnes, *Notes on I Corinthians* (New York: Harper and Brothers, 1848), p. 72.

2. *Did Ye Receive the Holy Ghost?* (Chicago: Good News Publishers, 1952), pp. 12–14.

3. "Christian Healing," mimeographed and distributed by Harvey Miller, Fairview, Penna.

4. *Notes on James and Peter* (New York: Loizeaux Brothers, 1947), pp. 60, 61.

5. *United Evangelical Action*, March, 1964.

6. For a two-sided discussion of "tongues," see articles on "Glossolalia in the New Testament" by Bastain Van Elderen and William G. McDonald, *Bulletin of the Evangelical Theological Society*, V. 7, Spring, 1964, pp. 53–68.

7. Consult Frank Farrell. "Outburst of Tongues: The New Penetration," *Christianity Today*, September 13, 1963.

8. For an appreciation of the background and scope of this "gift," read Morton T. Kelsey, *Tongue Speaking*, Doubleday, 1964. Rector Kelsey "is *not* a tongue speaker, although within his church a group of tongue speakers finds acceptance."

9. *I Believe in the Holy Ghost* (Minneapolis: Bethany Fellowship, Inc., 1965), p. 115.

10. Commenting on the clause, "But when that which is perfect is come," Barnes says, "The sense here is, that *in heaven* —a state of absolute perfection—that which is 'in part,' or which is imperfect, shall be lost in superior brightness." Lange says on I Corinthians 13:8–10: "Whatever may be the exegesis given this passage, the prevailing belief is that these gifts, especially those of a miraculous nature, were destined only for the apostolic period, and have already ceased. But this, certainly, it was not the intention of the Apostle to assert here. The time alluded to is undoubtedly that of 'the age to come,' ushered in by the second advent of the Lord."

11. Burton Scott Easton puts it thus:

...many gifts are for the present world only; faith, hope and love are eternal and endure in the next world ... even in heaven life will not be static but will have opportunities of unlimited growth. Never will the finite soul be able to dispense entirely with faith, while at each stage the growth into the next can be anticipated through hope. [*International Standard Bible Enc.* (Chicago: Howard-Severance Co., 1915), III, p. 1420.]

12. Many translations capitalize the "s" in verses 6 and 8, including Phillips, New English Bible, Worrell, Weymouth, Moffatt, Emphasized, Newberry, Berkeley, Rotherham and Darby.

CHAPTER NINE

1. Many spiritual believers experience this fact without knowing the doctrine:

An American Indian was giving his testimony in a gathering of Christian members of his tribe. He told of his conversion and of how in the beginning he felt as though he would never sin again; he was so happy in knowing his Saviour. But, he explained, as time went on he became conscious of an inward conflict, which he described somewhat as follows:

"It seems, my brothers, that I have two dogs fighting in my heart: one is a very good dog, a beautiful white dog, and he is always watching out for my best interests. The other is a very bad dog, a black dog who is always trying to destroy the things that I want to build up. These dogs give me a lot of trouble because they are always quarreling and fighting with each other."

One of his hearers looked up and asked laconically, "Which one wins?" The Indian instantly replied, "Whichever one I say 'Sic 'im' to." [H. A. Ironside, *Illustrations of the Bible* (Chicago: Moody Press, n.d.), p. 26.]

2. *Expositors' Greek Testament*, Ellicott. Barnes. Vincent. Newberry and Rotherham capitalize the "s."

3. Someone tells how a brother used this sword:

A well-known doctor of Switzerland, a Christian, had as his companion, in a compartment of a Paris-bound train, an infidel. The latter, knowing of the doctor's faith in Christ, began to argue with him about the Bible and Christianity. No matter what the infidel said, Dr. Malan replied with an exact quotation from the Scriptures. Never, not once, did he give his own opinion, nor did he try to explain the Scriptures in his own words. Time and again the infidel was thus met with the Word. Finally, in exasperation he exclaimed: "But I don't believe the Bible! What is the sense in your quoting it to me?"

The Swiss doctor answered with the words of our Lord: "If ye believe not that I am he, ye shall die in your sins" (John 8:24).

Ten years later, Dr. Malan received a letter from Paris. After a few introductory remarks, reminding the physician of the conversation on the train so long ago, the writer, the former infidel, wrote: "You simply used the Sword of the Spirit, and stabbed me through and through. Every time I tried to parry the blade, you gave me another stab with the Sword, until I realized that I was not fighting you, but God."

CHAPTER TEN

1. We follow the American Standard, Berkeley, Darby and other versions in omitting the Authorized reference in I Peter 1:22.

2. For helpful discussions of these perplexing verses, see Kenneth S. Wuest, *First Peter in the Greek New Testament* (Grand Rapids: Eerdmans Publishing Company, 1942), pp. 92–109; Albert Barnes, *Notes Explanatory and Practical* (New York: Harper and Brothers, 1847), V. on James–Jude, 199–206; J. N. Darby, *Synopsis of the Books of the Bible* (New York: Loizeaux Brothers, n.d.), V. V, 390f.; "Spirits in Prison" by James Orr in *International Standard Bible Enc.* (Chicago: The Howard-Severance Co., 1915), IV, 2456f; and "Who are the Spirits in Prison?" by William E. Banks in *Eternity*, February 1966, V. 17. No. 2.

3. *The Witness of the Spirit* (Grand Rapids: Eerdmans Publishing Company, 1959), p. 90.

CHAPTER ELEVEN

1. *The Ante-Nicene Fathers* (Buffalo: The Christian Literature Company, 1886), V. I, p. 5.

2. Ibid., pp. 52, 53.

3. Ibid., p. 27.

4. Ibid., p. 243.

5. Ibid., pp. 444, 5.

6. *A Manual of Church History* (Philadelphia: American Baptist Publication Society, 1904), V. I, p. 251.

7. Ibid., p. 185.

8. Ibid., p. 195.

9. *The Ante-Nicene Fathers* (Buffalo: The Christian Literature Company, 1886), V. IV, p. 27.

10. *A Manual of Church History* (Philadelphia: American Baptist Publication Society, 1904), V. I, p. 284.

11. Ibid., p. 285.

12. *The Ante-Nicene Fathers* (Buffalo: The Christian Literature Company, 1886), V. IV, pp. 252, 3.

13. Ibid., V. V, p. 641.

CHAPTER TWELVE

1. Moberly, quoted by Griffith Thomas, *The Holy Spirit of God* (Chicago: The Bible Institute Colportage Ass'n. 1913). p. 138.

2. Ibid., pp. 138, 9.

3. Herbert Lockyer, *All the Doctrines of the Bible* (Grand Rapids: Zondervan Publishing House, 1964), p. 79.

4. See Warfield in *International Standard Bible Enc.* (Chicago: The Howard-Severance Company, 1915), V. V, p. 3016.

5. W. T. Conner, *A System of Christian Doctrine* (Nashville: Sunday School Board of the Southern Baptist Convention, 1924), p. 264.

CONCLUSION

1. *The Holy Spirit of God* (Chicago: The Bible Institute Colportage Ass'n. 1913), p. 2.

2. See exposition of Romans 5–8 in Chapter VII and apply the ideas of "thirst" in Romans 5, "come unto me" in Romans 6 and 7, and "drink" in Romans 8 for a doctrinal basis of John 7:37.

3. *Man in the Process of Time* (Grand Rapids: Eerdmans Publishing Company, 1955), p. 27.

4. The following quotations from Griffith Thomas imply what I mean: "There is only one way of demonstrating Christianity as a supernatural religion, and that is by the constant insistence on the presence and work of the Holy Spirit." That is to say, "It is only as a 'dynamic' that Christianity will recommend itself to the life of today, and, according to the New Testament, this 'dynamic' is only possible by the grace and presence of the Holy Spirit." [*The Holy Spirit of God* (Chicago: The Bible Institute Colportage Ass'n, 1913), pp. 2 and 4.]

5. George S. Hendry, *The Holy Spirit in Christian Theology* (Philadelphia: The Westminster Press, 1965, revised and enlarged ed.), p. 153.

Bibliography

Biederwolf, William Edward. *A Help to the Study of the Holy Spirit.* Fourth Revised and Enlarged Edition. New York: Fleming H. Revell Company, 1903. Pp. 222.

Broomall, Wick. *The Holy Spirit.* Grand Rapids: Baker Book House, 1963. Pp. 211.

Criswall, W. A. *The Holy Spirit in Today's World.* Grand Rapids: Zondervan Publishing House, 1966. Pp. 193.

Clark, Dougan. *The Offices of the Holy Spirit.* Portland, Oregon: Evangel Publishers, 1945. Pp. 216.

Coltman, W. G. *The Holy Spirit Our Helper.* Findlay, Ohio: Fundamental Truth Publishers, 1946. Pp. 127.

Come, Arnold B. *Human Spirit and Holy Spirit.* Philadelphia: The Westminster Press, 1959. Pp. 208. Liberal in viewpoint, but stimulating.

Conner, Walter Thomas. *The Work of the Holy Spirit.* Nashville: Broadman Press, 1949. Pp. 196. Excellent.

Cumming, James Elder. *Through the Eternal Spirit.* Minneapolis: Bethany Fellowship, Inc., 1965 Edition. Pp. 203. A standard work; thoroughly scriptural.

Dalton, Robert Chandler. *Tongues Like as of Fire.* Springfield: The Gospel Publishing House, 1945. Pp. 127. Pentecostal.

Davidson, W. T. *The Indwelling Spirit.* New York, Cincinnati: The Methodist Book Concern, 1911. Pp. xiii, 340. A scholarly "attempt to describe the influence upon the human spirit of that Divine Breath...."

DeHaan, M. D. *Speaking in Tongues*. Grand Rapids: The Radio Bible Class, n. d. Pp. 29.

——*The Holy Spirit*. Grand Rapids: The Radio Bible Class, n. d. Pp. 35.

Dobbins, Gaines S. *Deepening the Spirit Life*. Nashville: The Sunday School Board of the Southern Baptist Convention, 1937. Pp. 151.

Dolman, D. H. *Simple Talks on the Holy Spirit*. London: Marshall, Morgan and Scott, n. d. Pp. 128.

Evans, Louis H. *Life's Hidden Secret*. London: Marshall, Morgan and Scott, Limited, 1959 Edition. Pp. 154.

Fant, David J. Editor. *Modern Miracles of Healing*. Harrisburg, Pa.: Christian Publications, Inc., 1953. Pp. 160. Personal testimonies of twenty-four well-known Christian men and women to the power of God to heal their bodies.

Fénelon, Francois de Salegnac de La Mothe (1651–1715) *Christian Perfection*. Edited and prefaced by Charles F. Whiston. Translated from the French by Mildred Whitney Stillman. New York and London: Harper and Brothers Publishers, 1947. Pp. xiii, 208.

Fitch, Mrs. May Wayburn. *The Healing Delusion*. New York: Loizeaux Brothers, n. d. Pp. 61.

——, Theodore. *Spiritual Gifts Being Restored*. Council Bluffs, Iowa, n. d. Pp. 80. Pentecostal.

Freeman, C. Wade. *The Holy Spirit's Ministry*. Grand Rapids: Zondervan Publishing House, 1954. Pp. 149. Compiled and edited. Messages by Billy Graham, W. A. Criswell, T. Lamar Mathis, Paul Brooks Leath, W. R. White, Stanley E. Wilkes, Warren Walker, E. Jesse Northcutt, R. C. Campbell, E. D. Head and Sidney W. Powell.

Greenfield, John. *Power From on High*. Third Edition. Warsaw, Indiana, 1928. Pp. 94.

Gordon, A. J. *The Holy Spirit in Missions*. New York, Chicago, Toronto: Fleming H. Revell Co., 1893. Pp. 241.

—— *The Ministry of Healing*. Harrisburg, Pa.: Christian Publications, Inc., n. d. Pp. v, 249.

—— *The Ministry of the Spirit*. Phoenix Edition. Philadelphia:

The American Baptist Publication Society, 1894. Pp. 229.

Gore, Charles. *The Holy Spirit and the Church*. New York: Charles Scribner's Sons, 1924. Pp. xiii, 366. Liberal; valuable as contrast to conservative viewpoint.

Graham, Billy. *Revival in Our Time*. Sixth Edition. Wheaton: Van Kampen Press, 1951. Pp. 156. Sermon on "How to Be Filled with the Spirit," pp. 105–121.

Harrison, Norman B. *His Indwelling: The Living Holy Spirit*. Sixth Printing. Minneapolis: The Harrison Service, 1928. Pp. 96.

Hendry, George S. *The Holy Spirit in Christian Theology*. 1965. Revised and Enlarged Edition. Pp. 168. Liberal.

Herring, Ralph A. *God Being My Helper*. Nashville: Broadman Press, 1955. Pp. xi, 139.

Holden, Stewart. *Fulness of Life*. London: Marshall, Morgan and Scott, 1955 Edition. Pp. 48.

Holverda, D. E. *The Holy Spirit and Eschatology in the Gospel of John*. Grand Rapids: Wm. B. Eerdmans Publishing Co., n. d. Pp. xiii, 141.

Horn, Neville. *A Spirit-Controlled Life*. Lincoln, Neb.: Back to the Bible Publishers, 1962. Pp. 94.

Horton, Harold. *Speaking With Tongues*. London: Assemblies of God Publishing House, n. d. Pp. 35.

—— *The Baptism in the Holy Spirit*. London: Assemblies of God Publishing House, n. d.

Hottel, W. S. *The Holy Spirit and the Christian*. No address, n. d. Pp. 15.

Ironside, H. A. *Holiness, the False and the True*. Oakland: Western Book and Tract Co.; New York: Loizeaux Brothers, Publishers, n. d. Pp. 142.

—— *The Mission of the Holy Spirit*. Oakland: Western Book and Tract Co., Inc.; New York: Loizeaux Brothers, n. d. Pp. 64.

James, Maynard. *I Believe in the Holy Ghost*. Minneapolis: Bethany Fellowship, Inc., 1965. Pp. 167.

Kellog, Howard W., and Brooks, Keith L. *Man, A Tripartite*

Being. Los Angeles: American Prophetic League. n. d. Pp. 16.

Kluepfel, P. *The Holy Spirit in the Life and Teaching of Jesus and the Early Church.* Columbus, Ohio: The Lutheran Book Concern, 1929. Pp. 145.

Kuyper, Abraham. *The Work of the Holy Spirit.* London and New York: Funk and Wagnals Co., 1899. Pp. xxxix, 664.

Lang, G. H. *The Rights of the Holy Spirit in the House of God.* Copies from the writer, The Woodlands, Walsham-Le-Willows, Suffolk, 1938. Pp. 26.

Larkin, Clarence. *The Spirit World.* Philadelphia: Rev. Clarence Larkin Estate, 1921. Pp. 158.

MacGregor, G. H. C. *The Things of the Spirit.* London: Marshall Brothers, 1898. Pp. vii. 79.

MacNeal, John. *The Spirit-filled Life.* Chicago: The Moody Press, 1896. Pp. 126.

——, C. H. *Sanctification, What Is It?* New York: Loizeaux Brothers, n.d. Pp. 22.

Matsler, Bertha Smith. *The Holy Spirit in Power.* Boston: The Christopher Publishing House. 1952. Pp. 63.

McQuilkin, Robert C. *What Is Pentecost's Message Today?* Columbia, S.C.: Columbia Bible College, 1931. Pp. 32.

Morrison, Henry Clay. *Baptism With the Holy Ghost.* Louisville: Pentecostal Publishing Co., 1900. Pp. 39.

Moody, D. L. *Secret Power.* Chicago: Moody Press, n.d. Pp. 125.

Murray, Andrew. *The Spirit of Christ.* London: Nesbit and Co., 1888. Pp. 394.

——. *The Full Blessing of Pentecost.* London, Edinburgh: Oliphants, Ldt., reprinted 1948. Pp. 127.

——. *Divine Healing.* Fifth Edition. London: Victory Press, 1952. Pp. 99.

—— *Absolute Surrender.* Chicago: Moody Press, n.d. Pp. viii. 97.

Mundell, George H. *The Ministry of the Holy Spirit.* Darby, Pa.: Maran-atha Publications. n.d. Pp. 95.

Ockenga, Harold J. *Power through Pentecost.* Grand Rapids: Wm. B. Eerdmans Publishing Co.. 1959. Pp. 176.

———. *The Spirit of the Living God*. New York: Fleming H. Revell Company, 1957. Pp. 128.

Pentecost, J. Dwight. *The Divine Comforter*. New York: Fleming H. Revell Company, 1963. Pp. 256.

Pierce, Samuel Eyles. *The Gospel of the Spirit*. Grand Rapids: Wm. B. Eerdmans Publishing Company, 1955. Pp. 104.

Ramm, Bernard. *The Witness of the Spirit*. Grand Rapids: Wm. B. Eerdmans Publishing Company, 1959. Pp. 140.

Redford, R. A. *Vox Dei: The Doctrine of the Spirit*. Cincinnati: Cranston and Curts; New York: Hunt and Eaton, 1889. Pp. 344.

Rice, John R. *The Power of Pentecost*. Wheaton: Sword of the Lord Publishers, 1949. Pp. 440.

Scofield, C. I. *Plain Papers on the Doctrine of the Holy Spirit*. New York, Chicago, Toronto: Fleming H. Revell Company, 1899. Pp. 80.

Simpson, A. B. *The Holy Spirit*. Two Volumes. Harrisburg, Pa.: Christian Publications, Inc., 1896.

———. *The Gospel of Healing*. Eighth Edition. New York: Christian Alliance Publishing Co., 1893. Pp. 281.

———. *Walking in the Spirit*. Harrisburg, Pa.: Christian Publications, Inc., 1886. Pp. 155.

Smith, Oswald J. *The Enduement of Power*. London, Edinburgh: Marshall. Morgan and Scott. Ltd.. sixth impression. 1951. Pp. iv, 113.

Stewart, James A. *Heaven's Throne Gift*. Philadelphia: The Continental Press, n.d. Pp. 194.

Sweeting, William J. *Studies on the Holy Spirit*. Denver: Baptist Publications, Inc., 1958. Pp. 160.

Thomas, W. H. Griffith. *The Holy Spirit of God*. Chicago: Moody Press, 1913. Pp. xvi, 303. Valuable.

Torrey, R. A. *How to Obtain Fulness of Power*. Wheaton: Sword of the Lord Publishers, 1897. Pp. 76.

Unger, Merrill F. *The Baptizing Work of the Holy Spirit*. Wheaton: Van Kampen Press, 1953. Pp. 147.

Versteeg, John M. *Perpetuating Pentecost*. Chicago: Willett Clark and Co., 1930. Pp. 207.

Walvoord, John F. *The Holy Spirit*. Wheaton: Van Kampen Press, 1954. Pp. xvii, 275. Theological.

Watkin-Jones, Howard. *The Holy Spirit from Arminius to Wesley*. London: The Epworth Press, 1929. Pp. 335.

Webb, Allan Becher. *The Presence and Office of the Holy Spirit*. Seventh Edition. London: Skeffington and Son. 1887. Pp. xi, 180.

Wildish, Harold. *Did Ye Receive the Holy Ghost?* Chicago: Good News Publishers, 1952. Pp. 62. Good.

Wilson, A. S. *Concerning Perplexities, Paradoxes and Perils*. Auckland: Scott and Scott, Ltd., 1932. Pp. 93.

———. *Faith's Fight*. Toronto: Rev. F. A. Robinson, Confederation Life Bldg., 1933. Pp. 195.

Wood, Skevington. *Life By the Spirit*. Grand Rapids: Zondervan Publishing House, 1963. Pp. 144, all on Romans 8. Thorough and Excellent.

Index of Persons

Scripture Index

6:3ff 170
6:4f 168
6:8 168
6:9 168
7:18f 200
7:19 91
9:8 .... 103, 169
9:10 57
9:14 .... 31, 169, 191, 193
9:26 123
10:7 31
10:10 .... 169, 192
10:14 169
10:15 169
10:19ff 103
10:22 .... 91, 169
10:26 12
10:26ff 170
10:29 .... 170, 190
11 18
11:3 10
11:5 83
11:32 19

JAMES
2 91
4:1ff 171
4:4 117
4:5 170
4:17 199
5:14f 97, 133

I PETER
1:2 171
1:5 66
1:11 171
1:12 171
1:23 165
1:23ff 55
3:18 172
3:18ff 172
3:21 165
4:14 172
4:17 199
5:6 200

II PETER
1:5 163
1:21 173
2:15 16
3 139
3:17f 162

I JOHN
3:23 173
3:24 .... 173, 174
4:1 173
4:1ff 134
4:2 173
4:13 174
5:7f 174
5:8 66
5:16 12

JUDE
17ff 175
19 .... 174, 175
20 .... 174, 175
21 139
22f 162

REVELATION
1:4 175
1:4f 177
1:5 176
1:10 .... 66, 176, 177, 178
1:12ff 201
1:20 177
2 and 3 165
2:7 176
2:11 176
2:17 176
2:29 176
3:1 .... 175, 177
3:6 176
3:7 66
3:8 95
3:13 176
3:22 176
4:2 .... 34, 176, 177
4:5 .... 175, 177
4:6 176
5:6 .... 175, 177
14:13 178
17:3 .... 34, 176, 178
19 201
21:10 .... 34, 176, 178
22 178
22:7 178
22:12 178
22:16 178
22:17 178
22:18 134
22:20 178